# FROM CONDOMS TO CABBAGES

# FROM CONDOMS TO CABBAGES

## An Authorized Biography of Mechai Viravaidya

Thomas D'Agnes

FROM **CONDOMS** TO **CABBAGES**

Published by Post Books
The Post Publishing Public Company Limited
136 Na Ranong Rd., Klong Toey
Bangkok 10110, Thailand
Tel: (662) 240-3700 ext. 1691-2
Fax: (662) 671-9698
postbooks@bangkokpost.co.th
www.bangkokpost.com/postbooks



Cover design and layout: Sataporn Kawewong
Editing: Hardy Stockmann

First published in Thailand in 2001
Printed in Thailand by Allied Printers
The Post Publishing Public Company Limited

Set in: Garamond and Futura

National Library of Thailand Cataloging-in-Publication Data
D'Agnes, Thomas
From Condoms to Cabbages: An Authorized Biography
of Mechai Viravaidya. — Bangkok:
Post Books, 2001. 420 pp.
1. Mechai Viravaidya. I. Title 926.1394
ISBN: 974-228-009-6

**For Leona, Heather and Katie,**
**the women in my life**

# ACKNOWLEDGEMENTS

*The idea for this book arose in September 1994, when Mechai was in Manila to accept the Magsaysay Award and I was living in Manila with my family. Mechai was kind enough to invite my wife, Leona, and me to attend the ceremonies and related festivities surrounding his receipt of that prestigious award. I have known Mechai since 1978, and learned much of what I know about population, family planning, and public health during the four years that I worked directly with him from 1978 to 1982. I was looking for an appropriate gift for Mechai, not only to celebrate his receipt of the Magsaysay Award and his impending 60th birthday in January 2001, but also to thank him for his friendship over the years. The best gift I could think of was to write his biography.*

Fortunately, I received copious assistance from Mechai's many friends and acquaintances when the time came to document his life. Jessie Melero and Mabel Jones, Dr. Ella's sisters and Mechai's aunts who live in Great Britain, were most generous to provide their personal written accounts of Dr. Ella's childhood in Scotland and the events surrounding her courtship with Dr. Samak. Both assisted immeasurably by proofreading the entire manuscript. Dr. Kunthorn Sundaravej and Col. Amphorn

Sundaravej, Mechai's first cousins, provided vivid descriptions of Dr. Samak's childhood as related to them by their mother, Utomporn Sundaravej, Dr. Samak's older sister; and their own recollections of life in Thailand prior to and during World War II.

The section on Geelong Grammar was enhanced by the accounts of Gary Hudson, Mechai's classmate at that esteemed institution, and Sandy MacKenzie, who attended Geelong Grammar several years before Mechai. Roger and Sue Wilson took time to audiotape and share with me their memories of Mechai as a student at Melbourne University.

Dr. Wanchai Ghooprasert, who is currently Deputy Governor of the Provincial Waterworks Authority, was the Director of the Planning Division when Mechai was Governor from 1983-85, a position that placed him strategically to be a resource person for that period. Dr. Montri Chenvidyakarn and Dr. Sondhi Tejanant, both of whom worked with Mechai when he was Minister in the Prime Minister's Office, supplied interesting background on the Prem and Anand Government periods.

My understanding of the macroeconomic implications of the Asian Economic Crisis in Thailand was enriched by Richard Pyvis, the director of CLSA Emerging Markets. Rolf Van Buren, who was Managing Director of Bangkok Glass when the TBIRD program was introduced, gave his personal account of the impact of TBIRD on his company. Dr. Gavin Jones was a young demographer working for the Population Council in NEDB when the Thailand's Population Policy was drafted, and was kind enough to describe events during that dynamic period.

During a consulting visit to Laos, Peter Fajans was kind enough to share with me his experiences working in the Cambodian refugee camps with CBERS in 1980. Chris Elias, who was then the country representative for the Population Council in Bangkok, hand carried a photocopy of the Population Council monograph on abortion in Thailand to me during a consultancy in Laos so I could get my facts on abortion straight. Henry David provided the background on Population and Development International (PDI), and helped to review the manuscript. Ian Fossberg helped with factual checking and pictorial arrangements.

I am particularly grateful to Tavatchai Traitongyoo and Sudha Chatchavalvong, who patiently recounted their long acquaintance with Mechai and supplied data about PDA and its affiliated agencies contained in this book. They are both good friends of long standing.

I am indebted to Dr. Allan Rosenfield and Dr. Malcolm Potts for their assistance with this book. In addition to their help reviewing the manuscript and continuous encouragement, both made themselves available for long interviews during busy trips to Thailand.

The contributions of Khun Nualnoi Visutkanchanachai deserve special mention. As a PDA employee of more than 25 years and Mechai's Executive Secretary since 1983, she is a walking institutional memory for PDA. She scoured PDA's pictorial archives for the pictures that appear in this book. She made arrangements for all interviews and made sure I arrived on time. She found resource documents whenever they were requested. This book would never have been completed without her.

My wife, Leona, was instrumental in the production of this book. She was the first person to review and edit each chapter, making the manuscript more readable in the process. She also assisted with the pictorial layout. Her patience and encouragement through the good times and bad kept me going.

Special thanks are accorded to Khunying Putrie Viravaidya, who made time in her busy schedule to be interviewed for this book. Her candid memories of Mechai as a child, and the events surrounding their courtship and marriage, were transcribed nearly verbatim in Chapter 5. She also researched the Royal Archives to find details about Phraya Damrong, Mechai's grandfather. The direct quote by King Vajiravudh upon Phraya Damrong's appointment as personal physician to the Queen Mother was a result of her research. Sujima (Looknoo) Viravaidya was also kind enough to share her memories of her father while growing up.

Finally, I would like to thank Khun Mechai for his cooperation in producing this book. He submitted himself to nearly 30 hours of taped interviews, during which he recalled some of the most intimate details of his past. On two occasions, he was so sick that I suggested we stop. He chose to continue because he knew that finding another opportunity in his busy schedule would be difficult. He put the library resources of PDA at my disposal. He hosted me during many visits to Bangkok to clarify details and collect more information. He was incredibly patient during the six years required to prepare this biography, especially during those lengthy periods when I was incommunicado in northern Laos. I hope this book will be an appropriate gift for his 60th birthday.

**Thomas D'Agnes**

# TABLE OF CONTENTS

# FOREWORD

*Genuine leaders are rare. Individuals who lead in more than one area are even more extraordinary. Mechai Viravaidya is such a person. This biography shows where Mechai came from, how he changed and how he made a great impact on his own country and, more broadly, on a global scale. Our complex and rapidly changing world needs great leaders, who are able to think about and conceive big ideas and help in their formulation and implementation.*

Mechai is one of very few national leaders to achieve high political office and nationwide fame, recognition and admiration by tackling some of the most intractable and important national and global issues. There have been politicians who have developed concerns about the environment, about population and family planning issues, about the tragic AIDS epidemic and have been advocates for action. But Mechai reversed this equation by tackling these kinds of issues before becoming involved with politics and attaining national and international prominence through direct programmatic involvement. Not only has he brought about profound changes in Thailand, but his open, fearless, common sense approach to problems that other leaders all too often avoid, has made him a model for other countries, both rich and poor.

Mechai first attained national and international prominence through his efforts in the field of family planning. He established a new organization in Thailand in the early 1970s called Community Based Family Planning Services (later the Population and Development Association — PDA) with the goal of delivering family planning information and services at the village level. He set out on a campaign to desensitize taboo attitudes about condoms and was so successful, with a humorous approach, that condoms in Thailand became widely known as "mechais". Not all families would have been pleased by this form of notoriety, but Mechai and his family accepted this in the good humor in which the initiative was developed. His program, working in close collaboration with the Ministry of Public Health's National Family Planning Program, helped in bringing education and services to the villages. He played a contributing role in the extraordinary success of the Thai national program, as described in the book.

But his impact was much broader than the family planning program. As the refugee issues resulting from the Cambodian and Laotian tragedies descended on Thailand, Mechai, through PDA, assumed a major role in the management of one or two of the largest refugee camps in eastern Thailand and brought order and efficiency to a previously chaotic situation. He entered government to help restructure the Provincial Waterworks Authority, building in new efficiencies and weeding out corrupt and dysfunctional practices of the past.

But perhaps Mechai's most lasting and important contribution both to Thailand and to global health has been his impact on the AIDS epidemic. With the sexual freedom and sexual tourism of Thailand, it was clear that AIDS would become a major problem and Mechai was one of the first Thais to recognize the critical nature of the threat. He chafed at the inactivity and inattention to the coming epidemic. He was totally impatient with the concerns about the potential impact of news about the epidemic on tourism, a major source of foreign income. He believed that the Ministry of Public Health, to which management of the epidemic was assigned, was too weak a ministry in Thailand (as it is in all countries) to manage an epidemic of this magnitude. Fortunately for Thailand, as the epidemic was gaining steam, a new interim technocratic government was installed after a period of political and military unrest, headed by Anand Panyarachun, with Mechai as a minister in the prime minister's office. Among other duties, he was assigned responsibility for a national program on AIDS. With the consent of Prime Minister Anand, a committee, chaired by the prime minister, was established with ministerial representation from the major ministries. Clear responsibilities were assigned to each ministry, including the Ministry of Public Health, under the watchful supervision of Mechai and the prime minister. As a result, the Thai Government and the private sector widely publicized the seriousness of the threat and the importance of safe sexual practices. Condom use became widespread and Thailand became one of the first countries in the world (along with Uganda in Africa) to see a decrease in the transmission of this tragic disease. The structure of national organization and the demonstration of clear and strong support from the top of government has been presented internationally as the model to replicate for serious national responses to this tragic worldwide epidemic.

Both of us consider it a privilege to have been involved with this unique and charismatic leader. The anecdotes about Mechai, a few involving each of us, are told in the story that Tom D'Agnes has so artfully presented in this book. Who can forget Mechai passing out condoms to parking lot attendants in lieu of cash, or young children blowing up condoms to see who could make the biggest balloon, or Mechai approaching one of the first visiting Vietnamese delegations after the war and handing the leaders condoms as a demonstration of the Thai approach to family planning and disease prevention.

Why read a book about someone with a strange name from an Asian country? It is because it is a fascinating story of a unique individual, with a remarkable set of parents, who had the genius to engage ideas and solutions no one has tried in quite the same way, and to do so no matter the prevailing opinions or criticisms.

**Allan Rosenfield, MD**
DeLamar Professor and Dean
Mailman School of Public Health
Columbia University

**Malcolm Potts, MD, PhD**
Bixby Professor of Population
School of Public Health
University of California, Berkeley

# INTRODUCTION

*In Thailand, a condom is called a "Mechai." In the rest of the world, Mechai Viravaidya is affectionately referred to as the Condom King. Most people might object to having their name become synonymous with a condom. But Mechai Viravaidya is not like most people. He thoroughly relishes the sobriquet and wears his crown proudly. He has used this simple but most anatomically suggestive contraceptive device to start a social revolution, turning the staid and conventional family planning establishment on its head in the process; and now uses it as his banner in his tireless crusade against HIV/AIDS. First there were condom-blowing contests, then T-shirts with condom shrouded anthropomorphic penises. Next came condom key rings followed by a Cabbages and Condoms Restaurant, and now multicolored condom floral bouquets. When it comes to condoms, no one has been more creative than the Condom King.*

However, to equate Mechai with condoms or family planning, or population control is to underestimate the man — and fail to capture his essence. What Mechai Viravaidya is all about is social and economic development — his relentless pursuit to improve the well-being of the poor, to create opportunities for them, to give them the tools to lead a more fruitful, productive, and fulfilling life. Mechai developed his vision for helping Thailand's poor in the late 1960s while working as a young economist for Thailand's National Economic Development Board. In the intervening years he has maintained that vision and pursued it resolutely. His achievements in family planning and AIDS prevention are a means to an end — the alleviation of poverty and injustice for the people of Thailand. Although he has become an international celebrity renowned worldwide for his achievements, his objective in the year of 2000 is exactly the same as it was in the 1960s — to help the underprivileged people of Thailand live a better life. He is not interested in anything else.

His story starts with his parents and their influence during his formative years. As a young boy, he was sent to Australia to study. For the next 11 years he was a stranger in a strange land that eventually became his second home, learning to fend for himself in an unfamiliar environment. Upon returning to Thailand, he serendipitously became a celebrity recognized throughout the country; and a development economist in a government agency writing newspaper columns about Thailand's rural development. In his spare time, he became a radio announcer and well-known television actor.

Impatient with the slow pace of change in government, Mechai tried electoral politics. Following his unsuccessful foray into politics, he moved to Thailand's family planning association where he developed his witty but outrageous approach to family planning education, which offended the establishment but delighted the Thai people. Finding this environment too stifling, he founded his own organization to promote family planning. Now he could do things his way, however unorthodox.

The organization he founded, called the Population and Community Development Association (PDA), was the vehicle Mechai used to pursue his vision for development. In the next 25 years, PDA would implement 134 projects with funds from 70 donor agencies. The projects were diverse — from family planning, appropriate technology, and refugee relief to environmental protection, AIDS control, and business development. The methods were unconventional but always entertaining.

Mechai's work with PDA was interrupted by occasional excursions into public service. He held executive positions in state-owned companies and senior positions in government. He served on the Board of Directors of public and private companies. He even made a successful comeback in electoral politics. Blessed by a dynamic personality, infectious entrepreneurial spirit, effective public relations strategies full of humor and wit, and concern for the common man, Mechai left his mark wherever he went.

Mechai's journey from condoms to cabbages — from his roots in family planning and population management to his ultimate objective of poverty alleviation and improved livelihood for Thai people — has spanned 34 years. Along the way, he has been alternately labeled a visionary, an iconoclast, a reformer, and a crusader. He is all of these. He is also a regular guy from modest origins who, in his early years, distinguished himself more by his athletic abilities than any outstanding attributes that would signal his future success. This book will shed some light on both Mechais. On one hand he was the compassionate son of a mixed marriage, the insular Thai boy going off to explore the wide world of Australia, the student who was more interested in sports and socializing than studying. On the other hand he was the development economist impatient with the slow pace of government-led development who evolved into the family planning iconoclast, the social reformer, the anti-AIDS crusader, and visionary leader.

# ABBREVIATIONS

| | |
|---|---|
| AIDS | Acquired Immune Deficiency Syndrome |
| ATI | Appropriate Technology International |
| BBC | Bangkok Bank of Commerce |
| BKKBN | National Family Planning Coordination Board of Indonesia |
| BMA | Bangkok Metropolitan Authority |
| BOT | Bank of Thailand |
| CBATDS | Community Based Appropriate Technology Development Services |
| CBD | Community Based Distribution |
| CBERS | Community Based Emergency Relief Services |
| CBFPS | Community Based Family Planning Services |
| CBIRD | Community Based Integrated Rural Development |
| CIDA | Canadian International Development Agency |
| CLSA | Credit Lyonnais Securities Asia |
| CPK | Communist Party of Kampuchea |
| DTEC | Department for Technical and Economic Cooperation |
| ECOCEN | Economic Cooperation Center for Asia and the Pacific |
| FBCB | First Bangkok City Bank |
| FIDF | Financial Institution Development Fund |
| FPPC | Family Planning and Parasite Control Project |
| GGS | Geelong Grammar School |
| GNP | Gross National Product |
| GTZ | German Technical Cooperation |
| GVS | German Volunteer Service |
| HIV | Human Immunodeficiency Virus |
| ICRC | International Committee for the Red Cross |
| IDU | Injecting Drug User |
| IEC | Information, Education, and Communications |

| | |
|---|---|
| IMF | International Monetary Fund |
| IPAS | International Pregnancy Advisory Services |
| IPPF | International Planned Parenthood Federation |
| IUD | Intra-uterine Device |
| IVS | International Voluntary Services |
| JOICFP | Japanese Organization for International Cooperation in Family Planning |
| KTB | Krung Thai Bank |
| MCOT | Media Communications Organization of Thailand |
| MOF | Ministry of Finance |
| MOPH | Ministry of Public Health |
| MOTC | Ministry of Transport and Communications |
| MP | Member of Parliament |
| MWA | Metropolitan Waterworks Authority |
| NEDB | National Economic Development Board |
| NESDB | National Economic and Social Development Board |
| NGO | Non-Government Organization |
| NPKC | National Peacekeeping Council |
| NPL | Non-Performing Loans |
| PDA | Population and Community Development Association |
| PDC | Population and Development Company |
| PDF | Population and Development Foundation |
| PDI | Population and Development International |
| PEA | Provincial Electricity Authority |
| PPAT | Planned Parenthood Association of Thailand |
| PTT | Petroleum Authority of Thailand |
| PTT-EP | Petroleum Authority of Thailand – Exploration Production |
| PWA | Provincial Waterworks Authority |
| PWC | PricewaterhouseCoopers |
| RSSI | Rural Small Scale Industries |
| SAP | Social Action Party |
| SEATO | Southeast Asia Treaty Organization |
| SEED | Student Environmental Education and Demonstration Project |

| | |
|---|---|
| STD | Sexually Transmitted Disease |
| TAT | Tourist Authority of Thailand |
| TBIRD | Thai Business Initiatives for Rural Development |
| TDRI | Thai Development Research Institute |
| TFR | Total Fertility Rate |
| TOT | Telephone Organization of Thailand |
| UNHCR | United Nations High Commissioner for Refugees |
| USAID | United States Agency for International Development |
| USFDA | United States Food and Drug Administration |
| VOLAG | Voluntary Agencies |
| WHO | World Health Organization |

# 1

## THE CONVERGENCE OF EAST AND WEST

*As the curtain fell on the 19th century, the British Empire under Queen Victoria had reached the pinnacle of its influence and power. From its isolated eyrie in the British Isles, Great Britain controlled a colonial empire stretching from the Atlantic ocean eastward through Africa, Asia, and Oceania. Besides being the era's economic and military superpower, its culture and language had pervaded every region of the empire, with its educational institutions the envy of the world. Rudyard Kipling was not exaggerating when he said that "the sun never sets on the British Empire."*

In the northwestern corner of the British Isles, a young man named David Anderson Robertson had just finished his eighth year of schooling at the Wade Academy in Dundee, Scotland, in 1889 at the top of his class. His father, John Robertson, a skilled tradesman and iron molder, and his mother, Jessie Anderson Robertson, were enormously proud of their son's accomplishments. In the Scottish tradition, they believed that a good education was one of the highest goals in life. They were determined that their children would receive the education they never had. When David won a tuition-free scholarship to the prestigious Wade Academy, the educational aspirations they desired for their offspring were being fulfilled in their first son.

David, however, was followed in quick succession by four more children in the Robertson household.[1] Educating all of them would be an expensive proposition, a burden that John and Jessie could not shoulder on their own. When David graduated from Wade Academy, his further schooling would be prohibitively expensive. Being the oldest of the five Robertson children and already the recipient of a good basic education, David decided that he should be the one to sacrifice for his younger siblings. On his own initiative, David left school and went to work as a telegraph boy in the local Post Office. His wages were used to put his three younger brothers and a younger sister through school.

Although the job seemed menial, it gained for David a foothold in the Civil Service, a respectable career which provided opportunities for travel and advancement. Later, he moved to Edinburgh, also as a telegraph boy. At the turn of the century Edinburgh was a cosmopolitan city and a world famous seat of learning. The University of Edinburgh was renowned as one of the foremost educational institutions in the world. Students from all over Europe and the British Empire flocked to Edinburgh to obtain the education that would propel their advancement at home. For David Robertson, circumstances precluded his entrance to Edinburgh University. If ever he had children, David decided, he would make sure that entrance to Edinburgh University would not be beyond their grasp.

By 1905 David was well entrenched in the Civil Service, which offered a practical alternative to formal education. He studied the civil service courses diligently, passed all the examinations, and became an Officer of Customs and Excise. This assignment catapulted him into the regular civil service career path, with its attendant rights and privileges. One of these was travel. A civil service career was renowned for the itinerant lifestyle it imposed on its employees.

David's would be no exception. After several more years in Edinburgh, he moved to East Anglia on the mainland of England, his first posting far from his native Scotland. While in the county of Norfolk, he saw "a beautiful girl on a bicycle, wearing a long tartan skirt, cycling along a Norfolk country lane," as he would later describe his future wife, Mabel Emma Girling. He decided then and there that she was the girl he would marry, which he eventually did, in London in 1910.

Mabel Girling was 10 years his junior. She came from an agricultural family in East Anglia. Her father was a tenant farmer and her mother was a domestic helper on the Lord of the Manor's estate. Mabel was clever at school but, like her future husband, had to leave school at the age of 14 after finishing eight years of education. She became a pupil teacher and monitor in the Foulsham School and then moved to Swannington where she became Infant Mistress in the Infant School. It was while working at the latter that Mabel met and married David Robertson.

Their first child, Isabella Mackinnon Robertson, was born in 1911 in Tullamore, Ireland, (which was then still part of Great Britain), where David had been posted the previous year. Ella, as she was called, was named after her father's maternal grandmother, Isabella Mackinnon.[2] The year 1912 brought another new posting for David, this time back to Scotland where in Birnam a second daughter, christened Mabel Girling Robertson but nicknamed Peg, was born. In 1916 the Robertson family made another move, this time to Haddington, East Lothian, 18 miles from Edinburgh, where the last of David and Mabel's three daughters, Jessie Anderson Robertson, was born in 1922.

The constant relocations were difficult for the three girls. They were never in one place long enough to make lasting friendships, being uprooted at a moment's notice when their father's career demanded it. This difficulty, however, paled in comparison to their upbringing as the children of David Robertson. He was a dour, autocratic man of Victorian disposition with a dominating personality. His wife and daughters feared his wrath, which could erupt without provocation. He was particularly strict with his daughters, allowing them no male companionship or friends. Although on the surface the Robertson family was decidedly middle class with perhaps a slight bias upward, they lived in an atmosphere of continuous subliminal stress caused by outbursts of anger which bred anxieties in the girls.

Nevertheless, David was determined that his daughters would have access to the very best education possible. Scotland was a male-dominated society at that time, and females were discriminated against in education and employment. When women first began to enter the formal labor force in early twentieth century England, it was primarily in low paying, menial jobs that men didn't want and in vocations such as nursing and teaching which were considered the natural domain of females. It was only in 1918 that women received the right to vote, and then only if they were over 30. Higher education and the professions were still, for all intents and purposes, the exclusive realm of men. But David insisted that no limits would be placed upon the educational horizons of his daughters, regardless of the prevailing attitudes of the time. While living in Edinburgh in 1925, he used some remote family connections to gain acceptance for Ella and Peg (and Jessie in due course) to the prestigious Edinburgh Ladies College, one of the leading schools for women.[3] He now had his daughters on the track to Edinburgh University and the quality of education they deserved.

This opportunity was a boon to his eldest daughter, Ella. She was a bit like her father, domineering with her siblings and aggressive with her peers, but without his unpredictable temperament. While she could sometimes be curt and abrupt, she was a genuinely kind and loving person who had great regard for others. Ella was 14 when she entered Edinburgh Ladies College, where she distinguished herself academically from the day she arrived. She had a slight stammer precipitated by the constant anxiety of living with her father's erratic temperament, a stammer which she later outgrew. She was intelligent and outgoing, and went from fourth year immediately to the sixth, skipping the fifth because her teachers thought it would be unnecessary for her. She had aspirations to become a physician because "then I won't have to take English anymore." But deep down inside, it was Ella's humanitarian proclivities that steered her toward medicine: as a doctor she thought she could help other people.

It was a happy day in the Robertson household when Ella was accepted into Edinburgh University in 1929 to study medicine. Major universities in Europe and the United States had just recently begun admitting women for advanced study in the professions. Now Ella would be studying at one of the most prestigious schools of medicine in the world.

On the other side of the world, in 1921 young Samak Viravaidya was preparing to depart Bangkok on the greatest adventure of his life. He had been given a King's Scholarship by King Vajiravudh to pursue advanced studies in Great Britain. As he sailed out of Siam on the month-long journey to England, he was leaving for the great unknown. Despite all the stories he had heard about Europe, he could not imagine life in a modern society surrounded by westerners, with their alien customs and unfamiliar foods. Furthermore, he was not sure when he would be returning to his country. But he was fully aware of the great privilege that had been bestowed upon him by receiving a King's Scholarship. When the time came and his studies abroad were completed, he would definitely be coming home to Siam to help the people.

Born in 1907, Samak was the first generation in Siam to grow up with routine exposure to western culture and society. His father, Huat, descended from a family in southern China that had migrated to Samut Songkhram in Siam in the 19th century to escape political upheavals plaguing China. Being a commoner, Huat had no surname, the custom in Siam at that time. Through sheer diligence and innate intelligence, Huat had risen from his humble origins to gain acceptance into Siam's first school for western medical training at Siriraj Hospital, where he excelled both academically and clinically.

After his graduation from medical school in 1898, Huat entered the Army Medical Corps, where he established a reputation as one of the Army's most qualified and astute practitioners of western medicine. At that time, western medicine and traditional medicine coexisted equally in Siam, with training programs available in both disciplines. Western medicine was in its ascendancy, however, so Huat's skills as a clinician and healer propelled him rapidly through the ranks. By 1904 he had become the Assistant Director of the Army Medical Corps; by 1909 he had become the Director. Then, in 1914, having achieved the rank of Colonel and having already been invested into the Civil Service hierarchy as Phraya Damrong Paetayakhun,[4] he became the Commander of the Army Medical Corps.

It was in his capacity as Commander of the Army Medical Corps that Colonel Phraya Damrong's name was presented to King Vajiravudh, who wanted to find a Siamese physician skilled in western medicine to serve as the personal physician to his mother, Queen Saovabha Pongsri. When King Vajiravudh ascended to the throne of the Kingdom of Siam as King Rama VI in 1910,[5] the country was emerging from the most vigorous period of reform and modernization in its history. During the reign of his predecessor, King Chulalongkorn (1868-1910), Siam not only weathered the surging colonial ambitions of the European powers both intact and independent, it also nurtured the institutional trappings of a modern nation state. For the first time in Siam's history, a state bureaucracy with cabinet style government centered in Bangkok exerted direct administrative control over the provinces. Modern tax, labor, and judicial codes were created to regulate the burgeoning public and commercial sectors. A military service patterned along western lines was developed to safeguard national security. A national rail network united the country. Siam's borders were recognized by its neighbors and the European colonial powers. Having assumed its present shape on the map, Siam was ready to transform itself into a modern nation.

In order to survive the political maelstrom of colonial Southeast Asia in the early 20th century, King Chulalongkorn recognized the need for educated administrators familiar with western institutions and culture. He urged his subjects to embrace education. The elite segments of Siamese society responded enthusiastically. Members of the Royal Family were the first to travel abroad and receive western education. Upon returning to Siam, they gravitated to the most influential positions in the bureaucracy by virtue of their superior education and skills. Even commoners among the elite were exposed to the outside world and culture, though not as extensively as the Royal Family. For the indigenous Siamese, a nationwide system of modern schools was built to provide compulsory primary education.

King Vajiravudh was well situated to advance his father's legacy of nation building. Having been designated Crown Prince by King Chulalongkorn in 1895, he had fifteen years to prepare for his role as King. Educated at Oxford with military training from Sandhurst, he was at the vanguard of the urbane elite educated abroad during King Chulalongkorn's reign. More the artist and intellectual than politician, he was unaccustomed to dealing with the entourage of royalty holding influential positions in his father's government. Gradually, he replaced them with talented and qualified commoners, who were promoted to prominent positions in his government.

When Phraya Damrong's credentials were presented to King Vajiravudh, the King was in no way deterred by his background as a commoner. First and foremost, he wanted a physician who was a "Siamese citizen who would have the utmost loyalty to the Royal Family. Among other things, the person would be required to have had experience and have a modern outlook of the world around him. He would have to be virtuous, possess good health and stamina, and have a satisfactory family life."[6] Prince Chirapravat, the Commandant of the Army Educational Institute who had recommended Phraya Damrong to the King, described him as an eminently qualified physician who had served the Prince for many years, had traveled to Europe twice in service to the Prince, and was a citizen of Siam whom he held in the highest regard.

In April 1917, the King promoted Colonel Phraya Damrong to the rank of Major General and appointed him in quick succession to the positions of Army Surgeon General and Personal Physician to the Queen Mother. There were many Personal Royal Physicians of various nationalities in service to the throne. As a rule, foreign doctors had previously been selected as Personal Physicians to the Queen Mother, who needed almost constant medical attention as her health deteriorated toward the end of her life. In fact, Phraya Damrong replaced Phraya Prasertsart Damrong, one Dr. E. Ryder, a British doctor who had passed away while serving as the Queen Mother's personal physician. As the first Siamese doctor appointed to this position, Phraya Damrong was given final authority in all medical matters involving the Queen Mother and could overrule decisions by any foreign doctor.

Phraya Damrong was indefatigable in his service to the Queen Mother. Morning, noon, and night, he could be seen in attendance at Her Majesty's bedside. When she traveled in town or up-country, he would be in her entourage. When the Queen was indisposed, his duty toward the Queen was always foremost in his mind, even to the detriment of his own health. King Vajiravudh was grateful to Phraya Damrong for the care and attention given to his mother. The King granted him many audiences to discuss the Queen Mother's health. In one of these it was recorded that the King advised Dr. Damrong "to be always aware that I have assigned you to be always with my mother, as she is my most valued treasure. I believe that a Siamese doctor will have unswerving loyalty to a member of the Royal Family over and above that which could be shown by foreign doctors. I admonish you to remember always that I have given you responsibility and authority to look after my mother. If other doctors prescribe any medicine or any course of medical action, they must have your approval, whether they be Siamese or foreign doctors."[7]

While still in the Army Medical Corps, Phraya Damrong's talents as a physician had been recognized by the Royal Family. Members of the Royal Family and their entourage regularly sought care at Phraya Damrong's home, and were sometimes "admitted" there if their illnesses required extended care. In 1911 a young orphan girl named Dek Ying Sangwalya,[8] who was being educated in the Dusit Palace under the sponsorship of Princess Valaya Alongkorn, was brought to Phraya Damrong to have a sewing needle removed from her hand.[9] She stayed at Phraya Damrong's home until he could surgically remove the needle and her hand healed. After her convalescence, she stayed on to live with Phraya Damrong and his wife, Khunying Sanguan,[10] and attended Satri Vitthaya School with their two eldest daughters, Chamnong and Utumporn. At Phraya Damrong's suggestion, Dek Ying Sangwalya attended nursing school at the age of 13, the youngest student in her class. Upon graduation, she worked at Siriraj Hospital for two years before receiving a scholarship to study nursing in the United States. While there, she and the other students from Siam who had made the journey to America with her, were met and taken care of by Prince Mahidol of Songkla, a half brother of King Rama VI. Royal permission was later granted for the Prince to marry Sangwalya, who subsequently became Her Royal Highness Srinagarinda, Princess Mother to King Rama VIII and to H.M. King Bhumibol Adulyadej of the present reign.

In recognition of Phraya Damrong's loyalty to the Royal Family and contributions to the country, King Vajiravudh gave him property in the Samsen section of Bangkok, had a home built in the classical style of the early 20th century, and presented him with an autographed photograph as a housewarming present. The King also gave him the surname "Viravaidya", which literally meant "brave doctor". Last names were just coming into fashion at this time in Siam. Having one was considered a sign of status. Having a last name conferred by the King of Siam was the ultimate honor. The family received a further honor when Queen Mother Saovabha Pongsri took their second daughter, Utumporn, into the palace to supervise her upbringing and education.

Due to the influence of both King Chulalongkorn and King Vajiravudh, education in general, and education abroad in particular, had become essential for advancement in Siamese society. While the Royal Family had been the first group to educate its offspring abroad, by 1910 common families possessing the resources were also sending their children for education abroad. Phraya Damrong and Khunying Sanguan wanted desperately to send their children overseas for their education, but like many people in their circumstances, they lacked the means to pay for it. Aware of these obstacles and anxious to find qualified people outside of the Royal Family circle, King Vajiravudh created a fellowship program called the "King's Scholars" which made scholarships available to common people as well as the Royal Family. The Viravaidya family was overwhelmed with joy and pride when their young son, Samak, received a King's Scholarship to study in England in 1921.[11] His ultimate objective was to study medicine at Edinburgh University in Scotland. At the time, Great Britain was considered to have the best educational institutions in the world and was the destination of choice for all Siamese students studying abroad. Edinburgh University was universally acclaimed as having the best medical school in Great Britain. Studying there would be a great opportunity for Samak.

As the youngest child in a family with two older sisters, Samak Viravaidya had been pampered as a child. With his pleasant disposition, courteous manners, and amiable personality, it was difficult for his sisters to do otherwise. As was natural for a child of his age, Samak emulated members of the aristocracy and the bureaucratic elite who frequented Phraya Damrong's clinic at the Viravaidya home. Many of them dressed in cosmopolitan clothing, spoke European languages, and lived in western-style houses with indoor plumbing. Sometimes, while attending the Mahatlek Luang School[12] young Samak could be seen dressed in knickers and a bowler hat. Nevertheless, Samak was an exemplary student with excellent grades. Influenced by his father, he became interested in medicine and wanted to study abroad.

During family trips through the countryside outside of Bangkok, Samak noticed that there was another Siam where people didn't dress in western clothes and live in splendid houses. In this second Siam, the people dwelled in crude structures without plumbing and practised subsistence agriculture as their ancestors had done for centuries before. They had little or no access to physicians like Phraya Damrong, and had even fewer opportunities to make their lives better. This paradox puzzled Samak. How could such wealth and opulence coexist with such poverty and deprivation? He could only think that if this situation was to improve, it would require people like himself, with access to better education, to bring about change. This made him more determined than ever to obtain higher education abroad.

When the opportunity came to study in England, Samak was only 14 years old. Sadly, his father was not there to share this proud occasion. During Phraya Damrong's service to the Queen Mother, a cholera epidemic had swept through Bangkok. As the senior physician within the Palace, Phraya Damrong's services were in great demand, as many members of the Royal entourage became sick and succumbed to this virulent disease. Commoners employed in the outer compound of the Palace were also being treated by Phraya Damrong. There was a custom at this time that no commoner should be allowed to die in the Palace. While examining his patients, he found one man, a commoner whose demise was imminent. Acting instinctively, Phraya Damrong picked up the man himself and whisked him outside the Palace compound, where the man expired shortly thereafter. In the process, Phraya Damrong had become infected with cholera, a highly contagious disease, and died shortly thereafter. He was 41 years old when he passed away.

Samak was devastated by his father's death. Phraya Damrong had been his role model and inspiration, the person who stimulated his interest in medicine and compassion for his fellow man. As he was preparing to depart on the greatest opportunity and adventure of his life, Samak's heart was heavy with sadness and longing for his father.

When Samak Viravaidya arrived at Edinburgh University to start his first year of medical school in 1929, he was overwhelmed by the school's physical presence and the history literally dripping from the ubiquitous spires crowning its stately buildings. Some of the greatest intellects of the western world had graduated from this university, and many of the foremost physicians of the time had done their training at the medical school. But the road to Edinburgh University had not been an easy one for Samak. When he arrived in England in 1921, he couldn't speak a word of English. Along with other students from Siam, he went to London first, where he met with members of the Siamese community and purchased clothing and items of necessity. Arrangements were made for him to live with a British family to learn English and to acclimate himself to life in the western world, which he did for the next eight years.[13] He had seen "farang"[14] before but now they were everywhere. The people lived in apartments and townhouses and worked in tall office buildings. The cities were a jungle of concrete — the streets, the sidewalks, the homes, the buildings — so different from verdant and tropical Bangkok. What trees remained were ornamental, placed strategically to break the monotony of the seemingly endless concrete.

For the Siamese palate, the food was tasteless. The pungent spices and subtle fragrances of Siamese food were missing from the bland meats and vegetables that were boiled or broiled until unrecognizable. And the potatoes! At every meal, without failure, there were potatoes — roasted, broiled, boiled, fried, mashed, scalloped, sauted, or souffled. No matter how they were prepared, they were still a poor substitute for rice, the Siamese staple of choice, which was virtually non-existent in Great Britain at the time.

Most of all, there was the climate. Try as he may, Samak disliked the cold and damp environment of temperate Britain, with its dreary skies and tempestuous oceans. Once the gray skies and rain descended in October, it seemed to Samak that the sun wouldn't shine for eight months. Living in a foreign country, speaking a new language, surrounded by strange-looking people who lived and worked in concrete fortresses, enduring horrendous weather — Samak began to wonder whether he had made the right decision to come to Great Britain to study. Maybe he should have stayed in balmy Bangkok with its tropical blue skies and coconut tree-lined beaches.

Nonetheless, like other students from Siam who came before him, Samak overcame these initial misgivings and eventually adapted to his new environment. The courteous and amiable boy from Siam had grown into a kind and affable man universally liked by his family, friends, and acquaintances in Great Britain. Soon Samak was speaking English well and fraternizing with the British people, whom he found polite and friendly beneath their rigid exteriors. He even came to like potatoes and boiled beef, though he would spice them up with chili and fish sauce if the opportunity arose. Eventually, his English language skills were adequate to complete his matriculations and he gained entrance into Medical School at Edinburgh University in 1929 at the age of 22.

If one envisions the lecture halls in the great nineteenth century universities of Europe, the image that comes to mind is steeply terraced, semicircular amphitheaters descending precipitously and converging on a small lectern where the omniscient professor expounded upon the great issues of the time. Edinburgh University matched the stereotype perfectly. There were nearly 100 students crammed into these lecture halls with Samak in his first year medical class. As he gazed across the lecture hall, he could see that most of his classmates originated from Scotland and Great Britain, but there were some from other European countries and several from British colonies in Asia and Africa. Samak immediately befriended two of these, Zan from Burma and Bokwe from the Gold Coast of East Africa (now Ghana). There were very few women in the class, but one of them, who seemed extraordinarily young to be in medical school, caught his attention. She was small and slim, with her brown hair cut stylishly short and pulled back demurely from her face. Although she was young, she seemed independent of character and determined in her studies. As he randomly surveyed his classmates, Samak Viravaidya made eye contact with Ella Robertson, and she with him. He decided he would like to meet her.

This would not be so easy, however. Color prejudice was rampant in Scotland, as it was in all of Britain at the time, and friendships between Asian men and western women were discouraged. All Asians of oriental descent were classified as "Chinese". In colonial Asia and Africa, the indigenous people were expected to step off the pavement when passing a white person on the street, such was the colonial arrogance that bred this racial discrimination in the British Empire. While the Mother Country was slightly more sophisticated, Asians were still treated with subtle condescension and perhaps covert disdain in Great Britain in the 1920s and 1930s. For her part, Ella also wanted to meet Samak. Beyond the superficial physical attraction, she was struck by his kindness, gentleness, and boundless congeniality. However, it was just "not done" for a girl to make the first move in a friendship with a male in the post-Victorian era. If Ella and Samak were to meet, he would have to make the first move.

Samak was quite an accomplished tennis player, and with his friends, frequented the public courts of Edinburgh in search of competition. Through his tennis network, he learned that Ella sometimes played tennis with her sister Peg at a local court near to her home. One day he conveniently arranged to turn up at the same time as Ella, and as luck would have it, got to play on the court adjacent to hers with his friend Zan. She and Peg couldn't help but notice how good they were, but were puzzled when errant balls from these skilled players kept straying on to their court. Each time, Samak came over to retrieve the ball, exchanging pleasantries with the two girls. Then, the stray balls seemed to confine themselves to Ella's side of the court. As the retrievals became more frequent, the pleasantries were extended a bit longer. By the end of the match, Samak's intentions had been made subtly clear. As Ella and Peg left the court, Peg was dispatched to arrange a meeting between Samak and Ella, which was achieved without incident. Ella immediately befriended Samak and the other foreign students attending medical school at Edinburgh University. And so began Samak Viravaidya's courtship with Isabella Mackinnon Robertson, which would culminate in their marriage in 1937. Their courtship was not easy nor without incident, with two major impediments. The first was the "color bar" prevailing in post-war Britain. When he arrived in Scotland, Samak had been classified as Chinese by the indiscriminate racial classification system used to categorize all non-white persons in Great Britain. The rank and file frowned upon relationships between Chinese men and Caucasian women. When Ella and Samak ventured out in public together, there were the inevitable stares and turned heads. Samak was concerned about Ella being seen with him, but Ella was not. In fact, she couldn't care less what others thought or what reactions her friendship with Samak provoked. She was a liberated woman years before the term became fashionable, contemptuous of traditional preconceptions of roles and expectations for women, and offended by racial stereotypes and prejudices which treated people as anything less than equals. After a while, Ella and Samak were oblivious to the rude glances, the snide comments, the whispered insults. They simply disregarded them.

The second impediment, equally ominous, was David Anderson Robertson. Ella's father was protective of his daughters, suspicious about any contact with males, much less with an Asian man. With his mercurial temper, it was not difficult to predict his hostile reaction to Ella's relationship with Samak. Fortunately, David's work took him away from home for long periods just as Ella entered medical school. And where David was conventional and xenophobic, his wife Mabel was more enlightened. She was kind, outgoing, full of charm, and sensitive to her daughters' social needs. While her husband was away, she welcomed Ella's foreign friends, including Samak, into the Robertson home.

Music was the mainstay of these gatherings. David Robertson had purchased a gramophone, quite a luxury in those days, so his family could listen to classical music. Instead, Ella and her friends found the latest hits from Broadway musicals and played them on the gramophone, something her father would consider sacrilegious had he known. The girls wore long-waisted dresses with short skirts, long beads, and the short hairdos that distinguished the twenties. The men, dressed neatly in casual suits, brought musical instruments and played around the Robertson family piano. There was singing and dancing — the Charleston, the Fox Trot, even the Tango. These "at homes", as they eventually became known, were quite popular at the Robertson's. Even neighbors started to attend. For a while, Mabel and her daughters were even able to have fun, something unheard of in the Robertson household. Except when David Robertson came home on leave. Then the "at homes" were suspended and the house returned to its usual dour state. If David ever learned about the gala festivities being held in his home during his absence, there would be hell to pay. But Mabel, Ella, and her sisters felt that what he did not know, he could not condemn.

During this period, Ella and Samak's relationship deepened. Being diligent and conscientious, Ella passed all her exams and graduated as Dr. Ella Mackinnon Robertson in 1933. After graduation, she spent 3 years in different hospitals practising medicine, gaining experience, making some money, but always staying in touch with Samak. For Samak, the road to graduation was more circuitous. First, he had to re-sit several of his exams, which delayed his graduation. Then, on June 24, 1932 a small group of middle level officials carried out a coup d'état in Bangkok which overthrew the absolute monarchy that had ruled Siam for a millennium. King Prajadhipok (Rama VII), who succeeded King Vajiravudh in 1925, quickly acceded to the demands of the coup plotters, and a constitutional monarchy was established to rule Siam on June 27, 1932.

The events of June 1932 had both political and practical significance for Samak. As the son of Phraya Damrong, he had grown up under the influence of a royal family with absolute power. With so many years of benevolent absolute monarchy, it was difficult for him to conceive how Siam could function without royal governance. However, the coup would have immediate practical ramifications for him. In the aftermath of the coup, some of the king's personal prerogatives were rescinded. Among these was funding for the King's Scholars, which was considered extravagant at a time of severe budgetary constraints at home. Accordingly, Samak lost his King's Scholarship and had to pay for his own schooling. His family helped some, but there was still a deficit that Samak had to finance himself. As a result, he was not able to finish medical school until 1936.

Ella's unwavering support for Samak was critical during these years. Although she and Samak were separated, her attachment for him never vacillated. Then, in 1937, they met for a holiday in Southport, a popular beach resort about 20 miles north of Liverpool serving the industrial area of Lancashire. The Robertson family had moved there in 1932. Ella had stayed in Edinburgh to finish her studies, but was now back with the family for a short vacation. Samak came to Southport[15] and stayed at the

Crown Hotel about 10 minutes walk from the Robertson home, the more convenient from which to meet Ella. All of this was taking place without the knowledge of Ella's father, of course, who would have vehemently disapproved. It was here that they made final plans to marry.

In April 1937 Samak Viravaidya married Ella Robertson in London, first at the Registry Office and then at the Siamese Legation[16] to Great Britain. Their plan was to return to Siam to live and raise their family. Samak would go first, as a ship's doctor to pay his fare, then Ella would follow several months later. She bade him farewell at a London station, then went back to Southport to tell her family.

Ella's mother and sisters were thrilled at the news of Ella's marriage to Samak. They knew Samak for the kind, gentle, and considerate man that he was, and knew he would make a good husband for Ella. Telling her father would be another thing.

When he heard that Ella was already married, to a Siamese gentleman no less, and would be leaving to join him shortly in Siam, he was furious. He remonstrated against the marriage, against Samak, against the conspiracy that had allowed this romance to take place under his nose without his knowledge. He tried, in vain, to persuade her not to go to Siam. But Ella was strong willed like her father. She was now 26 and would make the decisions affecting her life herself, and nothing her father said or did could dissuade her. Not to be outdone, her father threatened to disown her if she left. But Ella was firm in her resolve and eventually prevailed.

As the day for Ella's departure approached, her mother felt a particular sadness. Mabel had taken a considerable risk to open her home to Ella's friends while allowing Ella to see Samak during their "at homes" back in Edinburgh. In the process, she had grown to appreciate the vitality in her first daughter. Ella was clearly a maverick for her time, a woman who refused to be constrained by real or imaginary boundaries that either her father or society might want to place upon her. Just by entertaining a courtship with a "Chinese" man, she was challenging the norms society expected of her. Now she had married him and would travel to the other side of the world to be with him, to a place which most people in Edinburgh or Southport or even London didn't even know existed. When Ella boarded the boat, which would take her first to France and then on to Siam, her mother knew that she would probably never see this unique and spirited girl again, so rare was a trip to Siam in those days. As events transpired, she never did.

*Mechai's paternal great-grandfather, Capt. Choon, a captain in the Merchant Marine of Siam*

*Phraya Damrong and Khunying Sanguan, Mechai's paternal grandparent*

*Jessie Anderson Robertson,*
*Mechai's maternal great-grandmother*

*John Robertson,*
*Mechai's maternal great-grandfather*

*David Anderson Robertson,*
*Mechai's maternal grandfather*

*Mabel Emma Girling,*
*Mechai's maternal grandmother*

*Dr. Samak Viravaidya upon graduation from medical school, 1936*

*David Robertson with wife Mabel (right) and daughter Jessie (center)*

*Dr. Ella Mackinnon Robertson upon graduation from medical school, 1933*

*Dr. Ella and Dr. Samak in Scotland, 1936*

*Dr. Ella and Dr. Samak circa 1929*

*A student gathering at an "at home" at the Robertson residence. Dr. Samak is standing (far left) and Dr. Ella is third from left*

## NOTES:

1 The four ensuing children in the Robertson family were Andrew, Isabella, John, and Tom. Andrew and Isabella went on to Moray Teacher's Training College in Edinburgh; John attended the Herriot School for Boys and then went on to receive a B.Sc. and MA degree from Edinburgh University; Tom, the youngest, died of influenza in the 1919 epidemic at the end of the First World War. Except for John, David Robertson was instrumental in providing financial support for the education of all his siblings. Being quite bright, John had his Edinburgh education paid for by bursaries (tuition, room, and board) and scholarships for his tuition.

2 Isabella Mackinnon was the wife of David Anderson and the mother of Jessie Anderson, who was David Robertson's mother.

3 David Robertson's father was a cousin to the Scot's poet, John Logie Robertson, who had taught English at the Edinburgh Ladies College. The headmistress had a soft spot in her heart for the poet, which David used to his advantage to gain acceptance for his three daughters into the school despite long waiting lists. The school is now known as the Mary Erskine School and celebrated its tercentenary in 1994.

4 There are six honorary, non-hereditary civil service hierarchical titles for commoners, both Thai and foreign, which can be given by the King. In ascending order, these are 1)Khun, 2) Luang, 3) Phra, 4) Phraya, 5) Chao Phraya, and 6) Somdej Chao Phraya. The term "Phraya Damrong Paetayakhun" literally means "Damrong the most capable doctor". For purposes of accuracy, he should always be referred to using the full title, "Phraya Damrong Paetayakhun". For purposes of literary convenience, he will be referred to only as "Phraya Damrong" in the remainder of this book.

5 Thailand was known as Siam until 1938, when the name was changed to Thailand, meaning "land of the free".

6 This was the actual terms of reference for Phraya Damrong's appointment as personal physician to the Queen Mother.

7 From the writings of Nang Amorndarunrak Viravaidya (Utumporn Sundaravej), about her father Phraya Damrong Paetayakhun (Huat Viravaidya) from the Royal Archives.

8 The term "Dek Ying" is the Thai term used to designate a female child coming from a commoner background.

9 Dek Ying Sangwalya was washing a piece of needlework while a student at the Satri Vitthaya School when a needle that was carelessly left by another student near the water jar became embedded in her hand. She was immediately taken to Phraya Damrong's house at the Army Medical Corps near Chana Songkhram temple, where she stayed until Phraya Damrong could operate and remove the needle after three attempts.

10 Phraya Damrong's wife was invested with the Most Illustrious Order of Chulachomklao 4th Class in 1911, and she became entitled to add the honorific "Khunying" to her given name, Sanguan.

11 Samak was not the only, nor even the first, member of the Viravaidya family to receive a scholarship to study abroad. The elder daughter, Chamnong, had received a scholarship from Prince Mahidol of Songkla (who was the father of H.M. King Bhumibol Adulyadej, the present King of Thailand) to study nursing in Massachusetts before 1920.

12 It was the custom in Siam that every king would build a great temple to leave as his legacy. King Vajiravudh decided to build the Mahatlek Luang School, which would eventually come to be known as the Vajiravudh School, as his legacy instead of a temple. Attend-

ance at the Mahatlek Luang School was considered a great privilege, and many of the future leaders of Thailand would receive their elementary education there.

13 Between 1921 and 1929, Samak attended the Friends' School, Saffron Walden. He then went to Loughborough College to qualify for university. Both of these institutions are in England. He did not live in Scotland until he attended medical school.

14 The term "farang" literally derives from the Persian "Feringhi" meaning foreigner. It has been in use since the Ayutthaya period, when Pharsi Persians came to trade with Siam. In its modern usage, the word "farang" came to embody the diminutive and marginally pejorative connotation with which the Thai refer to all persons of western or Caucasian ancestry.

15 Because of the color bar which prevented free movement of non-Caucasians in Great Britain at this time, Siamese students had to get permission to go to any new place, ostensibly to protect them from exposure to "adverse attitudes", but actually to restrict their free association with white Britons. Southport was evidently acceptable, since Samak was able to go there without specific permission.

16 Although Siam had formal diplomatic ties with Great Britain since the reign of King Mongkut (Rama IV), it maintained a Siamese Legation in Great Britain, rather than an embassy, until after the Second World War, when the Siamese legations around the world were upgraded to embassies.

## 2

# INSTRUCTION AND DEMONSTRATION

*When Samak returned to Siam in 1937 as Dr. Samak Viravaidya, he could hardly recognize the country he had left behind. Profound changes had buffeted the country in the intervening 16 years. Not only was Siam now governed by a constitutional democracy, but an insidious militant nationalism was beginning to rear its head. The old order, where a courtly and benevolent monarch ruled the country, was gone for good. For the first time in over 150 years, there was no sitting King in Siam. With his fellow students from Siam studying in Great Britain, Samak had followed the momentous events overtaking his country from afar, discussed their impact, and debated the consequences for the country. Now he would be able to assess the situation first hand.*

The reign of King Vajiravudh ended in 1925 upon his premature death at age 44. He was succeeded by his youngest brother, King Prajadhipok (Rama VII), the 76th of King Chulalongkorn's 77 children and the last surviving son of Queen Saovabha Pongsri. Without the luxury of the extended apprenticeship enjoyed by King Vajiravudh, he was unprepared for the challenge that fate had suddenly cast upon him. Unfortunately, King Rama VII inherited the throne at a time when the Kingdom's finances were in disarray, a situation that was exacerbated when the Great Depression reached Siam in 1930.[1] Popular dissatisfaction with economic conditions among the educated elite and the slow pace of political reform, especially during the reign of King Vajiravudh, led King Rama VII to explore avenues for popular participation in government. By early 1932, he had even asked his advisors to draft a provisional constitution that would introduce some measure of representative government.

Events soon overtook the King's overtures toward participatory government. A small group of intellectuals, primarily educated in France and led by the lawyer Pridi Phanomyong and the soldier Phibunsongkhram had become imbued with socialism and popular democracy during their studies abroad. As students, they began discussing a plot to overthrow the absolute monarchy and upon their return began to put the plan into action. Their opportunity came in 1932. The financial dislocations caused by the Great Depression necessitated draconian budget cuts, layoffs of civil servants, salary reductions, tax increases, and currency devaluation. During this period, public perceptions of official indecisiveness and greedy public officials shattered the government's credibility. Taking advantage of the chaos, young radicals led by Pridi and Phibunsongkhram joined older moderates identified with General Phon Phahonyothin, forming a group called the "Instigators". On June 24, 1932, they launched a coup which toppled the monarchy.

In the interests of national unity and preservation of the Kingdom, and to guarantee safety for members of the Royal family taken hostage during the coup, King Prajadhipok acceded to the demands of the Instigators and returned to Bangkok as the Constitutional Monarch of Siam,[2] ending 150 consecutive years of absolute monarchy under the Royal House of Chakri.

Over the next five years, a semblance of representative government was established in fits and starts, interrupted by occasional coups. General Phon Phahonyothin emerged as the visible leader of the post-revolution government. But real power rested with Lieutenant Colonel Phibunsongkhram. In October 1933, a provincial army under Prince Boworadet marched on Bangkok and nearly toppled the government. Only a vigorous counterattack led by Lieutenant Colonel Phibunsongkhram thwarted the insurrection. With the government enjoying strong popular support during the crisis, Phibunsongkhram was hailed as a conquering hero.

As it would for the next half century, the military now exerted a dominant influence over the government. While the People's Party which engineered the 1932 revolution ostensibly governed the country, the military was in control. Military spending was increased dramatically, not only for the aggrandizement of the military but also to bolster Siam's armed forces in the face of rising militarism worldwide in the 1930s. As the western democracies withered in the face of fascist regimes in Germany, Italy, and Spain, the militarized ultra-nationalist states became a model for Siam. Close relations were forged with Japan, which was pursuing its extraterritorial ambitions in China, and was emerging as the dominant power in Asia. Authoritarian leaders like Hitler and Mussolini were glorified by the media, while western values and culture were vilified. Where Siam once reached out to embrace the values of the west under King Chulalongkorn, it now withdrew into a cocoon of nationalism and xenophobia. The brunt of this intolerance was directed toward the ethnic Chinese in Siam, but there was a clear anti-foreign and anti-Western sentiment in the policies and propaganda of the government.

Relations between King Prajadhipok and the new government were strained after the revolution, and deteriorated further. The King was unhappy with the direction government policy was taking, especially with its propensity for autocratic excess. For its part, the government suspected the King's complicity in the 1933 insurrection under Prince Boworadet. While in England for medical care in 1935, King Prajadhipok abdicated his throne without designating a successor. In his abdication letter, the King said he was willing to give up his powers to the people, but not to those who went against the will of the people. Invoking the Law of Succession promulgated by King Vajiravudh in 1924, the National Assembly sent a delegation to Switzerland to ask the ten-year-old Prince Ananda Mahidol, the son of Prince Mahidol and Princess Srinagarinda,[3] to reign as the eighth king of the Royal House of Chakri. The new King was studying in Switzerland, and would be represented by a Council of Regents for the next 11 years. Within three years, Siam had moved from an absolute monarchy to a constitutional monarchy, and now to the absence of royalty in the country for the first time in hundreds of years.

While these momentous political changes perplexed Samak, he had more practical considerations that required his attention when he arrived in Bangkok. His family was not aware that he was married, and Ella would be arriving within several months. His immediate concerns were to inform his mother, Khunying Sanguan, about his marriage, find acceptable lodgings, and begin practising medicine.

Ironically, the discrimination that Samak and Ella faced in Scotland would now have its mirror image in Siam. Coming from a good family with connections to the monarchy, it was naturally expected that Samak would marry a Thai woman of suitable rank. His mother and sisters, all strong and domineering women, were disappointed when they learned of his marriage to a farang. Samak was unwavering in the face of their opposition, just as Ella had been when confronting her father. His wife would be joining him in several months whether they liked it or not. If they chose to accept her, he would be glad to bring her to the house. If not, he would make alternate arrangements.

Dr. Ella Viravaidya arrived in Siam in 1937, about three months after Samak. After a short sojourn in France to attend the Paris Exhibition, she caught a steamer in Marseilles which wound its way through the Suez Canal and on to Southeast Asia. As she traveled south and then east, Ella's emotions and anxieties were similar to those Samak had experienced as he left Siam 16 years earlier. She was leaving the familiarity of home, family, friends, and culture — an environment she had never left in her 26 years — for the unknown awaiting her in exotic Siam. Her only frame of reference was the graphic descriptions Samak had painted for her, rich in their imagery of culture and royalty. Unlike Samak, however, who was part of a larger community of Siamese systematically seeking their education abroad, with an organized network waiting to receive them upon arrival to ease their transition to western life; there was no similar legacy of Scottish women who had made a comparable journey. Apart from Samak, Ella knew no one in Siam. She would be on her own, a stranger in a strange land left to fend for herself. But as she passed from the dreary climate and harsh landscapes of Europe into the azure waters of Asia, she noticed an appealing warmth and simplicity among the people. She felt an immediate attraction for Asian people which eased her fears somewhat.

But nothing calmed her more than the sight of Samak waiting at the pier as Ella disembarked from the ship in Bangkok. Reunited after a three-month hiatus, he whisked off his wife to meet his family at their home in Samsen. Her reception was cordial. Khunying Sanguan and Samak's sisters had resigned themselves to this new member of the family, but it would take time for them to adapt to having a foreigner in their midst. Ella and Samak moved right into the Samsen home, where Samak's older sisters, Chamnong and Utumporn and their families, were also living. In the intervening months prior to Ella's arrival, with Samak living at home with his mother and older sisters, he had fallen into a routine much as he had as a child. Once his wife arrived, she immediately recognized the need for independence from this sibling dominance, creating friction that hastened their eventual departure from the Samsen residence.

This was immediate and total immersion into Siamese life for Ella. She was now living with Samak's family in the Thai style, dealing with family responsibilities and their concomitant internecine politics. Then she had to learn the Thai language, with its seemingly unrecognizable sounds and indistinguishable tones. Simultaneously, Ella was exposed for the first time to Thai food, as alien to the European palate as the bland food in Great Britain had been to Samak.[4] Everything was hot, spicy hot. The assorted, delicate spices that characterize Thai food assaulted and awakened dormant taste buds dulled by a lifetime of boiled beef and potatoes. This food would take some getting used to, she acknowledged. And finally, there was the heat. Under the best of circumstances and for the most seasoned of travelers, Bangkok's climate is oppressively hot. For Ella, accustomed as she was to the cool weather of temperate Scotland, Bangkok's heat and humidity were overwhelming. Worst of all, it was inescapable. Modern conveniences like air conditioning were non-existent in the Bangkok of 1937. Frequent showers with tepid water were the only relief for the unbearable heat. Ironically, she would eventually learn to love Bangkok's climate, preferring it to the climate in her native Scotland.

Adjusting to life in Siam would not be easy for Ella, but she and Samak had decided to live and raise their children there. She was committed to staying in Siam, never entertained thoughts of returning to Scotland, and would make the sacrifices that were necessary. But there was one compromise she would never make. "I live in Thailand, my children and husband are Thai, but I am a Scotswoman. I am not Thai," she reiterated frequently. She would not pretend to be Thai. She was Ella MacKinnon Robertson (now Viravaidya), a Scotswoman, and would stick with what she was comfortable with, being herself. Just as adamantly, she insisted that her children be raised as Thai, be given Thai names, and develop a Thai identity. These two principles would consistently govern Ella's behavior throughout the fifty years she lived in Thailand.

But the sacrifices and compromises would not only be at a personal level. Discrimination and prejudice would once again stalk Ella and Samak, this time from an ultra-nationalist Thai society intolerant of westerners and decidedly opposed to mixed marriages. The xenophobic sentiments of the Phibunsongkhram government had a definite anti-Western bias. The rude glances and snide comments they had endured in Scotland would now be repeated in Siam. Discrimination spilled over into the work place. Upon his return to Siam, Samak was appointed as a lecturer at Chulalongkorn Hospital and Medical School. However, because he had a foreign wife, he was never given a permanent position on the faculty despite his exceptional qualifications, remaining only a temporary employee during his ten years at Chulalongkorn. Paradoxically, Ella became the Nurse's Doctor at Chulalongkorn, the first female physician there and a foreigner to boot. In spite of the nationalist excesses of the time, some western skills and values were still appreciated.[5]

Ella and Samak continued to live with Samak's family until 1940. By then, their first daughter, Sumalee, was born and they needed more space, both physically and personally. So they moved out to the country, to Soi Aree (now Soi 24) off Sukhumvit Road, where they rented a small cottage. Land was cheaper and space more plentiful around Soi Aree. There were other advantages to this remote location. The political climate in Siam was becoming increasingly intolerant, and an isolated sanctuary had certain distinct advantages for the Viravaidyas.

As the 1930s drew to a close, the situation in Siam, indeed in the world, became progressively bleaker. War in Europe seemed inevitable. Unanswered German aggression in Rhineland and Sudeten graphically demonstrated the weakness of the western democracies in the face of persistent German hegemony. In Asia, Japan was in the ascendancy. Having had its way in China, it was preparing to extend its Zone of Peace, Security, and Prosperity to Southeast Asia. In December 1938 General Phibunsongkhram became the Prime Minister of Siam, overtly assuming the mantle of power he had wielded behind the scenes during the previous five years. The Phibunsongkhram Government took an abrupt turn to the right. It vigorously encouraged Thai nationalism while deriding Chinese enterprise and western values. It strengthened the military, cultivated closer political and economic linkages with Japan, and mobilized the country for a war that seemed increasingly inescapable. In 1939 it changed the country's name from Siam to Thailand, ostensibly to signify Thai, as opposed to Chinese, supremacy in the country, but also to exhibit the linguistic connection Thais had with other Tai speaking peoples beyond their borders. In the process, the cult of Phibunsongkhram was erected. His pictures and slogans became ubiquitous, his accomplishments were glorified, his shortcomings minimized.

When war broke out in Europe, Thailand maintained official neutrality with a clear tilt toward Japan. As the German Panzer Divisions swept across Europe, the western colonial powers collapsed in their wake. The resulting vacuum created opportunities for Thailand, which Phibunsongkhram was quick to exploit for his nationalist and extraterritorial ambitions. In 1893, the

French had humiliated Siam by forcing it to cede all of Laos east of the Mekong River to French Indochina. This was a festering wound that Phibunsongkhram and the Thai people yearned to avenge. Their chance came in 1940. When France fell to Hitler's armies in June 1940, the puppet Vichy Government set up by the Germans to govern France was not able to consolidate control over France's colonial empire, especially in Asia where Japan now prevailed. Phibunsongkhram stepped up his irredentist claims for the territories seized earlier by the French. In November 1940, Thailand invaded Laos and Cambodia and occupied the disputed territories. Japan intervened and forced a settlement which ceded major portions of Laos and Cambodia back to Thailand.

The Thai war with French Indochina was immensely popular in Thailand. It restored national pride while redressing a territorial grievance smoldering in the national consciousness for 50 years. Even Ella and Samak, neither of whom was either a nationalist or Phibunsongkhram apologist, were swept up in the euphoria. When their second child, a son, was born on 17 January 1941, they named him Mechai, which literally means "victory", to commemorate Thailand's triumph in the French Indochina War.

If nothing else, Mechai Viravaidya was a typical and very ordinary Thai boy. Even though his mother was a Scotswoman, he was being raised as a Thai, had a distinctly Thai name,[6] spoke Thai, went to Thai schools, practised Thai customs, and learned the Buddhist religion[7] just like the other boys in his social circles. That was the way his mother wanted him raised. His passions were chicken raising, fun, and adventure. His father, Dr. Samak, raised chickens in their home on Soi 39 Sukhumvit, so it was natural for his son to adopt the avocation. Mechai fed the chickens, cleaned the pens, collected the eggs, then sold them. He had one major weakness, though, which boded poorly for any future aspirations he may have had as a businessman. He was averse to taking money from people, especially from people he knew. When it came time to collect money for the eggs, Mechai was too embarrassed to take his customer's money and ran away. Dr. Samak, who was paying for the upkeep of the chickens, quickly recognized that his son's weakness made the business unsustainable, and encouraged Mechai to stick to domestic chicken raising.[8]

An incident that occurred when the boy was seven left an exceptionally strong impression on him. Dr. Ella was taking her young son Mechai shopping in Bangkok's Chinatown. As they prepared to cross the street, she stretched out her hand, which Mechai grasped reflexively and led her across the street. He was a man, she told him (albeit only a seven-year-old one), and it was his responsibility to lead his mother as they ventured out on the streets. In fact, she was leading him, but she wanted to teach him leadership and independence. With their shopping finished, Dr. Ella and Mechai got into their car to return home. While stopped at a red light, an old Chinese women struggled across the road carrying a hap, a bamboo pole at the ends of which two baskets laden with fruit were precariously balanced. Slowed down by the sheer weight of her cargo, she was still in the middle of the road when the light turned green. The car next to them immediately began tooting its horn to rush the old woman along, impatient to be on their way. Dr. Ella was appalled by this insensitive behavior. "Mechai," she told her young son, "this is such a pity. This woman is old, she is poor, she is working so hard. These people have cars, they are rich, yet they still try to rush this woman along. If they had any decency, they would get out of their cars and help her rather than tooting their horns at her. If these people, who have been blessed with education and wealth, won't help this poor old lady, who will?" It was something he would never forget.

As Mechai got older, his predilection for fun and adventure eventually led him toward sports and athletics. When it came to sports, Mechai was a natural. He was ambidextrous and blessed with extraordinary hand-eye coordination. He was also a perfectionist. He would practise until he mastered the sport. Whether it was rugby, soccer, fives, squash, badminton, or tennis, he played them all. While he may have had no stomach for taking money when selling his eggs, he had the killer instinct when the chips were down in sports. As the clock ticked down in a close game, he wanted the ball and knew what to do when he got it.

Unfortunately, his obsession with perfection in sports did not extend to the classroom. The educational system in Thai schools in the 1940s stressed rote memorization. The teacher spoke dogmatically and the students regurgitated the lesson verbatim and unchallenged. Mechai just couldn't learn that way. From his earliest recollections, his mother had instructed him using reason rather than fear. If she either forbade or allowed him to do something, she always explained why and encouraged him to question her when he disagreed. Rather than say, "Mechai, you must eat your eggs," she would tell him "Mechai, you must eat your eggs because they will help you to grow big and strong." When she took him to buy shoes, she would always tell him to buy the best shoes because "it is better to spend more and get good quality shoes that are good for your feet and will last a long time. Cheap shoes may be inexpensive and look good, but they'll bugger up you feet." When Mechai got to school, he thought his teachers would instruct as Dr. Ella had done. Unfortunately, this wasn't the case, a situation that would plague Mechai throughout his scholastic life. He would never be an exceptional student within the traditional system of education.

Soon after Thailand's war with French Indochina, its diplomatic relations with the West deteriorated as its association with

Japan tightened. Phibunsongkhram was the most immediate beneficiary of the war. Already Prime Minister and Supreme Commander of the Armed Forces, he was promoted to the rank of Field Marshal, Admiral of the Thai Fleet, and Air Force General. Field Marshal Phibunsongkhram, as he became known, knew that war in the Pacific was inevitable. His dilemma was how to prevent Japanese colonization of Thailand. The western powers, with pressing security concerns of their own, could certainly provide no balance to the Japanese. Armed resistance, though nationalistically popular, was militarily impractical. On December 7, 1941 while the Japanese simultaneously attacked Pearl Harbor, Guam, Midway, the Aleutians, Hong Kong, and the Philippines, the Japanese also invaded Thailand at nine points. Realizing that armed resistance was suicidal, Field Marshal Phibunsongkhram negotiated a cease fire that allowed Japan passage through Thailand in return for Japan's recognition of Thailand's independence and territorial integrity.

In hindsight, this was the best deal Thailand could expect. Throughout the Second World War, it was the only country in all of East and Southeast Asia that remained fully independent and not cruelly occupied by the Japanese. Within the government and the military, there was also strong sympathy for the Japanese war aims, and a conviction that Japan could win the war. Thailand quickly concluded a military alliance with Japan and in January 1942, declared war on the United States and Great Britain. The Thai Minister in Washington, M.R. Seni Pramoj, refused to deliver the declaration of war and set about forming a Free Thai Movement.[9]

Whether Phibunsongkhram's actions were taken because of support for Japan or as the best way to protect the Thai people is difficult to ascertain. Although Japanese soldiers did occupy Thailand, they did not unduly interfere with the daily life of the people. They did, however, establish prisoner of war camps on Thai soil and, as the war progressed, interned westerners living in Thailand. This situation now placed Dr. Ella in grave danger. She resigned her position at Chulalongkorn Hospital and, with their children Sumalee and Mechai, she and Dr. Samak moved to a remote site on an acre of land on Soi 39 Sukhumvit Road far from the presence of the Japanese soldiers. She had to remain in hiding and move about surreptitiously until the end of the war for fear of being interned.

Dr. Samak, on the other hand, continued his work at Chulalongkorn Hospital and volunteered to provide medical care to British soldiers in the prisoner of war and internment camps. His familiarity with and acquired affinity for all things British combined with his innate propensity to alleviate suffering made Samak a natural for this service. In return, the British prisoners adored Samak, not only because of the competent medical care he provided them, but also for the solicitous and benevolent manner in which he insisted they all be treated while under his care, a welcome respite from the cruel and inhumane treatment British prisoners customarily received from their captors. Samak questioned them incessantly about affairs in England, especially in Southport where Ella's family now lived. Since the outbreak of hostilities in 1941, Ella had no news of her family nor they of her. She was desperate to learn of their safety, and to assuage their concerns about hers. Samak's patients were the only link they had with events in England. Fortuitously, several of his patients who either escaped or were repatriated, contacted Ella's family when they reached England with a message that she and Samak were fine, and to express their eternal gratitude for the care they had received from Samak. From 1941 until the cessation of hostilities in 1945, these surreptitious messages carried by prisoners of war were the only contact Ella had with her family back in England.[10]

When the war ended, Ella and Samak could finally get down to the business of raising their family in more or less normal conditions. Despite its association with the Axis powers during the war, Thailand was treated relatively fairly by the Allies in the post-war period,[11] allowing the government to focus its efforts on rebuilding the country. For their part, Ella and Samak built a "temporary house" on their land on Soi 39, which eventually became the Viravaidya compound, where they would live comfortably for the rest of their lives.

Mechai loved the life of a country boy. He could raise his chickens unfettered, swim in the "klongs" (canals) of rural Bangkok, shoot slingshots with his many friends (he was remembered as an ace shooter), and indulge his voracious appetite for sports in the wide open spaces around Soi 39.[12] Every summer and school holiday, however, his mother insisted that he spend a period of time living with Dr. Samak's older sister and her family in urban Bangkok. Because of her determination to raise her children as Thai, she wanted him to experience life with a Thai family where Thai was spoken all the time and Thai traditions and customs were strictly followed. This arrangement suited Mechai just fine. In addition to his country life, he also got to spend time living and playing with his cousins in downtown Bangkok, where they could explore food stalls, the trams, and the markets with their colorful vendors and shops — all the hustle and bustle of a city which was absent back in Soi 39. For him it was the best of both worlds.[13]

The demands of formal schooling eventually cramped Mechai's otherwise idyllic lifestyle. He started at the Wattana Pre-school in 1948, continued in the Bangkok Christian College until 2nd grade in 1950, then entered the prestigious Vajiravudh Boarding School in 1951, where Dr. Samak had also studied as a child. For Mechai, primary school education had one ultimate objective — preparing him for the day when he would take up his studies abroad. Beginning with his grandfather, Phraya Damrong Paetayakhun, the Viravaidyas had been going abroad. His father had spent 16 years studying abroad. For the children of Samak and Ella Viravaidya, studying abroad was a foregone conclusion. From his earliest recollections, Mechai just naturally assumed that, when the time came, he would leave his home and his family, travel to some unknown country, and continue his studies there as his father had done before him. The prospect neither frightened nor intimidated him. It was simply a family tradition.

Vajiravudh Boarding School was to prepare Mechai for the obstacles he would eventually face abroad. Although a mere 30-minute drive from his home, his parents could visit him only on weekends and he could only return home once a month. When they visited Mechai, Dr. Ella and Dr. Samak would bring him clean clothing and food — primarily eggs, milk, and canned beef. Mechai would immediately sell off the eggs and milk to his classmates and use the proceeds to buy sweets, something his parents never provided. He was ten years old when he entered Vajiravudh. If boarding school would make him homesick, he would experience it there first.

Mechai thoroughly enjoyed his time at boarding school, the freedom it afforded him, the camaraderie his classmates provided and, most of all, the extensive opportunities to engage in sports. At Vajiravudh Mechai was exposed to organized, competitive sports for the first time and thrived. Now he had coaches who could teach him the rules and feed his desire for perfection. Mechai played rugby, fives, tennis, and squash at Vajiravudh and excelled at all of them. By the time he left Vajiravudh at age 13, he was an accomplished athlete.

Academics, on the other hand, was a different story. Vajiravudh's traditional, authoritarian teaching methods didn't suit Mechai. Consequently, he viewed the classroom purely as an adjunct to the athletic field, the place he would go when he was not playing sports. Not surprisingly, his academic record there was undistinguished. If a subject appealed to him, he did well. If it didn't, the results could be quite different. Each term Vajiravudh gave awards to the student from each class who excelled in each subject. Except for English, Mechai was never in the running for any of these awards. Because his mother was Scottish and spoke English with him in the home, his classmates expected him to at least receive the award for excellence in English. And every term, when the award was announced, another student would receive it. Then, in his final term at Vajiravudh, the award for Excellence in English was awarded to Mechai Viravaidya — because the top student was sick and could not sit the exam!

But during his childhood, the real learning for Mechai would take place in the home, with Dr. Ella and Dr. Samak as the teachers. Dr. Ella would use reason to instruct him. Dr. Samak would demonstrate. When reasoned instruction was followed by demonstration, as his parents did, learning came easy to Mechai. Together, they would have the greatest impact on his personality and values.

Dr. Ella was his moral compass. From her Mechai developed his social conscience and learned to care about other people, especially the less fortunate, regardless of race. After the war, she became a very prominent and respected pillar of the expatriate community in Bangkok, especially among British women who had married Thai men. But she adamantly refused to join the British Club in Bangkok despite numerous invitations because it withheld membership from the Indian Ambassador. She would have nothing to do with an organization that discriminated by race.

She also imbued her son with the importance of honesty and integrity. For her, honesty came from inside oneself. "You are not wrong only if other people catch you out," she intoned. "You must know yourself when you are wrong. Honesty starts from inside. You need no evidence from the outside." One event really impressed this teaching on Mechai. After the war, when Dr. Samak had become Director of the Thai Tobacco Monopoly Hospital,[14] he sent his private jeep to the shop that repaired the hospital's vehicles. When the jeep was returned, Dr. Ella was suspicious when no payment was requested.

"How much did the repair cost?" she asked Samak.

"It was done for free," he replied. Dr. Ella was furious.

"This cannot be free. They are repairing it for free as a favor to you. This may look like an innocent gift, but it should not be so. You can be accused of corruption for this. Either you pay them the fair market price for those repairs, or you cancel all your repair contracts with that company immediately." Dr. Samak paid them straight away; and young Mechai learned a lesson he would never forget.

She also ingrained in Mechai the importance of modesty and principle. Dr. Ella never praised her children to others, and loathed it when others extolled their children's virtues publicly. For Dr. Ella, actions spoke louder than words. When she opened her own private medical practice after the birth of her third child, Sunya, she refused to sell drugs directly from her clinic, as was the custom among physicians in Thailand at the time, recognizing it for the conflict of interest it was. "I am a doctor," she said. "If I sell drugs, it will affect the way I treat my patients." Instead, she referred her patients with a prescription to a drug store so that she would not be involved in that monetary transaction. For Dr. Ella, it was a matter of principle.

Where Dr. Ella instructed Mechai in the meaning of a social conscience, Dr. Samak demonstrated and personified the values she was trying to inculcate in her son. He labored tirelessly to alleviate the suffering of the British prisoners of war and internees. When he opened his private practice, patients who were not able to pay were treated free. He was always caring and solicitous toward his patients; and considerate and understanding with his friends, his acquaintances, and especially his children.

An incident from Mechai's childhood illustrates Dr. Samak's approach toward raising and educating his son. At the tender age of eight, Mechai began to develop an innocent interest in the anatomy of the opposite sex. He was particularly interested in the female breast, and wanted to see one first hand. A young and curvaceous nursemaid employed to care for his younger brother, Sunya, seemed a likely candidate to satisfy Mechai's curiosity. She would bathe every day in the secluded area behind the house — a most auspicious opportunity, he thought, to observe her breasts. Following several reconnaissance missions to the bathing area, Mechai found a concealed perch atop an adjacent tree that would afford him an unhindered view through the window and into the bathroom. One day, as the maid entered for her daily bath, Mechai climbed up the tree to have a peek at her breasts. Unfortunately, he was quickly noticed, not only by the maid but by other household staff as well. Shrieks and screams engulfed the compound. Mechai was quickly apprehended by the maids for his transgression, roundly reprimanded, and detained in his room. There would be hell to pay, he was told, when his parents came home and were informed of his malfeasance.

Mechai was frightened and disoriented. What seemed to him like an innocent adventure had gone wildly out of control. When his parents returned from work and were informed of the day's events, Dr. Samak immediately went to see his son. Mechai was surprised when his father calmly queried him about what had happened.

"I was just curious to see what a woman's breasts looked like," Mechai replied innocently. "Climbing that tree and watching the maid bathe seemed like the best way for me to do that."

"Wait here for a minute," his father replied. "I think I can help you." Several minutes later, Dr. Samak returned with a Gray's Atlas of Anatomy from his medical school days, where every part of the human anatomy was graphically and colorfully illustrated. He showed his son what a female breast looked like, not only from an external view but also from a lateral view; he showed Mechai what a breast looked like cut in cross-section, in sagittal section, antero-posterially, and postero-laterally.

"If you want to know more," his father said, "just come to me or read the book." Mechai was incredibly relieved by this unexpected turn of events. His fear was replaced by inquisitiveness as he eagerly learned about the entire female anatomy, not just breasts. Dr. Samak had turned a terrifying and traumatic experience into an educational and productive one for him. This was how Mechai liked to learn.

In the Viravaidya family, Dr. Ella was the stable and stoic parent, not overly affectionate with her children but always a gentle and caring mother. She was the one who taught her children how to survive in a world that could be hostile and sometimes cruel. Although not at all domesticated, she knew how to run her household. She was known as a stern and aggressive woman who didn't suffer fools gladly, characteristics no doubt inherited from her father. She had a sharp tongue when the occasion warranted, whether with her children, her domestic help, or her peers. But beneath her sometimes gruff exterior, she was really a soft-hearted, principled, and charitable person, who encouraged her children to always be considerate toward others.

Dr. Samak was the gentleman and patrician father, kind-hearted and generous almost to a fault,[15] and loved by everyone.

He took his children on holidays, to the beach, horseback riding, on boat trips through the klongs of Bangkok, to the temples, to fly kites, and to learn how to drive. He was always the fun parent, who was there when they needed him and always took them places. As Mechai portrayed his parents in retrospect years later, "My father relaxed in an armchair to study. My mother sat straight up to study."

As parents, they lived by the dictum "spare the rod and spoil the child". Mechai was certainly no paragon of good behavior all the time, so they had to use the rod liberally with him. His expertise with the slingshot would sometimes be turned on birds or other animals. And he got the rod. His mischievous pranks around the home were not always as innocent as his pursuit of a glimpse of the maid's breasts. And he got the rod. On one occasion, Dr. Ella was administering a beating to Mechai with a slipper when, in an effort to evade further punishment, he shouted back to his mother, "You can't use a slipper to hit me. Thais think its bad." To which she responded, "I'm not a Thai." And continued the beating unabated.

The post-war period was fraught with uncertainty for Thailand. Damaged by its tilt toward Japan during the war, it desperately sought closer ties with the victorious Allies. With the military discredited by its wartime alliance with Japan, civilian politicians seized the reins of government through democratic elections. For a time, it seemed that democratic institutions, political parties, and stable civilian leadership might become rooted in the country. However, a series of forgettable and ineffective civilian leaders were unable to marshal the popular support necessary to govern the country and stabilize the economy.

Two events in 1946 terminated any hopes for continued civilian leadership through democratic means. First, Phibunsongkhram was exonerated for his wartime association with

Japan, and resurrected as a force to be reckoned with in Thai politics. Then, on June 6, 1946, King Ananda Mahidol, who had returned to Thailand only six months earlier, was found shot dead in his bed. The entire incident was handled ineptly by Pridi Phanomyong's Government. Eventually, he was forced to resign and leave the country. While traveling abroad, Pridi formed associations with nationalist groups in Vietnam, Laos, Cambodia, and Indonesia, groups which by this time had clear communist connections. When Pridi returned to Thailand in 1947, the civilian government he had left behind was tottering and ineffectual.

In order to restore order and forestall any communist infringement on the country in the person of Pridi, the army staged a coup d'état and seized control of the government. The coup's instigators — Phibunsongkhram and Sarit Thanarat — installed Khuang Aphaivong as Prime Minister, lest Thailand be censured internationally if a military government took power. Like its predecessors, the Khuang Government was ineffective and tainted by its association with Pridi and his supporters. As the threat of communism undermined other colonial regimes in Southeast Asia, and with Communist insurgencies threatening the Nationalist government in China, western distaste for a military dominated, strongly anti-Communist government in Thailand dissipated. Always the opportunist, Phibunsongkhram ousted Khuang from power and became the Prime Minister of Thailand with the approval and support of western nations.

Only three and a half years after resigning in disgrace, Phibunsongkhram was back in charge, reconstructed as an anti-Communist crusader surrounded by hostile and restive neighbors. Through a clever balancing act, Phibunsongkhram would maintain control of Thailand for the next nine years, dressing his military government with the trappings of a parliamentary democracy, and casting it as an anti-Communist bulwark against the increasingly insidious advance of communism. The Cold War had arrived in Thailand by 1948. Phibunsongkhram would use it adroitly to extract recognition and substantial financial support from the West.

For post-war Thailand, though, the Viravaidya household was hardly a typical one. With two physicians bringing home an income, money was not an overwhelming concern for the family. What money they had was for their children's education first, and for their comfortable lodgings in suburban Bangkok only secondarily. English was spoken liberally in the home. Although Dr. Samak and Dr. Ella spoke English together, Dr. Samak spoke with his children in Thai only. Dr. Ella spoke with the children in English, but they responded in Thai. Consequently, as a young boy growing up in Bangkok, Mechai could understand English but he couldn't speak it or write it. As the time approached to go abroad for school, this posed something of a problem. While at Vajiravudh, he certainly didn't distinguish himself in his English language studies. So after finishing Grade 5 at Vajiravudh, he was withdrawn to attend Mrs. Sherwood's School, a small 15 student school for expatriate children opposite Christ Church in Bangkok, to learn to speak English in preparation for going abroad. This was his first extensive exposure to farang other than his mother.[16]

Sumalee was the first Viravaidya to go abroad for her education in 1951. Like her father, she was sent to England, to the Friends School, Saffron Walden.

"Why are you sending a girl away to school?" friends asked.

"Because she is the oldest," was Dr. Ella's standard response. "Boys and girls are both human, they are the same. Sumalee is the oldest. She goes first." Dr. Ella, after all, had bucked the system to become a physician when few women even finished secondary school. Like her father before her, she would make sure that her daughters received the same educational opportunities as men.

Unfortunately, post-war England was no country club. The country had been devastated in the war, and by 1950, when Sumalee went there to study, the country was still suffering shortages. Food was being rationed in England then, and sometimes there was not enough for the students to eat. When Sumalee returned to Thailand for the summer after her first two years abroad with tales of hardships in England, Dr. Samak decided that this was no place to send Mechai. He started looking for other countries where his son could get a good education abroad. One obvious choice was Australia. It was close to Thailand. The fighting in World War II never reached Australia. In fact, the country was experiencing a post-war boom. There was plenty of food, the economy was flourishing as Australia provided raw materials and manufactured goods for the European and Asian countries ravaged during the war, unemployment was low, and there was lots of fresh air and wide open spaces. This seemed like an environment where Mechai could thrive. But neither Dr. Samak nor Dr. Ella knew anything about Australia. So they decided to find out.

Dr. Samak began inquiring among his friends. A close friend, Luang Pisut Isarasena, sent his oldest son to a school near Melbourne called Geelong Grammar School, and showed Dr. Samak some brochures. Dr. Samak was impressed by the school's impressive architecture and the neat verdant campus. As he inquired further, he found that another respected friend, M.L. Dej Snidvongse, had also sent his son to Geelong Grammar School and was extremely pleased with the entire educational experience it provided. He learned that two former Prime Ministers, Khuang Aphaivong and M.R. Seni Pramoj, also had sons who attended Geelong Grammar School. Everywhere he investigated, the name Geelong Grammar School was recommended again and again — an excellent school with a long history of quality education. Dr. Samak had heard enough. Geelong Grammar School it would be.

In 1953 a movie which showcased Australia came to Bangkok. Father and son went to see the movie. Mechai couldn't believe his eyes. Australia seemed so modern and clean. Everything was big, and everyone so happy. This was his first exposure to what has become a lifetime involvement with Australia.

In January 1954, when he was 13, knowing nothing about the country except for what he had seen in a movie, Mechai Viravaidya set off for Australia to continue his studies at Geelong Grammar.

*Dr. Ella with Sumalee (left) and Mechai (right)*

*Mechai at Vajiravudh*

*(Left to right) Mechai, Dr. Ella, Marissa, and Dr. Samak*

*The Viravaidya children circa 1955 (left to right) Sunya, Sumalee, Marissa, and Mechai*

*Dr. Samak with Sunya (left) and Mechai (right), 1958*

## NOTES:

1 When King Prajadhipok ascended to the throne, Siam had a budget deficit that was 14% of total revenue. His first act as king was to trim the royal budget by 40% and reduce the civil administration. The spending cuts he introduced relieved the immediate crisis. By the late 1920s, balanced state budgets accompanied a wave of prosperity that temporarily muted political criticism.

2 King Rama VII accepted a letter from a naval party representing the "Instigators" at the Klai Kangwol Palace in Hua Hin on June 24 demanding his immediate return to Bangkok by ship. He declined and returned to Bangkok the same day via the Royal train. In his reply to the ultimatum from the conspirators, King Prajadhipok wrote "I have received the letter in which you invite me to return to Bangkok as a constitutional monarch. For the sake of peace; and in order to save useless bloodshed; to avoid confusion and loss to the country; and, more, because I have already considered making this change myself, I am willing to cooperate in the establishment of a constitution under which I am willing to serve. Furthermore, there is a possibility that, if I decline to continue in my office as King, the foreign powers will not recognize the new government. This might entail considerable difficulty for the government."

At his personal residence in Sukhothai Palace, he received a delegation from the coup plotters who handed him a full fledged constitution for his signature. He refused to sign, considering it a draft only, and even added the word "provisional" to the draft. The document signed by the King on June 26 granted a provisional constitution only. The first permanent constitution was granted on December 10, which is considered Constitution Day in Thailand.

3 The same Princess Srinagarinda who, as Dek Ying Sangwalya, had lived with the Viravaidya family during her convalescence following the surgical removal of the sewing needle from her hand.

4 In 1937, Asian food, apart from the occasional Chinese restaurant, was virtually unknown in the west, a function of the cultural imperialism the European powers still exerted over their colonies. In her later years, as Thai food and restaurants became ubiquitous in the smallest towns of Europe and the United States, Ella would always be amazed at the insatiable appetite westerners demonstrated for Thai food.

5 Although Thailand in the late 1930s was definitely anti-western, this bias was not consistently exercised. A series of 12 "Cultural Mandates" introduced in 1939 adopted a western calendar, encouraged people to live along modern lines, and required them to dress in a modern fashion. For the Thai, nothing was monolithic, which explains why Ella could be appointed to the staff of Chulalongkorn Hospital in an era of intolerance and racism.

6 In her determination to raise her children as Thai, Ella insisted that her four children had uniquely Thai names — Sumalee, Mechai, Sunya, and Marisa. They were never given or called by western names either, as was frequently the case among Thai children of mixed parentage. Interestingly, none of them were given nicknames which Thai people customarily give their children, such as "mouse", "pig", or "fatty". According to Thai custom, if you call a child by a pretty name, the devil will take the child. If, on the other hand, the child is given an unflattering diminutive, it will make the child less attractive to the devil. Dr. Samak, with his western upbringing, gave little credence to such superstitions.

7 As a child, Mechai was raised as a Buddhist. When he went to Australia to study at Geelong Grammar School, he studied and practised the Anglican religion, the practice at that school. Neither Dr. Ella

nor Dr. Samak were absolutists about religion. They wanted their children exposed to many religions, but imposed none. They felt that their children should be free to choose the religion that most suited them when they were old enough to decide for themselves.

8 Mechai's reticence to charge money had one notable exception. As a child, Mechai hated to get injections. When he was sick and had to have an injection, he would charge his mother 50 baht to give him an injection, and his father 100 baht. He found that this remuneration reduced the discomfort substantially. The higher price charged to his father accounted for perceived higher pain associated with his father's injections. He described his father's techniques of giving injections as similar to "throwing a dart".

9 The Thai resistance movement during World War II, called the "Seri Thai" or Free Thai Movement, was led by M.R. Seni Pramoj in the United States, Pridi Phanomyong in Thailand, and also had a base in England. The resistance movement was extremely active and provided intelligence and access to Thailand for Allied agents during the war. Unlike resistance movements in other countries, it did not take an active role in military resistance to the Japanese, in large measure due to Allied reluctance to engage the Japanese beyond their front lines in Burma. For an excellent synopsis of the Seri Thai Movement during World War II, see John B. Haseman's *The Thai Resistance Movement During the Second World War*.

10 Unfortunately, this channel of communication could only carry messages one way, from Siam to Great Britain, otherwise Dr. Ella would have heard that her mother died of cancer in 1943 and her father died of heart disease in 1944. She only learned of her parent's demise after the war, when normal communications were restored, and her sisters had the unenviable task of informing her.

11 As it had done so successfully in the past, Thailand skillfully balanced the interests of the Axis and Allied powers to obtain a

reasonable peace settlement. As Japan's eventual defeat became apparent in late 1944, the Phibunsongkhram Government was forced to resign and was replaced by a civilian government under Khuang Aphaivong but directed by Pridi Phanomyong acting as regent for King Ananda Mahidol. In an effort to curry favor with the Allies, Pridi offered the services of his Free Thai Movement to resist the Japanese. Although the Allies declined the offer, they acknowledged the Free Thai Movement's vigorous opposition to the Japanese, which certainly worked in Thailand's favor in the immediate post-war period. When the war ended in August 1945, the British, angered by Thai annexation of British territory in Malaya and its acquiescence in Japan's use of Thai territory to invade Burma and Malaya, attempted to impose harsh terms upon Thailand. Seni Pramoj, the wartime ambassador to the United States who had personally neglected to inform the Americans of Thailand's declaration of war, became the post-war prime minister and lobbied for US support to moderate the British demands. Although the land annexed from Britain in Malaya and from France in Laos and Cambodia was returned, Thailand managed to ameliorate the most extreme Allied peace terms, was admitted to the United Nations in 1946, and emerged in the post-war years with a decidedly pro-western foreign policy.

12 For current residents and visitors to Bangkok, it must be absurd to hear the areas around Soi 39 Sukhumvit described as "wide open spaces". Today its narrow streets are dotted with high-rise apartment buildings, office buildings, and shopping centers that dwarf the occasional, remaining residential compounds, having been consumed in the urban sprawl of Bangkok. In the 1940s, however, urban Bangkok extended only to Ratchadamnoen Avenue. The area around Sukhumvit Road was still rice paddies and orchards.

13 This episode demonstrates how strong Dr. Ella's convictions were that her children should be raised as Thai. Her relationship with her sisters-in-law had never been close, perhaps due to the cool

reception she had received when she first arrived in Thailand, or because they never accepted their brother marrying a foreigner. An incident that occurred in 1938 when she first met Khunying Sanguan, who was quite ill at the time, may also have been a cause. At Khunying Sanguan's request, Ella was brought in to see her. In a poignant manifestation of her acceptance of her daughter-in-law, Khunying Sanguan took her cherished ruby ring from her finger and placed it upon Ella's finger. Ella was overwhelmed with emotion at this gesture. Immediately upon leaving the room, Samak's older sister confronted Ella and said, "My mother is very ill and doesn't know what she is doing. Please return the ring to me." Ella was crushed with disappointment, but obediently surrendered the ring. Although this incident undoubtedly created friction between Dr. Ella and her sister-in-law, she never demonstrated any overt animosity or antagonism toward her for it, even to the point where she insisted that Mechai spend summers with her and her family. Dr. Ella only confided this story to Mechai in later years after her sister-in-law had passed away, and acknowledged how much it hurt her.

14 Dr. Samak was one of the founders of the Thai Tobacco Monopoly Hospital and its first Director. Because of his benevolent treatment of British prisoners of war, Dr. Samak had a legion of admirers back in Great Britain after the war who felt tremendous gratitude toward him. As an expression of their gratitude, several joined together and sent medical equipment and supplies to him in Thailand after the war. He used these to establish the hospital. After several years in his position as Director, what he thought were trusted subordinates maneuvered politically to have him removed. Dr. Samak never imagined that there would be those in his retinue who would betray him, and was too much of a gentleman to fight back. As this drama unfolded, Dr. Ella would relate events to Mechai. He resolved that he would never let this happen to him. This lesson served him well when he worked in bureaucracies and organizations in the future. Unlike his father,

Mechai would vigorously fight the internecine bureaucratic battles during attempts to unseat him.

15 Dr. Samak's unbridled generosity were sometimes a source of friction between him and Dr. Ella. After the death of Khunying Sanguan, the Viravaidya house in Samsen had been bequeathed in its entirety to Dr. Samak, in accordance with Thai custom. When he left the house to live in Soi 24 and then Soi 39, he allowed his sisters and their families to remain there. When the house was eventually sold, he gave his sisters an equal share in the proceeds. Over time, Dr. Ella was confounded by his inability to say no to any request. On one occasion, when Samak and Ella were struggling to find the resources to send their children abroad for schooling, Dr. Samak's older sister approached him with a request to borrow money to send her son abroad. If not, he might be drafted. Dr. Samak struggled with this dilemma, because his resources were limited. Finally, he had to say no to his sister. "I would really like to help, but I have my own children to educate," he told her. Dr. Ella was relieved. Samak had finally said "no".

16 Mechai's first real exposure to farang was at the Bangkok Sports Club, where his father would take him occasionally during summer holidays. It had a pool and many sporting facilities used by expatriates in Bangkok, so he loved to go there. Prior to the Sports Club, any swimming Mechai did was in the klongs around Soi 39. When swimming in the klongs, the boys would customarily bring along some soap and bathe at the same time. When Mechai saw the swimming pool at the Sports Club for the first time, he was astonished by the clear blue water. Just perfect for bathing, he thought. He had brought his soap along in anticipation of a good bath and, after frolicking in the water, he pulled out the soap and started sudsing up, much to the consternation of the pool maintenance staff and the Sports Club's manager. On subsequent visits to the Sports Club, he was frisked for soap.

# 3

## DOWN UNDER

*Today there is a direct flight from Bangkok to Melbourne on Qantas Airlines, nine and a half hours flying time in the comfortable confines of a Boeing 747-400 jet. In 1954 to reach Melbourne and ultimately Geelong Grammar School, Mechai had to travel for three full days, flying on a Qantas Airlines Super "G" Constellation four engine propeller plane via Singapore, Jakarta, Darwin, Sydney, and finally Melbourne. For his first overseas excursion, Mechai was taking the circuitous route.*

When he left Bangkok for Melbourne in late January 1954, 13-year-old Mechai Viravaidya was accompanied by two 18-year-old Thai boys from Vajiravudh also on their way to study in Australia. Stated more accurately, Mechai was escorting them as their spokesman and translator, because he at least spoke a modicum of English while they spoke none. Considering the embryonic level of Mechai's English, this was a loose interpretation of the term "translator". Their first stop was Singapore. Prior to arrival, they had to fill out immigration documents, presenting Mechai with the first independent test of his English language skills. He was stumped by the very first item on the immigration card, the blank space next to the word "Christian Name". Mechai still didn't remember how to write his name in English. Fortunately, Dr. Ella had anticipated this dilemma, and provided Mechai with a card where not only his name was written in English, but his address, nationality, age, date and place of birth.

After what seemed like an eternity, they arrived in Singapore and proceeded immediately to the Raffles Hotel. Singapore was a steamy Southeast Asian city, quite similar to Bangkok in those days, but with a colonial ambiance exemplified by the Raffles. The tall Gothic columns and whitewashed walls, the Singapore Slings in the Raffles bar, and the "punkah wallahs" that ventilated its rooms,[1] were reminiscent of a colonial period that was rapidly coming to an end in Singapore. After a shower, Mechai and his friends came down to dinner and, by chance, met a Thai Maitre'd. "What a great country Thailand is," he thought. "Everywhere I go, people speak Thai." Dr. Samak had recommended that he order lamb, since he would be eating so much of it in Australia, he might as well get used to it immediately. When the waiter, who didn't speak Thai, came to get his order, Mechai ordered "sheep meat", a direct translation from Thai, where any meat is described by the animal from which it is derived. After some explanation abetted by hand signals and sign language, the waiter brought him a plate of broiled mutton. The gamy odor overwhelmed him, and he nearly vomited. If this was all he could eat in Australia, Mechai figured he would be pretty hungry.

The following morning the group got on the same Qantas Super "G" Constellation and spent another eternity flying to their next destination, Jakarta, for a long stopover, then on to Darwin, on the northern coast of Australia. Assuming that he had reached Australia and therefore his destination, Mechai prepared to disembark from that wretched plane and travel by road to Geelong outside of Melbourne. He figured that, like Thailand, Australia had only one airport, with the remainder of his travel by land transport from there. He was surprised to find that any country had more than one airport, and that this trip was far from over.

After stopping for showers in Darwin while the plane was cleaned, the intrepid travelers took off at midnight for the eight-hour red eye flight to Sydney, where Mechai's protégés were jettisoned. Then Mechai still had to get on a domestic flight to Melbourne. After three days on a plane, he was exhausted when greeted by Mr. Douglas Fraser, a teacher at Geelong Grammar, and his son Michael at the Melbourne airport.

But his odyssey still wasn't over. By car they traveled 70 km. southwest of Melbourne to Corio, where the Geelong Grammar campus was located. It was the dead of summer in Australia. The weather was hot and dry and all the vegetation parched. The panorama looked desolate, with nothing but long, dry grass and stones along the road and everything colored in varying shades of brown and yellow. As he surveyed the arid landscape, so bleak compared to tropical and verdant Thailand, Mechai thought of all the odious "sheep meat" he would have to eat, and became uncertain at the prospect of having to spend his formative years in this god-forsaken place.

Mechai's feeling of discomfort, however, lasted for exactly the time it took to drive from Melbourne to Corio. When he first saw the spectacular campus of Geelong Grammar School, dotted with red brick buildings and surrounded by lush green fields with the Youyang Mountains in the distant background on one side, and nestled against the gentle waters of Corio Bay on the other, his spirits soared. Geelong Grammar School was situated on an 800 acre plot of land. It had six full-size football fields, a nine-hole golf course, a 500-meter shooting range, 11 hard-court tennis courts, two grass courts, a yacht club, and a rowing club. In addition to the classrooms and boarding houses, there was an Art School, Music School, Military Cadet Corps, carpentry shop, mechanics shop, gymnasium, and swimming pool. "What a great place this is," Mechai thought, "far too good for study." For him Geelong seemed more like a grand country club than a school.

Mechai had arrived one week before classes commenced, so Douglas Fraser, who was also the headmaster of Barwon House where Mechai would reside, invited him to stay at his home with his family until school started. To introduce Mechai to his new environment, Michael Fraser along with the children of several other teachers like "Clock" Spears, Barney Hutton, and James Darling, took him on bicycle excursions to explore the school grounds and environs of the Corio countryside. The vistas, fragrances, flavors, and resonance of Corio captivated Mechai. Beyond the sepia-colored landscape, he found a wilderness of wide open spaces and sheep as far as the eye could see.

Back at the Fraser house, he was introduced to the western diet. In Mrs. Fraser's skilled hands, "sheep meat" was prepared in a variety of succulent, and in Mechai's opinion, eminently edible dishes. There were a cornucopia of temperate zone fruits, all crispy and fresh, like cantaloupe, rock melon, apples, strawberries, and grapes, which he had previously seen only as rare, imported products to Thailand. In the mornings, cornflakes smothered with fruits were the breakfast fare. No rice for breakfast in Australia. In the evenings, Mechai and his new mates would raid the refrigerators of several housemasters, finishing the remnants of the days meals. During the days they would play and explore in the cool, clean air, a pleasant change from humid and steamy Bangkok. Dr. Samak had told Mechai to immerse himself in the culture at Geelong, to do everything the other boys did, and not to use his being Thai as an excuse for not participating. In that first week, Mechai did just that and liked what he saw. Although he knew it would be years before he would see his family again, he wasn't homesick at all. Geelong seemed like a country club to him.

The other students arrived and classes began the next week. Mechai started Geelong Grammar in the Second Form, the last year of Junior School.[2] He was the first Thai and only Asian in the Junior School at Geelong at that time.[3] He felt like he had been transported into another world, where life as he knew it was turned on its end. In his first letter home to Dr. Ella, he was struck by the fact that "this place is filled with farang," not realizing that, here, he was the outsider. Nor did this bother him in the slightest. After all, he was used to seeing white people; his mother was Scottish. But unlike Thailand, here he would have to adapt to the farang, to learn their language and customs, to eat their foods, to pulsate to their rhythms, if he were to survive in Australia. This prospect didn't intimidate Mechai at all. His father had done it. His sister had done it. He would do it, too.

Geelong Grammar School (GGS) began its life as the all male Church of England School in 1855.[4] It has been co-educational since the 1970s. Today it has four campuses with a student population of 1600, making it the fourth largest boarding school in the world. Numbered among its distinguished alumni are Prince Charles of England, Kerry Packer, Rupert Murdoch, John Landy, members of Royalty from Thailand, Malaysia, and Brunei, and Mechai Viravaidya. Geelong was established as a boarding school in the true English tradition replete with mandatory studies of the Anglican religion and the house system of boarding.[5]

When Mechai arrived in 1954, Geelong Grammar had two campuses.[6] The main campus at Corio housed the boarding school and day school facilities. The second campus, at Timbertop, was conducting a unique and innovative educational experiment that has not been duplicated to this day. All students aged 14-15 entering the Senior School at Geelong had to spend a full year at the Timbertop campus, in the mountainous wilderness at the foot of Mt. Timbertop over 100 km. northwest of Melbourne. The facilities at Timbertop were purposely kept spartan and austere. The boys had to live and study in this simple, rustic environment where they had to do everything for themselves except cooking and teaching. Living in units of 12, they had to find and chop their own wood and transport it to the campus, serve food, wash dishes, and clean toilets, all done on a two-week rotational basis. If they didn't do it, it didn't get done. On weekends beginning on Friday afternoons, there was hiking and trekking in the mountainous hinterlands of eastern Victoria. The Headmaster at Geelong Grammar from 1930 to 1961, Sir James Darling, had established Timbertop "to provide an opportunity for teenage boys to learn and live together, often under simple and arduous circumstances; to gain self confidence and to appreciate their immediate natural environment."[7] Timbertop was a place for the Geelong boys to develop self-reliance, independence, and character, like an educational "Outward Bound" before the concept became popular.

Darling had more practical, parallel motives for developing the Timbertop experience. In 1952, Geelong Grammar had reached a point where it had to either contract or expand. Contraction would have meant higher fees for fewer students. Expansion involved prohibitive capital investment in classrooms, dining and boarding facilities beyond the school's means. Creation of the Timbertop year allowed Geelong to expand with only the modest investment required to build the unpretentious facilities at Timbertop, with only marginal staff costs since the boys did everything themselves. With one whole year's class off at Timbertop, there was space for 150 additional students in the school's existing facilities at Corio. Although Darling has always been hailed as a visionary for creating the Timbertop experience, his decision made educational and business sense.

Years later, reflecting upon their time together with Mechai at Geelong, his classmates were amazed at how quickly and completely he adapted to Australia and how easily he fit in. His father's advice to "do as the other boys did" certainly helped him to blend in. Also, being adept at sports in Australia's sports conscious society didn't hurt. Within 12 months, his English was up to standard, clearly benefiting from his total immersion in the language. Perhaps equally helpful in improving his English was his regular correspondence with his parents. Every student in the Junior School was required to write one letter per week to their parents and show it to their Master in Charge. When he first arrived, Mechai would write in Thai. In those weeks when he was too lazy to write anything, he would just scribble some Thai characters and numbers on a piece of paper and give it to the Master in Charge who, not being able to read Thai, thought it a quite proper letter. Soon thereafter, he began writing letters to his parents in English, beginning what would become a continuous six-year mutual correspondence. Dr. Ella would always write back using the same format. The first part of her letter contained news from home; the second part corrections of the English in his previous letter. Just as when he was a child, she used reason to instruct him. In one letter, he wrote, "it is raining down very heavily," the verb form "raining down" being a direct translation from Thai. In her response Dr. Ella wrote, "Mechai, it always rains down. It never rains up. If you just say that it is raining, people will understand." Although they were separated by a continent, Dr. Ella would continue to be a principal source of instruction for Mechai, mostly through her letters, a benevolent influence that she would exert upon him for the rest of her life.

During that first year at Geelong, Mechai began a tradition that not only hastened his adaptation to Australia, but was instrumental in engendering the powerful attachment to Australia that he maintains to this day. Because Geelong was primarily a boarding school, it was customary for all the boys to return home to their families during the holidays. This luxury, of course, was not even an option for Mechai. With the Easter holiday of April 1954 approaching, all the boys were preparing to return home except Mechai. Then, a young boy boarding in the same house as Mechai in the Junior School named Rory Treweeke asked Mechai "What are you doing for Easter?" The question puzzled Mechai, because he thought Easter was a person and he was chagrined for having unknowingly neglected him. "I don't even know who Easter is," was Mechai's ingenuous reply. So Rory explained, and invited Mechai to spend the Easter holiday at the Treweeke farm, referred to as a "station" in Australia, called Petherton in Mt. Bryan north of Adelaide in the state of South Australia.

This vacation was a seminal event for Mechai. The city boy from Bangkok got to see what life was like on a functioning sheep and wheat station in rural Australia. Mechai was astonished by what he saw and did there. There was sheep shearing, fishing, picnics by the lake, and excursions to see kangaroos. There was also life with the Treweeke family — Rory's parents Hamlin and Mary, and his sister Katie. He was taken into their family like one of their own children, experiencing the warmth and camaraderie of their family unit, but also subjected to the rigor and discipline of life on a farm. They became like foster parents to him. Rather than spending the vacation alone back at Geelong, he was living a true Australian experience.

Mechai spent the May school holiday that year with the Treweekes at their second station called Calooma near the township of Dirranbandi in the southernmost part of Queensland bordering the state of New South Wales. The September holiday was split between Geoffrey Ripper's family in Melbourne and Peter Carey's family in Bacchus Marsh. For the Christmas holiday, he was back with the Treweekes in Queensland. This pattern would continue in various permutations and with assorted classmates during his six years at Geelong. By the time he was finished, Mechai had visited a greater variety of places than most Australians see in a lifetime, and was exposed to the intricate mosaic of Australian life. These holidays remain a warm and joyous memory for Mechai, and in his opinion, hastened his adaptation to Australia more than any other stimulus. That these opportunities were made available to him was purely serendipitous (although Mechai suspects that Doug Fraser was instrumental in arranging the invitations). In his continuing relationship with Geelong, he is trying to get similar opportunities integrated into the curriculum for overseas students at Geelong.[8]

Mechai's adaptation to Geelong was not entirely social. He also had to make an academic transition from the rigid Thai school system, with its emphasis on rote learning, to a more open learning environment where students were encouraged to explore and challenge. Plus, all his lessons were now in English. Compared to Thailand, Mechai found education at Geelong more interesting and the learning more applied. Classroom work was complemented by field visits, where the students could see how the theory they learned in class worked in real life.

But Geelong Grammar School in 1954 was by no means a liberal academic institution. Its regimentation typified the traditional English boarding school. All students wore uniforms. There were classes until 3:00 P.M. every day, with after school activities alternating between community service and sports. There was a compulsory study period at night. In the Senior School, there was even military training once per week. Discipline was strict. If the offense warranted, there was caning by the Housemaster. For the most egregious offenses the caning was sometimes administered by Sir James Darling himself, who was said to have a deliberate back swing, smooth stroke, and excellent follow through when wielding the cane. For less serious offenses, there was detention doing odd jobs around the campus. Like all boarding schools, Geelong had its rules, which the boys found more confining as they got older. If you operated within the rules, life at Geelong was good. If you transgressed, you paid for it.

Although Mechai clearly preferred Geelong's academic environment to the one he experienced in Thailand, he still faced some subjects which, either because the teacher did not stimulate him or the subject left no room for creativity, were drudgery rather than a pleasure. His real passion remained sports. In this realm, Geelong was like nirvana for him. Sporting activities were ubiquitous. He played on the Geelong Grammar first team in cricket, tennis, Australian rules football, and rugby against other schools. He also participated in inter-house competitions in cricket, tennis, rowing, field hockey, rugby, swimming, track and field, and Australian rules football.

Mechai was also a very respectable boxer, winning the mosquito weight boxing title his first year at Geelong, and the flea weight boxing title in the following year. Outside of the ring, he could box using his hands and his feet in the traditional Thai kick-boxing style. During that first year at Geelong, while still a newcomer to the school, Mechai would occasionally get teased by the other boys. Because his English still wasn't fluent, he was often tongue-tied when trying to respond to their taunts. Once, a classmate named David Lester was teasing him relentlessly and he just couldn't respond verbally, so he delivered a roundhouse kick, Thai boxing style, and landed it in his tormentor's mid-section, dropping him to the ground with a cracked rib. To acknowledge this hitherto unknown prowess, the other boys gave him the nickname "Meat Axe". Mechai had established himself as someone who could not be pushed around and the other boys respected him for that. Also, because they now knew what the consequences were when "Meat Axe" got riled, the teasing pretty much subsided thereafter.

By the end of 1955, Mechai was feeling quite comfortable in this new country. The environment at Geelong, the sports, the camaraderie with his classmates, the holidays with friends cavorting in the Australian bush, the hunting, fishing, and horseback riding — all of these had combined to turn this very typical Thai boy into an Australian lad. At the end of his second year at Geelong, Mechai made his first trip back to Thailand. Sumalee was back from the UK so the whole Viravaidya family was reunited.[9] He was overjoyed to see his family after two years. He brought a cricket bat, balls, and gloves to teach Sunya, then only nine, how to play the game. Much time was spent at the Bangkok Sports Club with old friends, where Mechai displayed his evolving tennis skills. He enjoyed himself immensely while in Thailand. But when the time came for him to return to Australia, he was eager to get back to continue his new life there. Plus, when classes began, he would be entering his Timbertop year, the adventure every Geelong Grammarian waited for. When it came time to get on that Qantas Super Constellation for the arduous journey back to Melbourne, Mechai was the first to board the plane.

The Timbertop campus had nine dormitories, called units, in February 1956, sufficient to accommodate 118 boys. The units were really just long huts with 12 beds with a desk beside each, a sitting room with fireplace, two lavatories, and two showers. The campus also contained a kitchen, a dining room cum chapel and meeting room, sanatorium, masters quarters, and classroom block, all with no central heating. The only heat they got came from the fireplaces. There was also a water boiler, which when properly stoked with wood cut by the boys, provided them with hot water. In the warm months of February to April, this was not particularly inconvenient. However, when cold weather and snow blanketed the mountainous region around Mt. Timbertop, warmth became a precious commodity. Hot water was like gold. The boys would climb into their bunks at night with whiskey bottles filled with hot water to get warm. In the morning, the boys would shout "first up" to get into the shower for their allotted three minutes while the hot water lasted.

Mechai remembers his Timbertop year as "survival training with education mixed in." E.H. Montgomery, the Headmaster at Timbertop, was a strict but highly respected disciplinarian whom the boys called "Basher" because he ran Timbertop with an iron fist; but who allowed them the freedom to venture off on their own and develop independence. The first group of boys attended Timbertop in 1952. Mechai's class was the fifth group there, so the facilities were still quite lean. From the minute the boys arrived, they had to work to survive — sweeping the units, disposing garbage, serving food, and most importantly, finding and chopping wood for fuel. They quickly learned that under difficult circumstances, cooperation abetted their survival while dissension jeopardized it. Strong bonds of friendship and teamwork formed among the boys. During the week, school work and chores occupied all their time. There were no organized sports, something Mechai dearly missed. Cross-country running was the only sporting activity, with two runs per week compulsory. On the weekends there was hiking in uncharted wilderness around Mt. Timbertop and adjacent peaks. Treks of several days were not uncommon, to places like Sheepyard Flat, Howqua River, Mt. Stirling, and the Crosscut Saw. They would carry sugar, tea, cheese, biscuits, bread, butter, chocolate, lamb chops, and sausages with them for their meals. They carried the food, along with sleeping bags and tents, in their backpacks. If they didn't carry enough food, they went hungry. If they didn't collect wood, they went cold. When they reached their destination, the incomparable vistas, serenity, and feeling of collective achievement made the hardships seem worthwhile.

Despite the inconveniences, Mechai thoroughly enjoyed his Timbertop year. His appetite for natural surroundings, whetted during vacations with the Treweekes or the Careys, was now satiated by the boundless wilderness around Timbertop. The campus had a dark room, one of its few amenities, which Mechai used to indulge a fledgling interest in photography. The chores and rigor reinforced friendships with classmates who shared the experience. Self-confidence, independence, and self-reliance — qualities which the Timbertop year sought to nurture — quickly became apparent in Mechai.

Timbertop lacked one essential for Mechai — organized sports. Physical activity was confined to hiking and running, neither of which Mechai was particularly enamored with and both of which he would do only the minimum of. However, with all the work required from the boys just to exist, plus their regular classes, there was no time for competitive sports. Reluctantly, Mechai abandoned his tennis, cricket, and football for the year and plunged into the Timbertop experience.

When he returned to Corio the following year in 1957, Mechai decided to make up for lost time. He was now 16 years old with the upper body strength and speed that come with physical maturity. Hiking and running in the Timbertop wilderness was tolerated for one year. This year he would concentrate on sports.

Concentrate on sports is exactly what he did. There were the old standbys — cricket and Australian rules football. He was proficient at both, played on all inter-house competitions, and competed on teams that played other boarding schools. His passion, however, was tennis. His coach at Geelong was Frank

Sedgman, a former Wimbledon and Australian Open champion. With a schoolmate named Michael Lockhart, he played incessantly. The more he played, the better he became. He loved to practise. When Michael Lockhart or other worthy opponents were not available, he would just hit the ball against a wall, over and over, to perfect his stroke and sharpen his game. During holidays that year, Mechai and Michael played in tennis tournaments in Melbourne. In 1957 and 1958 they won the Schools Doubles Championship at Geelong. When he returned to Thailand in 1957, he won the National Junior Doubles Championship of Thailand with his friend Manop Pongsatat. In 1958 Mechai won the Geelong Singles Championship.

1957 was a great year for Mechai, as he fully indulged his passion for sport. Everything was going so well for him — until his final exams came along. Then he realized that, with his overwhelming preoccupation with sports, he had not devoted enough time to his studies. In Geelong's rigorous academic environment, this could be problematic, as Mechai learned when he failed his final exams in some subjects and had to repeat his Leaving Certificate year.

Obsession with sports was not the only reason Mechai failed his Leaving Certificate year. With two parents who were physicians, he entertained thoughts of studying medicine. So he took preparatory courses in science and math. Math was just not his strength. Although he was slightly better at physics and chemistry, these subjects didn't interest him. If there was one constant about Mechai's approach to academics, it was that if a subject didn't interest him, he didn't apply himself. Given the choice between his studies, which bored him, and sports, which excited him, he would always choose sports. Now he had the grades to prove it.

This situation posed a dilemma for Mechai. First, he had to repeat his Leaving Certificate year at Geelong. He didn't want to fail again. This was cold reality staring him in the face at 17 years of age. Dr. Ella put his predicament in the clearest perspective. "Mechai," she wrote to him in one of her regular epistles, "if you fail your Leaving Certificate again, you won't be able to graduate and go to university. Then your only alternative will be to return to Bangkok and become a bank clerk." For Mechai, this admonition conjured up images of him sitting behind a desk in some bank wearing a green visor, with a bulky calculator to his right and a bookkeeping ledger in front of him, adding up rows and columns ad nauseam. "My God," thought Mechai, "that's the last thing I want to become." He decided to change his ways.

As he would do so often during his studies in Australia, indeed as he would throughout his life, Mechai demonstrated that when he had his backside to the fire, he could perform and produce. First of all, he abandoned any aspirations of becoming a physician and dropped his math and science classes. Perhaps courses like history, economics, and the social sciences would appeal to him more. Second, he would prioritize academics at the expense of sports. This was a most difficult pill for Mechai to swallow. He couldn't abandon sports altogether, of course. It was too integral a part of his life. In 1958, he eventually won the singles and doubles championship in tennis at Geelong. But sports would be kept in perspective and schoolwork would now take precedence.

Finally, his mid-year holiday during the 1958 school year would have to be spent studying rather than vacationing with his classmates and their families. Since his first year at Geelong, without interruption, Mechai continued to spend school holidays with friends all over Australia. After every holiday, Dr. Ella would assiduously correspond with the families, thank them for their kindness and generosity toward her son, and even arrange subsequent holiday visits. This was vintage Dr. Ella, always looking out for Mechai's welfare. There was no shortage of invitations. Mechai was a personable and well-mannered young man by this time and the families loved to have him as a guest. But in 1958, Mechai spent his mid-year holiday at the home of John and Anne Knox, his guardians in Melbourne,[10] studying for his exams. Leaving no stone unturned, he even had special coaching to prepare for his exam papers. Nothing was left to chance.

This strategy worked perfectly. When exam time came, Mechai whizzed through his Leaving exams and passed them all with ease. He could now move on to his Matriculation year at Geelong in preparation for university.

The sixth form at Geelong Grammar was called the Matriculation year. Unlike Mechai, most students entered Matriculation after one year of Leaving at the age of 17. Matriculation prepared students for entrance into a university. Although it could be finished in one year, most students preferred to do two years of Matriculation to add breadth and depth to their preparatory work, and also to take administrative roles in the school, such as becoming house prefects. Geelong's boarding school style discipline was more relaxed for the Matriculation students, who were allowed academic and social freedoms commensurate with their physical and emotional maturity.

Mechai entered his Matriculation year on a high. He had overcome the adversity of repeating his Leaving year and was now rejoining his classmates in Matriculation without the pressure of failure hanging over his head like the previous year. Moreover, he had proved his academic mettle. When the chips were down, everyone knew that Mechai could produce.

An added responsibility in 1959 was the arrival of Mechai's younger brother, Sunya, at Geelong Grammar. Unlike Mechai, Sunya had not attended boarding school in Thailand and this was his first time away from home. He was only 12 years old when he arrived in Australia and predictably homesick. He would look to his older brother for emotional support to ameliorate his loneliness, something Mechai was pleased to provide. He picked Sunya up at the airport and took him to the DeWolf's home, where Mechai was spending the holidays, to begin his orientation to Australia. Sunya entered Geelong in the second year of Junior School and like Mechai, boarded at Barwon House. Sometimes, he would just wander up to the Senior School to be with Mechai. For Mechai, it was a pleasure to have his younger brother around, and he did what he could to ease Sunya's transition to Australia. They would spend the next seven years in Australia together. Sunya was an excellent student and went on to study medicine at Melbourne University and became the second Thai physician to graduate from that prestigious institution. Dr. Ella always said that the difference between Mechai and Sunya was that, with Mechai she always said "Don't forget to study your lessons." With Sunya she said "Don't study too much."

Since entering Senior School, Mechai had been boarding at Perry House. He'd always been close with his housemates, but their bonds of friendship really congealed during Matriculation. Mates like Gary Hudson, Brian Wawn, Ian Brown, and Jamie Kinnear became fast friends with Mechai, and these friendships persist unabated to this day. With the relaxed discipline they now enjoyed, the boys spent more time off-campus, mostly in Melbourne, where they assembled at the homes of friends to socialize and carouse. Wherever they ventured, they went as a group from Perry House. They began to see what life would be like after Geelong Grammar.

Mechai was 18 years old when he entered his Matriculation year in 1959. Already a mature young man, he had grown to become exceptionally gregarious and socially competent. He possessed excellent interpersonal skills, and loved to be with other people. Almost without exception, other people found him courteous, gracious, sociable, and well-mannered. He was popular with Australian girls and enjoyed their company. Australian women found his rugged, swarthy, Eurasian good-looks combined with his polite manner quite attractive. Plus Mechai had one quality that enhanced his appeal. He had an amazing rapport with parents, especially the mothers. He enjoyed spending time with his friend's parents, talking with them to satisfy his inquisitiveness about their culture. As a stranger in a foreign setting, he took nothing for granted. Wherever he went, he would always bring a gift for the mothers. If food was being served, he would help out in the kitchen, set the table, help with the dishes. If invited to a house for dinner, he would always follow up with a thank you note to the parents, which enhanced his standing immeasurably. The mothers loved him, and so did their daughters. His friend Roger Wilson observed that "he was so popular with the girls that the rest of us looked like bounders in comparison."

During these years, many of the attributes that would contribute to Mechai's success began to manifest themselves. He had such extraordinary interpersonal skills that his friends knew, even then, that Mechai was a special person. His creative imagination was evident in the tasteful and appropriate gifts he would always bring for parents, or in his suggestions for spicing up parties and social occasions. Interestingly, his ability to invent catchy slogans that appealed to common people, an ability he would raise to an art form during his career, first became apparent while at Geelong. Each Sunday after dinner and before Chapel, the boys had an hour of free time. Rather than studying, most listened to "The Hit Parade". One Sunday, there was an advertisement for a slogan competition for Page Barker's Scurf and Dandruff lotion. The prize was an electric shaver, quite a desirable gadget in those days. Mechai's interest was piqued by the slogan competition. Afterwards, in chapel, while semi-comatose from a particularly boring sermon, he heard the preacher refer to "the wonders of the world". This struck a chord. Using the back of his hymn book, he began scribbling slogans, and finally came up with this ditty:

"Of the wonders of this world, I have little notion.

But the wonder of your hair is Page Barker's Scurf and Dandruff Lotion."

He sent it into the radio station.

Several weeks later, when the boys were again listening to "The Hit Parade" rather than studying, they heard an announcement that Mechai Viravidtchthya (the announcer couldn't come close to pronouncing "Viravaidya") had won the slogan contest. Mechai didn't believe it until his electric shaver arrived in the mail, and he began hearing his slogan in advertisements for Page Barker's Scurf and Dandruff Lotion. A sloganeer was born.

Things went so well for Mechai that year that he passed his Matriculation in one year and moved on to university. Academics was no longer a problem. Though never an outstanding student, Mechai now kept up with his classes and passed all his exams. He continued his obsession with sports, though modulated to accommodate his studies. He became a house prefect in Perry House, supervising the younger boys and providing them with a role model. When it came time to select a university, Mechai had one dream — Melbourne University. It was the university of choice for every Geelong Grammarian, indeed for everyone in Victoria. It was recognized as one of the finest universities in Australia. Mechai never considered going anywhere else.

There were two problems. First, he had to decide what to study. Then he had to get accepted. He couldn't study medicine, law wouldn't do, the arts didn't suit him, and math was certainly out of the question. So he decided to study commerce. Today, it is extremely difficult to be accepted into commerce at Melbourne University. Next to medicine, it is probably commerce which has the most rigid entrance requirements. In 1959, when Mechai applied, commerce was not very popular and competition for entrance was not as fierce. Because he had passed all his Matriculation year exams, Mechai was accepted into Melbourne University, and commenced his studies there in February 1960.

The city of Melbourne was booming in February 1960 when Mechai took up residence at Medley Hall to attend university. It was a modern city that maintained a traditional rural flavor. A freeway system was being constructed and new buildings dotted the city center. Yet trams still ferried people around its clean and orderly environs. It was a cosmopolitan city, with large Greek, Italian, and Eastern European immigrant populations. It was a pleasant and inexpensive city, with a balanced mixture of urban and rural life. Most of all, it was an outdoor city. People in Melbourne seemed to live their lives outdoors. Picnics, barbecues, sporting events, and beach excursions were the favorite pastime of Melbourne's residents. They especially loved sporting events. It was not a dynamic or vibrant city because few people actually lived in Melbourne's downtown area. Most commuted into the city and returned home to its suburbs after work. Except for restaurants and movie theaters, Melbourne essentially closed down at 6:00 P.M.

When Mechai arrived at Melbourne University, he was no stranger to the city. He had spent many holidays there with friends. His guardians, the Knoxes and later the DeWolfs, lived there, so Mechai could be found in Melbourne whenever Geelong was not in session. During the summer holidays of 1958 and 1959, he worked for the Coca Cola Company doing "specials" — delivering chairs, tables, and Coca Cola for parties in private homes all over the city.[11] This job took him into every nook, cranny, and back alley in Melbourne, where he could see how the people really lived. He knew Melbourne well and felt comfortable living there.

His new life as a university student also suited Mechai well. After six years leading a cloistered life in an Anglican boarding school, he and his classmates were overjoyed with the freedom university students had. There was no compulsory religious education, no dedicated study time, no chapel services, and no disciplinary rules. At Melbourne University they could come and go as they pleased. With his mates from Geelong like Gary Hudson, Brian Wawn, Rory Treweeke, Dickson Robinson, Trevor King, and Ian Brown, plus new friends like Roger Wilson, Tony Kosky, Roger Knott, Billy Wood, and Dick Park, the group had the freedom to spread their wings. This they did with great gusto, often to the exclusion of their studies.

It was not surprising, then, that it took Mechai five years to finish a three-year course in commerce at Melbourne University.[12] He failed subjects in his second and fourth year which had to be repeated. Accounting and statistics, compulsory courses in the commerce program, were his nemesis. Only after passing these two subjects in 1964 did Mechai receive his degree. It wasn't lack of intelligence that slowed him down. It was lack of interest in his courses, and a heavy social schedule that left him little time for study — a replay of his failed Leaving year but this time on a grander scale.

His first year, while boarding at Medley Hall and a non-resident at Trinity College, actually went quite well. He passed all his exams and moved on to his second year. He didn't really like Medley Hall though. The place was bleak and depressing, and he felt like he was slumming. For his second year he moved to a new residence at International House in 1961, where his social life blossomed but his grades went south. Mechai described his time at International House as "his bridge, poker, and lecturing year". During his second year at Melbourne University, Mechai became involved in extracurricular activities. He joined the Thai Students

Association and traveled around the state of Victoria lecturing about Thailand. He also started doing radio programs on Radio Australia. But according to Mechai, "my most important and time consuming extracurricular activities were bridge and poker."

International House was renowned as the focal point for bridge playing at Melbourne University. When Mechai arrived, he felt right at home. He had always been an avid small stakes poker player, but now he became fascinated with bridge. With his buddies, they would play bridge incessantly. On one occasion, Mechai and his friend were playing bridge at International House when all the electricity in the house went out and darkness consumed them. Instinctively, the boys picked up the cards and tablecloth, set up right outside under the street lights, and continued the game without missing a bid.

A favorite pastime of Melbourne University students at that time was the pub crawl. In this activity, the participants would visit a number of Melbourne pubs within a specified time period, having a drink at one pub and then moving on to the next. When they weren't playing cards, International House students could frequently be found on pub crawls. One time, Mechai and his Malaysian friend Mat Awang had to go to the university to take the final statistics exam for which they were not well prepared. So they decided to go on a pub crawl on their way to the exam site. It took them several hours to cover the five kilometers between International House and the exam site, stopping at several pubs on the way. This is not the best way to go to an exam, but in view of their inadequate preparation, Mechai and Mat Awang figured they had nothing to lose. When Mechai received the results from that exam, the only mark he got was for spelling his name correctly. Even that he attributed only to luck.

Then, of course, there was sports to occupy his time. And his social life. Although not as fanatical about sports as he was while at Geelong, Mechai remained a keen and avid sportsman. He played for the Melbourne University Ping Pong team, and played tennis and football with the Old Geelong Grammarians.[13] While at university, though, even sports played second fiddle to his social life. As he got older, Mechai grew progressively more outgoing and sociable. He had a natural ability to communicate and was extremely comfortable in the presence of others. His friends found him genuinely caring, thoughtful, and considerate, attributes seldom demonstrated by Australian men in those days.

Mechai's wit and keen sense of humor, which he would subsequently use as his most potent weapon in his campaign to desensitize family planning in Thailand, also surfaced during this time. He possessed an innate ability to make people laugh, finding humor in even the most mundane places. He would do magic tricks that served primarily as a vehicle for his light banter and joking. Whether satirizing, extemporizing, or criticizing, he could do it with humor. Although principally amiable, his sense of humor could also be mischievous, which he demonstrated at the wedding of his good friend, Roger Wilson.

Roger had invited Mechai to be a Groomsman in his wedding party. On the morning of the wedding, Mechai approached Roger and, with his most serious demeanor, said,

"You must allow me to clean your shoes before your wedding. It's an old Thai custom." Roger protested, but Mechai insisted that it was Thai tradition (which he made up), and he would be terribly upset if Roger didn't conform. So Roger gave Mechai his shoes.

A short while later, Mechai returned with Roger's immaculately shined shoes, and continued,

"Now you must allow me to put the shoes on your feet. It's an old Thai custom. I will be insulted if you refuse." By this time, Roger knew that it was useless to protest further, so he just sat back and allowed Mechai to put his shoes on for him.

Roger was feeling quite satisfied with this Thai custom as he entered the chapel to meet his fiancé, Sue Broadway, for the wedding ceremony. He now had impeccably polished shoes, compliments of his good friend Mechai, to go along with his white tie and tails. He looked positively dapper, he thought. As the ceremony began and he knelt at the altar, Roger could hear stifled laughter from the assembled guests, which continued throughout the ceremony. Curious at the source of this laughter, Roger glanced at Mechai, whose mute response connoted innocent ignorance. It was only later that he learned that Mechai had painted the word "HELP" on the sole of his left shoe, and "ME" on the sole of his right shoe in big white letters. While Roger Wilson knelt piously at the altar for his wedding, the soles of his shoes broadcast the message "HELP ME".

With so many distractions, it was not surprising that Mechai failed his courses that second year at Melbourne University. For his third year in 1962, he left International House and took a flat at Royal Parade in Carleton directly opposite the university. His roommate that first year, Somsak Adithepworaphan, was a respectable cook and taught Mechai some of the intricacies of Thai cooking. When Somsak left, Ian Brown moved in and their flat became a cross-roads for the social life of a wide variety of friends and acquaintances who would drop in at all hours of day and night because there was always something going on. On special occasions, Mechai would prepare Thai food for his friends. Having left Thailand at age 13, Mechai had little appreciation for the wide range of flavors and textures that constituted Thai cooking. Plus his cooking skills, learned from Somsak, were rudimentary at best. As a result, Mechai's Thai food bore only a dim resemblance to the real thing. But his friends, certainly no connoisseurs of Thai cooking, loved everything he served up.

On one occasion, however, Mechai did experience a subtle racial slight which he only learned about much later. Mechai was dating a girl who had invited him to her house for dinner after a football match. When her father met Mechai and saw that he was of Asian descent, he suggested that his daughter and Mechai have dinner in the kitchen rather than in the dining room where meals were regularly taken. This didn't particularly bother Mechai because he ate in the kitchen all the time. When it was time to eat, he wasn't too choosy about the premises.

At this same time, Mechai was invited by Sir Robert Knox, a Geelong Grammarian and relative of the Treweekes', to help out as a liaison officer during the visit of Their Majesties the King and Queen of Thailand to Australia, an invitation which Mechai was quick to accept. In this capacity, he made the acquaintance of Sir Morris Nathan, the Lord Mayor of Melbourne. Mechai and Sir Morris got along famously. Sir Morris offered Mechai a summer job as a supervisor at his camp (where Mechai subsequently worked) and invited him to the races at the prestigious Flemington Racing Club in Melbourne. Attendance at the races was a big social event in Melbourne, with women sporting elegant hats and formal gowns and men decked out in top hat and tails. So with rented top hat and tails, Mechai found himself seated in the VIP section, called the Members' Stand of the Flemington Racing Club.

Coincidentally, the girl's father, who had made Mechai eat in the kitchen only one week before, was an avid race fan and happened to be attending the races that day. Only he was seated in the turf benches while Mechai was in the Members' Stand. When he spotted the girl's father, Mechai went down to cordially greet him. The girl's father, more than a little surprised to see a nattily attired Mechai in the VIP section, asked how he came by those seats. "The Lord Mayor invited me," was Mechai's candid reply.

The next time Mechai went to the girl's house for dinner, the table was beautifully laid out in the dining room, with the finest china and silverware. Mechai had a great meal.

These descriptions of Mechai's university days may sound quite carefree, but they must be interpreted within the historical context in which they occurred. Australia was a prosperous country with seemingly boundless potential in the early 1960s when Mechai attended university there. It had been spared the land war in Asia during World War II which had devastated its neighbors, leaving it with an intact industrial infrastructure that could manufacture goods for the devastated countries of Asia and Europe. It had vast natural resources that were voraciously sought by the emerging industrial economies of Japan and Europe. Unemployment was low and incomes were high. Graduates from prestigious schools like Geelong Grammar and Melbourne University were viewed as assets to any organization thus in high demand, regardless of their grades or the number of years it took to graduate. Employers were literally knocking on their doors to hire them.

Consequently, there was not a lot of pressure on Mechai and his friends to perform. Life was free and easy for them, and the opportunities were vast. They just went through a natural evolutionary process — boarding school, university, a good job, a prosperous life. University was like a right of passage, a credential for entrance into a select club. They could afford to goof off, to be irresponsible, to fail a course, to repeat a year; because they would eventually pass and a job would be waiting for them.

Nor was Mechai quite as insouciant as this description implies when compared to his friends. He always maintained a little more decorum during parties; he stopped playing cards a little sooner. He applied himself a little more academically, took advantage of opportunities just a little more. He was more considerate and thoughtful than the others, more generous and caring, more sociable. While he was certainly no paragon of virtue, he was really behaving just like the average university student in Australia in the 1960s. After all, that is what he was.

In order to sustain himself in his bachelor lifestyle at Royal Parade, Mechai required some modest financial resources. His parents covered room, board, and tuition for four years. Beyond that, Mechai had to work to obtain spending money. From 1958 until he finished his Bachelor's degree in 1964, Mechai worked in odd jobs every summer holiday like everyone else in Australia to earn extra money. The kind of work he did was less important than the money he made doing it. He worked at Coca Cola for two years doing specials. While at Coca Cola, he became a "jockey" parking delivery trucks in tight spaces after all deliveries were made and the trucks returned to the yard. For a time he worked on a road repair crew. He worked one year at the Crestnet Knitting Factory wrapping and shipping goods. Another summer found him at AIG/AIA Insurance Company scrutinizing lapsed insurance policies. He labored in the Shares Department of Dunlop Rubber Co., and even worked as a supervisor taking care of children in the Lord Mayor's Camp. But the best money he made was going out to rural districts with no sewage outside Melbourne emptying night soil cans. These jobs introduced Mechai to working class people with less education from different backgrounds, people he could never meet at exclusive schools like Geelong Grammar or Melbourne University. He really liked these people, mixed with them comfortably, and enjoyed their company. It was an important part of his education.

As Mechai began his fifth year at Melbourne University in 1964, he decided that five years was quite enough time to earn a Bachelor's degree. This year he would apply himself to his studies to complete his degree. There were just two subjects impeding his graduation — accounting and statistics. They were also his worst courses. Mechai hated to learn by rote memory, which is how he approached accounting and statistics. His poor grades in both subjects were not surprising. So he tried a different approach. He tried to understand and rationalize the principles of accounting and statistics rather than memorize them. The results were amazing. When exam time came, he knew both subjects so well that he finished the exams in half the time. Mechai's first reaction was panic. "What have I done wrong?" he thought as he laid down his pencil. "Everything seems to add up." It did. He scored high on his exams that year and graduated from Melbourne University with his degree in commerce at the end of 1964.

Thailand was his home. His parents had made it eminently clear to him that he had been sent abroad for his education so that he could return home, help his country, and do some good. Although he had returned to Thailand sporadically during his time in Australia,[14] he grew more anxious to return as the years progressed. Mechai loved Australia, considers it his second home, and maintains strong associations with the country and its people to this day. But he was a Thai. Dr. Ella and Dr. Samak had taken great efforts to raise him as a Thai. Even 12 wonderful years in Australia could not dilute that allegiance. When he completed his contract with the RAAF in December 1965, it was time for him to return to Thailand. Mechai Viravaidya was going home.

*Geelong Grammar School cricket team, 1959. Mechai is seated in the middle row far right*

*Mechai at Timbertop*

*Mechai the cricketer at GGS*

*Timbertop accommodation unit*

*Mechai in wedding attire at Rory and Joan Treweeke's wedding, 1963*

*Rory and Joan Treweeke leaving Trinity College chapel. Mechai and Ian Brown as groomsmen are right of Jaon*

*Rory Treweeke (left) with Roena Clark and Mechai (right) at a polo match in Adelaide*

## NOTES:

1 Even after electricity was introduced to the Raffles, the hotel retained the punkah wallahs to ventilate its larger rooms in the colonial style: "by wiggling their big toes which were tied to a sheet of white cloth hanging from the ceiling. They could keep going even when asleep." See "Punkah Hotels," *The Economist*, May 3-9, 1997.

2 In the Australian school system, Junior School is roughly analogous to a middle or junior high school. Students complete the Junior School at approximately 14 years of age. The Senior School comprises five years and is roughly analogous to High School. Mechai spent six years at Geelong Grammar, one in the Junior School and five in the Senior School. The years he attended and the terminology used to describe the programs in which he enrolled are shown below:

| Year | Mechai's Age | Program/School | Form |
|---|---|---|---|
| 1954 | 13 | Junior School | 2nd |
| 1955 | 14 | 1st yr Senior School | 3rd |
| 1956 | 15 | Timbertop | 4th |
| 1957 | 16 | Leaving | 5th |
| 1958 | 17 | Leaving | 5th |
| 1959 | 18 | Matriculation | 6th |

3 The first Thai to attend Geelong Grammar was M.R. Kasem Samosorn Kasemsri in 1947. He went on to become a distinguished diplomat, Thai Ambassador to the United States, Deputy Prime

Minister, and Minister of Foreign Affairs. M.R. Kasem Samosorn entered Geelong in the Senior School. The first Asian to attend Junior School at Geelong was Charles Ho from Singapore.

4 The town of Geelong was a sleepy, pastoral, frontier town situated 70 km. southwest of Melbourne when gold was struck at Ballarat in 1851. Located 86 km. Inland, Ballarat was most conveniently approached from Geelong. By 1855, when Geelong Grammar School was established as the Church of England School, Geelong was a bustling mining town of 20,000 people, with an additional 30,000 miners in its hinterlands. Strategically located at the gateway to the mining region, it was competing with Melbourne as the hub of Victoria's economy. Influential figures in the community lobbied for and received government grants to convert Geelong's Church of England School into Geelong Grammar School, with educational programs modeled on the English boarding schools. Geelong Grammar School prospered in Geelong until 1914, when it was moved across Corio Bay to its present site at Corio facing the bay. The appointment of Sir James Darling as Headmaster in 1930 revolutionized the school. Darling's rich experience in the English public school system combined with his entrepreneurial instincts, led Geelong Grammar School on a quest for excellence that transformed the school into a premier academic institution, a reputation it enjoys to this day. He recruited new staff and raised the standard of scholarship. He restructured the schools finances and put them on a sound footing. He introduced the Timbertop experiment. The innovation that most invigorated Geelong Grammar School was the introduction of co-educational instruction. It started as an exchange with the Hermitage, a boarding school for girls, in 1970. In 1972, 33 girls entered the fifth and sixth form, Geelong Grammar's first female students. Subsequently, the "most famous boys school in Australia" (given that seal of royal approval after the enrollment of Prince Charles) was a co-educational institution. For more about the history of Geelong Grammar School see Weston Bate, *Light Blue Down Under — The History of Geelong Grammar School.*

5 In the "house" system, students of various ages from several forms board together in a single house. Although classes are taken with students from the same form, discipline, study and camaraderie are fostered by the house. Loyalty is to one's house first and foremost. In Geelong, inter-house sporting competitions were frequent and fierce, the battleground upon which Mechai would make his reputation.

6 There were actually two other campuses, one in the township of Geelong called Bostock House for younger boys, and Glamorgan in Melbourne for day scholars, but these were minor in comparison to the Corio and Timbertop campuses.

7 Sir James Darling was probably the most colorful and memorable Headmaster in Geelong's history. When he arrived in 1930, Geelong was experiencing some financial difficulties. When he left in 1961, it was renowned as one of the premier boarding schools in Australia. For an in-depth depiction of this interesting character, see *Richly Rewarding — An Autobiography*. Sir James passed away in 1993.

8 Mechai was elected to the Geelong Grammar School Council in 1995, the first Asian member of the Council. From his position on the Council, he continues his close association with Geelong Grammar School.

9 This is the last time the whole Viravaidya family would be together until all the children had finished their education more than 20 years later.

10 Throughout his years at Geelong, Mechai always had a host family in Melbourne, who were almost like surrogate parents to him. They would look after him, monitor his grades, and provide a home environment for him on short holidays. John and Anne Knox, Rory Treweeke's aunt, were his primary guardians for five of his six years there. When they left Melbourne in 1959, Peter and Petra DeWolf

became his guardians for his final year at Geelong. John Knox and Peter DeWolf were Old Geelong Grammarians.

11 The trucks that delivered "specials" for Coca Cola had a driver and a jockey. The driver navigated Melbourne's streets and the jockey delivered the goods. Mechai worked as the jockey on his truck. The driver was a medical student at Melbourne University named Julian Metzner. Julian was a Catholic, one of the first Catholics Mechai had ever met in Australia, since he lived primarily within the Anglican confines of Geelong Grammar. At Geelong Grammar, he had been taught that Catholics were ogres, papists, all left-handed, and ate no meat on Friday. But Julian was a good old boy, just like Mechai and his friends at Geelong. This episode reinforced for him Dr. Ella's counsel that he should never have preconceived notions about other people, regardless of what he had been told or read. He should accept people for what they are, and make his own judgments.

12 Ironically, Mechai was awarded an honorary Doctorate in Laws at Melbourne University many years later, only the second Thai to receive an honorary doctorate at that prestigious institution. The first was H.M. King Bhumipol Adulyadej. In his acceptance speech Mechai said, "I am sure one reason this award is being given to me is because it took me so long to finish my degree here and I had to pay so much money in tuition, that I was one of Melbourne University's largest contributors at that time."

13 The Old Geelong Grammarians, affectionately referred to as "The Old Boys" in those days, were alumni from Geelong Grammar who continued to fraternize through sports, fund-raising, or social service. Other boarding schools, like Melbourne Grammar, had similar alumni associations, and sports competitions among them were spirited affairs which Mechai rarely missed. Since Geelong Grammar became co-educational in the 1970s, the Old Geelong Grammarians are now referred to with the

more politically correct appellation "The Old Boys and the Old Girls".

14 Between 1954, when he arrived in Australia, and 1965, when he returned to Thailand, Mechai only visited Thailand three times: in 1955, 1957, and 1960. When he returned to Thailand in December 1965, he had been in Australia for six years straight without visiting Thailand.

## 4

# THE RISING STAR

*In many ways, Mechai's return to Thailand from his studies in Australia resembled Dr. Samak's homecoming from England 30 years earlier. Both had been abroad for extended periods, spent their formative years in English speaking countries, and returned to Thailand immeasurably transfigured by momentous historical events.*

In other ways, they were quite different. Where Dr. Samak had been a King's Scholar returning to his country with distinguished professional credentials, Mechai had completed his university degree in commerce uncertain of his mission and the direction of his future. Where Dr. Samak had closely followed the political changes his country experienced in the 1930s, Mechai, who was barely a teen when he left Thailand, was unaware of the tectonic shift in the political winds that buffeted Southeast Asia during his absence.

When Mechai arrived in Bangkok in December 1965, Thailand was a front-line state in the Second Indochina War convulsing Southeast Asia, more popularly referred to as the Vietnam War. Over 200,000 American troops were propping up a shambolic military regime in Saigon and pursuing a land war in South Vietnam. Extensive US aerial bombardment of key industrial and military installations was intrinsic to a strategy intended to bomb North Vietnam either into submission or at least to the negotiating table. Neighboring Laos was teetering on the brink of a civil war that submerged the country in chaos. Thailand was a critical player in all of these affairs, first as a bulwark against communist encroachment and a domino to be propped up at all costs; second, as a strategic base for prosecuting the air war; and finally, providing troops for the fighting, primarily in Laos but also in Vietnam.

A new facet of Thailand's political life was its strategic relationship with the United States. In the midst of post-colonial turmoil in Southeast Asia, with the looming communist specter already engulfing China, North Korea and North Vietnam to the north and threatening Indonesia and Malaysia to the south, Thailand was viewed as an independent, stable, and powerful ally essential to the Cold War policy of containment. The United States had strategic interests in supporting a pro-Western, anti-Communist, market-oriented Thailand, both economically and militarily. By 1969, there were 46,000 US military personnel stationed in Thailand. Huge air bases in Udon Thani, Phitsanulok, Nakhon Ratchasima, and Utapao were staging points for B-52 raids on Vietnam and Laos. Part of the US Seventh Fleet was stationed in the Gulf of Thailand, prepared to intervene militarily anywhere in the region. Between 1951 and 1975, US$ 2.5 billion in military assistance flowed from the US to Thailand, equivalent to 54% of the Thai military budget. An additional US$ 627 million of US development aid fueled development of infrastructure, agriculture, irrigation, and education. Thailand was awash in dollars. In the period 1959-69, GNP growth averaged 8.6% per year, almost double its performance in the 1950s. The economy boomed.

Thailand's transformation from an indifferent ally of a defeated Japan to the focal point of the West's Cold War strategy in Southeast Asia was a classic example of shrewd political maneuvering, opportunism, and luck. The second Phibunsongkhram Government quickly exhibited its pro-Western foreign policy by being the first Asian country to send troops to fight in Korea. Conversely, demand for Thai commodity exports created by the Korean War stimulated the Thai economy. As communist governments gained control in China (1949), North Korea (1953), and North Vietnam (1954), the West in general but the United States in particular increased its reliance on Thailand for regional stability. In 1954, it became the cornerstone of the Southeast Asia Treaty Organization (SEATO). As Thailand's geo-political importance grew, the torrent of foreign aid gushed, with the military as the main beneficiary. Discredited and demoralized after World War II, the Thai military quickly regained its pre-war prominence in the 1950s.[1]

With the Cold War providing a convenient cover for its frequent coup d'état and authoritarian excesses, the Thai military maintained its pre-eminence for the next 30 years. Phibunsongkhram was toppled by a military coup d'état in September 1957, replaced by another ineffectual, self-serving civilian government. When the government proved itself incapable of acting on urgent domestic and international priorities, the military under Field Marshal Sarit Thanarat stepped in and reimposed its control. Sarit's government exercised authoritarian control but was committed to development. Also, appreciating the integral role of the monarchy in Thai society and the respect that the Thai people had for it, he supported a more active role for the monarchy under H.M. King Bhumibol Adulyadej.

When Sarit died in 1963, his hand-picked successor, General Thanom Kittikachorn, took over the government. He was assisted by General Praphas Charusathian as Deputy Prime Minister and Minister of the Interior, who wielded considerable power within the government. The Thanom-Praphas Government engineered even closer military and economic ties with the United States. This alliance was considered essential because the Vietnam War was heating up, and Thailand had genuine security concerns. The North Vietnamese made no secret of their intentions to "liberate" all of Indochina. The Laotian Crisis of 1960-62,[2] which destabilized Thailand's entire northeastern border, amplified the military's paranoia. When the United States offered its assistance to directly defend Thailand against foreign encroachment, its rapid acquiescence was understandable. Thailand's deepening involvement in the Indochina War by 1966 was the logical progression of these events.

Mechai was completely unaware of these current events and political intrigues prior to returning to Thailand in December 1965. Indeed, in this respect he was just like most Thai people in 1965, for whom the Vietnam War was just a sideshow that had little direct impact on their daily lives. Mechai was just happy to be back with his family and friends. His parents had built him a small apartment on top of their garage, a vantage point from which he could pursue his one overriding concern — finding a job to support himself. Although inclined to work in government, he had no real mission that he aspired to. As far as Mechai was concerned, he had no exceptionally strong points with which to sell himself. He just wanted to get a job and get on with his life.

There followed an interlude of several weeks when Mechai took some time off to scout job opportunities and see friends. As frequently happens, luck played a big part in his job search. Also, with Thailand's booming economy, demand for university graduates with degrees from western universities was high. In short order Mechai had three job offers. The first was at the Ministry of Commerce in the Insurance Division. The Permanent Secretary of the Ministry of Commerce had met Mechai when he was President of the Thai Students Association at Melbourne University, where Mechai had done some simultaneous translations of his speeches. Unbeknownst to Mechai, the Insurance Division was proposed by the Permanent Secretary because it was the fast track to advancement in the Ministry of Commerce. For Mechai, however, insurance seemed boring. He envisioned himself sitting in some dilapidated government office examining claim forms, much as he had done while working for AIG in Australia. In his mind, this was one step up from being a bookkeeper. He politely turned the job down.

His second offer was in the private sector with Shell Oil Company. They needed someone fluent in Thai and English, a qualification which Mechai fit perfectly. This was a rather lucrative offer compared to working for the government, so Mechai needed to give it some consideration. He consulted Dr. Ella, his moral compass, to see what she thought about this opportunity.

"Mechai," she advised him, "if you work for Shell, you will make a lot of money, you will play golf, you will have time off, you will live a good life. But if people like you work only for money, who will help the poor? That's not what we educated you for. We educated you to help other people." This advice made Mechai pause and think. His first thought was about the old woman carrying the heavy baskets across the road when he was seven years old. Dr. Ella's advice then was exactly the same as her advice now. "If people who had been blessed with education and wealth don't help the poor, who will?" Mechai had received every advantage in life. His parents had provided him with a good education at great personal sacrifice. His mother had made very clear how she would like him to repay that debt, by helping the poor. He certainly couldn't do that working for Shell Oil. He rejected the job offer.

His third option would indirectly give him an opportunity to fulfill his mother's wishes. Dr. Samak was acquainted with the

Permanent Secretary of the National Economic Development Board (NEDB),[3] Prayad Buranasiri, and asked him whether he had any positions for which Mechai might be suited. NEDB was a relatively new government agency created in 1961 to coordinate the vast resources that were now pouring into Thailand for its economic development. The Secretary General offered Mechai a position in the Evaluation Division of NEDB. The Evaluation Division was responsible for reviewing all development projects and evaluating their impact upon the economy and people of Thailand. Mechai knew nothing about development, but was attracted by the broad scope and potential this job offered. He also saw the possibility of fulfilling his mother's wishes, to help other people. He decided to accept the position with NEDB.

During this job-hunting period, there occurred a very serendipitous episode that would have a significant impact upon Mechai's life. In January 1966, Thailand was being swept by a Miss Universe Beauty Pageant mania. Miss Thailand had just been crowned Miss Universe, and together with the first runner-up Miss USA, was making a triumphal return to Thailand replete with ticker tape parades and myriad guest appearances. One of Mechai's distant aunts knew the official chaperone for Miss Universe. She was looking for escorts for the two beauty queens as they made their rounds of guest appearances. She knew Mechai had some free time, so she rang him up to see if he was interested.

Mechai possessed the two qualifications required of an escort — he had the free time to spare and he spoke English and Thai. He knew nothing about beauty pageants and beauty queens. But he accepted the offer nonetheless. For its amusement value alone, this opportunity held great promise.

As an official escort to Miss Universe and her first runner-up, Mechai had to accompany them to all appearances and special events, chat with them a bit during intermissions, and provide them with pleasant company. All of these Mechai did with admirable poise and aplomb. On the third night, he was escorting Miss Universe to an appearance near the Foreign Ministry. During a break in the action, he asked for her autograph.

"Khun Phook (her nickname), the woman who does my laundry at home would like to have your autograph. When she heard that I would be with you, she asked me to get it."

Miss Universe was pleased to oblige, but neither she nor Mechai had any paper.

"Why don't you sign it on my cuff?" Mechai retorted as he pulled up his jacket sleeve. "When she washes my shirt, she'll see your signature."

Miss Universe found this unorthodox suggestion amusing. So she signed her autograph on the cuff of his white shirt sleeve. All of a sudden, flash bulbs started popping when a swarm of photographers descended upon them as Miss Universe signed Mechai's cuff.

The next morning, that picture was splashed across the front page of every newspaper in Bangkok. Seeing a chance to sell some newspapers, the press had manufactured a story casting Mechai as a contender for Miss Universe's affections, competing with her beaux, who was a dashing Thai Army officer. They called him "The Dark Horse" for Khun Phook's affections. That there was no substance whatsoever to this story did not discourage the press for one second. All they cared about was selling newspapers.

And did it ever sell newspapers! The story stayed on the front pages for days. For his part, Mechai became an instant celebrity overnight. Everywhere he went, people recognized him. "There's Mechai!" was the ubiquitous greeting he received whenever he ventured out. Restaurants called to offer free meals and nightclubs invited him for free entertainment if they could hang his picture on the wall. Girls would wait outside his house to see him. Even Dr. Samak didn't dare go to his normal Rotary Club meetings for two weeks to avoid the media frenzy.

Mechai was overwhelmed, and more than a little discomfited, by his sudden popularity. One day he was no one — unknown, unrecognized, and happy. The next day everyone knew him, people gaped at him, they called out his name. He felt like an animal in a zoo. He had lost that most precious commodity, privacy. Now he was a public figure. Celebrity has its price.

He didn't know quite how to handle this situation. He certainly didn't revel in it. Mechai was perfectly happy being unknown and carefree. Anything that would hasten a return to his former obscure existence was desirable. So he did the only thing he thought sensible. He just stayed home all the time. With time, he thought, the furor would blow over.

And so it did. But not before it had transformed his life. Once you become an overnight sensation, people don't forget who you are, even if you stay in hiding for a while. Only when the time came for him to commence his work at NEDB did Mechai emerge from his seclusion. When he arrived at NEDB, people were hanging from the rafters to get a glimpse of him. On his first field trip, to the South of Thailand, he was met by the Governor's wife and provincial authorities arranged for the press to meet him. For Mechai, life would never be the same.

The Sarit-Thanom Governments' commitment to economic development required a government infrastructure to promote economic growth and manage the stability of the economy through investment promotion, budget control, fiscal and monetary management, and development planning. The National Economic Development Board (NEDB) was established to coordinate centralized economic planning. Originally designated the National Economic Development Council, it was consolidated in 1961 into the NEDB, reporting directly to the Prime Minister. Its main function was formulation of five-year development plans. Its first plan for the period 1961-66 emphasized infrastructure investment in irrigation, transport, electric power, and education; and encouraged economic growth in the private sector.

Like Mechai, most of NEDB's key mid-level staff were educated largely at western universities and spoke good English. Unlike Mechai, most had specialized training in current development thinking — that growth could be achieved through spontaneous efforts of the private sector, bolstered by a friendly environment encouraging foreign investment, fostered and assisted by supportive government policy. Mechai had no idea what the current development thinking in Thailand was when he joined NEDB. However, with his background in commerce and economics, he had the tools to learn. His learning would have to be done on the job.

The Evaluation Division provided the perfect classroom for his education in development. Because NEDB coordinated development planning in all sectors, the Evaluation Division had to evaluate projects in every sector. Mechai had to travel widely and frequently. He visited every region in Thailand — North, Northeast, Central, and South — to evaluate projects to build roads, dams, ports, schools, irrigation systems, power plants, telephone systems, airports, water supplies, highways, and railroads. Through these trips, Mechai came to understand what development was, how development worked, and very frequently how it didn't work. He found development to be an intensely captivating subject. He had actually stumbled upon something that really interested him.

During his extensive travels with NEDB, Mechai came to know and understand Thailand and its people. Several things made a strong impression upon him. Born and raised in Bangkok and educated abroad, Mechai had really never seen Thailand. Now he explored every corner of the Kingdom and met the real Thai people. Thailand's diversity astounded him. The rugged North was blanketed by an impenetrable range of densely forested mountains which provided Thailand with some of the richest hardwood forests in the world. The Meo, Yao, Lahu, Lisu, Akha, Khamu, and Lue hilltribes that inhabited the North, with their colorful tribal garb and medieval customs, were nomadic farmers who emigrated to Thailand from southern China. The hilltribes practised slash and burn agriculture to grow upland rice and opium, the region's largest cash crop. The Golden Triangle, one of the world's most prolific opium producing regions formed by the confluence of Burma, Laos, and northern Thailand, was a fiefdom unto itself, impervious to the administrative control and development efforts of any of these countries.

Northeastern Thailand, by far the largest and most populous region, was also its poorest. It was inhabited by the Isan people of Lao origin and dominated by the Mekong river basin. The arid climate in its high plains allowed only one rice crop per year, and the region was alternately buffeted by floods and droughts. Central Thailand was the country's rice bowl. The rivers draining the northern mountains combined with the fertile alluvial soils of the central flood plain to provide three rice crops for its industrious farmers. In southern Thailand, which bordered Malaysia, fishing supplemented farming as a source of food, and Islam supplanted Buddhism as the dominant religion. Thailand was not a monolithic country, Mechai soon learned, but a potpourri of ethnic groups, religions, cultures, topography, and climate. If development programs were to be successful, they would have to be tailored to the realities in each region.

Mechai was also struck by the ubiquitous poverty. Despite Thailand's impressive annual growth and the massive infusion of foreign aid, the vast majority of Thai people remained depressingly poor. The rural people, who comprised 85% of the population, lived in small village groups with wooden homes elevated on stilts to protect against flooding. Electricity, clean water, and sanitation were non-existent in many areas. Average caloric intake barely met minimum standards, and insidious forms of mild and moderate protein energy malnutrition compromised the people's health status and sapped their productivity. Infectious diseases were rampant, and vector borne diseases like malaria were out of control. One in ten children born would die of diarrhea, respiratory infections, tetanus, or malaria before they reached one year of age. Agriculture accounted for 27% of Thailand's Gross National Product. Fully 70% of Thai households obtained their income from farming.[4] Yet many farmers still practised subsistence agriculture. And those who did enter the cash economy were easy prey for the landowners and middlemen who dominated marketing, distribution, and credit. The Thailand that Mechai saw was a classic example of maldistributed, trickle-down development where the elites siphoned off the cream and left only crumbs for the people.

There was one other observation that Mechai made again and again during his travels. In every sub-district he reached, in every village he visited, there seemed to be so many children. At first, this observation was purely subjective. When he arrived in a village, hordes of children would greet him. When he visited a rural-development project or drove through small towns, young children could be seen everywhere. Young village women would be carrying one and sometimes two infants. The image of a mother breastfeeding an infant while two others tugged at her sarong was repeated over and over. When he asked women how many children they had, responses of seven or ten were the rule rather than the exception. And usually one or two of these had already died. Although he was still a fledgling development economist with little knowledge of demographics, Mechai knew that all of these children would have to be fed, clothed, housed, educated, and eventually employed. In the economic geography course he took at Melbourne University, there was a theory that posited that there is no population problem, because food production was increasing and new land could be put into cultivation. What he saw in rural Thailand was the exact opposite. Common sense told him that overpopulation had deleterious implications for Thailand's development. This was one area, he decided, that would require further study.

On every trip to the provinces, rather than just listening to the glowing rhetoric and soothing palaver that government officials spewed forth so effortlessly in support of their projects, Mechai would spend most of his time talking to the villagers who were supposed to be the beneficiaries. He wanted to see development from their perspective, to understand how they viewed the changes it wrought, and to really appreciate how these projects affected their lives. Their responses were most enlightening. Although they were the target of these development projects, the people were never consulted in advance and didn't seem to be reaping any benefit from them at all. If a power plant were to be built in their area, the local people would only find out about it when the engineers came to survey the sites. Villagers displaced to build dams supplying electricity to cities would never receive any electricity themselves. Rather than being beneficiaries of development, these rural villagers were more like an excuse for lavish development projects that benefited the urban middle and upper classes and corrupt government officials. The whole system seemed perverse.

Through his travels, his discussions with the people, and the inferences that he drew from these, Mechai came to the conclusion that development is a disturbance in the social and economic life of the people, no matter how well it is done. The more people you have, the more the benefits are diluted. To do it correctly, the people needed to be consulted first, and enlisted as partners. To introduce change, it must be done gently and gradually in a way that is both understandable and palatable to the local people for whom it is intended. Most importantly, if population growth wasn't curbed first, it would negate all the gains from development. This was certainly not how development was being done in Thailand circa 1967. Maybe, Mechai thought, he could do something to change that.

Between 1966 and 1968, Mechai continued his extensive travels to evaluate development projects for NEDB. This was a period of intense intellectual and emotional growth for him, resulting in a seismic transformation in his personality. Thailand's development was a subject that profoundly interested him and to which he was prepared to devote his intellectual capital. His travels had introduced him to the people of Thailand. He had come to know their poverty and hopelessness, but also to appreciate their spiritual beauty, gentle simplicity, unquestioned integrity, and boundless generosity. These people were poor, and the system was not helping them. Trapped between the usurious middlemen and landowners who oppressed them at every opportunity, an apathetic rural bureaucracy indifferent to their plight, and massive development investment that not only bypassed them but frequently handicapped them, the rural agricultural people of Thailand, in fact, had the deck stacked against them. As his mother so often told him, "If people like you don't help the poor, who will?" Now Mechai realized how he could combine his interest in economic development with a more noble mission — to help Thailand's disadvantaged poor. In the future he would devote himself to working for the people. And NEDB was the platform from which he would pursue both his interest and his mission.

After each of his field trips, Mechai had to write a report in English and Thai assessing the status of the various development projects he visited. Writing reports in English was no problem for him. Writing them in Thai was a different matter. Mechai had not written in Thai since 1954 when he left for Australia. While he could certainly speak Thai fluently and could still write respectably, he could not write in the lofty bureaucratic style required for an NEDB report. He desperately needed some help to improve his reports.

Fortunately for Mechai, that help arrived shortly after he joined NEDB, when Tavatchai Traitongyoo was also appointed to NEDB's Evaluation Division. Unlike the other staff in the Evaluation Division, Tavatchai was a recent graduate of Thammasat University in Bangkok, came from a decidedly middle class family, and lacked fluency in English. Although Tavatchai was intelligent and eminently capable, the Chief of the Evaluation Division had an unspoken bias for foreign trained graduates. Consequently, Tavatchai was continually overlooked when choice assignments were passed around. Mechai found this treatment unfair and unacceptable. For him, merit was the only yardstick by which a person should be measured. When judged by that standard, Tavatchai scored very respectable grades.

When he joined NEDB, Tavatchai had already heard of Mechai through the Miss Universe story. When he saw him for the first time, he thought Mechai was a foreign expert in NEDB because he spoke such good English and looked like a farang. Tavatchai was apprehensive about meeting Mechai. Being a local graduate, he thought that a famous personality like Mechai would have little use and less time for someone like him. After all, the other foreign trained staff in the Evaluation Division came from rich families, and were not interested in a common person like Tavatchai. Why should Mechai be any different?

Quite to the contrary, Mechai and Tavatchai immediately gravitated toward each other after meeting. Tavatchai found Mechai to be an ordinary guy like him. Unlike the other staff, whose families provided them with expensive cars, Mechai drove around in a beat up jeep that seemed a prime candidate for the junk heap. Mechai was always courteous and respectful toward everyone, including Tavatchai. And he was committed to his work. Soon they started traveling together. Tavatchai was moved by Mechai's compassion for the people, by his dismay at the appalling conditions in which they lived, and by his determination to do something about it. Mechai was impressed with Tavatchai's intelligence, his innate understanding of the people, and his common sense and good judgment. Mutual respect developed. They became close friends.

Mechai and Tavatchai also found that they possessed complementary skills and weaknesses. When it came time to write their assessment reports, they decided to collaborate. For Mechai's reports, Tavatchai would write the Thai version and for Tavatchai's reports, Mechai would write the English. Their reports were outstanding. In the process, Tavatchai taught Mechai to write impeccable Thai, a skill that would be essential for his future work in population and development. Mechai and Tavatchai became the perfect team. They remain so to this day.

Mechai's first two years at NEDB were a time of hard work and intense study. He read prodigiously. He learned about the different sectors that contributed to the Thai economy — commerce, housing, energy, education, health, transport, defense, agriculture, forestry, and foreign affairs. He studied macroeconomics, how Thailand's monetary policy, fiscal policy, trade policy, regulatory framework, and labor markets impacted the economy. He studied the microeconomics of the rural farmer, especially their exploitation by landowners, merchants, middlemen, and banks.

He familiarized himself with foreign affairs, especially with the Indochina War that embroiled Thailand's neighbors, the threats it posed to Thailand's security, and the distortions the huge US military and economic presence in Thailand had upon its economy and social fabric. Most importantly, he learned about demographics and population growth, about the impact of overpopulation on the health and nutritional status of the Thai people, and its ramifications for Thailand's economy.

The more he read and learned, the more astute his evaluation reports became. The more he traveled and observed, the more critical he became not only of the development projects he was evaluating, but of Thailand's development in general. Within NEDB, he became more outspoken about perceived misguided development policies. He was impatient with the pace of change that the government was willing or able to deliver. He became an outspoken advocate for intensified population control as an integral component of Thailand's development policy. Within the bureaucracy Mechai was increasingly labeled as a brash activist who would make his positions known, however unpopular and regardless of the consequences. He could afford this luxury because his work was simultaneously being recognized for its insight and quality. His positions were being taken seriously, his recommendations heeded. Mechai was soon acknowledged as one of the rising young stars in NEDB.

In 1968, Mechai proposed that NEDB prepare a "Report to the Nation" on the progress of Thailand's development. Rather than producing a thick, densely written report that would only collect dust on bookshelves, he proposed a series of terse articles directed at the development establishment suitable for newspaper publication. He wanted to present his ideas in the public arena, to become a player in the public debate on development. The proposal eventually reached the Secretary General of NEDB, who was intrigued by the idea and asked Mechai to prepare it. His "Report to the Nation" was subsequently published in the *Bangkok World*, Bangkok's leading English language morning newspaper. The editor liked the report and asked Mechai to write a series of articles.

In one of his evaluations of development projects, Mechai produced a report critically evaluating a development project which chronicled not only its shortcomings but the persons responsible for them. The Deputy Secretary General of NEDB, who was reviewing Mechai's reports, called him in for a talk.

"Mechai," he began as he tossed the report on the table, "you have written a factual report outlining the deficiencies of this project. But you cannot write these things in an official government document. It would upset too many people in the responsible Ministry, leaving us with implacable opponents there who are even more resistant to the kinds of changes you recommend. If you want to write these things, it should be done with a velvet glove rather than a jagged ax."

These words struck a responsive synapse in Mechai's brain. He had been insensitive to the subtle nuances of internecine politics within the government bureaucracy. The Deputy Secretary General was right. Mechai now realized that many things that needed to be said could not be said in official government documents because they would ruffle too many feather and upset too many friends. Also, if he wanted to criticize, it should be done constructively. There had to be a better forum for him to present his ideas on development.

This reminded Mechai of the offer he had received from the editor of the *Bangkok World*. It was an English language daily whose readership represented the audience Mechai wanted to reach — educated development professionals from domestic universities, government ministries, and international agencies. The editor of the *Bangkok World* had liked his "Report to the Nation" and wanted Mechai to write a regular series of similar articles. Mechai was intrigued by the idea of a weekly column, and decided to accept the offer. He immediately consulted with the Secretary General of NEDB to seek his advice and approval. The Secretary General recognized the value of Mechai's work and the contribution it could make to the development dialogue in Thailand. He authorized Mechai to proceed, but cautioned "Just don't use your own name as the author, don't indicate any connection to NEDB, and if anyone asks me, I will tell them I don't know anything about it." Mechai was out in the cold on his own on this one.

The first weekly article appeared in the *Bangkok World* in March 1968 under the pen name "GNP". Mechai chose that sobriquet as the abbreviation for "Gross National Product", symbolizing the economic development perspective his articles would portray. But he also chose "GNP" because backward it spelled "PNG" which stood for "Persona Non Grata", something he would become if it was discovered that he was the author of these articles.

Under the guise of GNP, Mechai produced a weekly treatise on Thailand's development for the next four years. He wrote on every topic imaginable.[5] There were articles on Bangkok's traffic and urban blight, foreign trade and the balance of payments, irrigation, drought, tourism, the war on middlemen, the impending economic supremacy of Japan, civil service reform, corruption, the perils of prebendalism,[6] agriculture, transportation, commerce, the energy sector. He wrote about the US presence in Thailand, and as early as 1968 was projecting the adjustments that would be required by the US withdrawal. Every year there would be an analysis of the Thai economy and the government budget. He even advanced his assessment (quite pessimistic) on the consequences for Thailand of the Nixon-Agnew victory in the 1968 US presidential election. Special attention was reserved for what was becoming his favorite topic — population management to support economic development. He sympathized with the supporters of birth control who were lobbying for a population policy in the face of opposition from a pro-nationalist military government anxious to maintain the supply of recruits for its military adventures. He was a vocal proponent of a National Family Planning Program that would give the people access to the contraceptives they needed to control their fertility and limit family size.

The GNP articles provided Mechai with the perfect forum to disseminate his ideas about Thailand's development. GNP soon became required reading for the development literati in Bangkok. His writing style was crisp and concise. He used humor to modulate his criticisms, satire to mask them. When the situation warranted, he could be complimentary and supportive. Because so much of Thailand's development at the time was foreign controlled,[7] Mechai used GNP to present a distinctively Thai angle on development. Thailand was being flooded with US development assistance and personnel. With it came US technical experts, who were becoming ubiquitous in the various government ministries. There were even ex-Texas Rangers, resplendent in their Stetson hats, serving as Public Safety Officers in the Ministry of Interior. Thai government officials were being sent to US universities for advanced training, and returning with American ideas about development. GNP provided a welcome yet trenchant counterpoint to this foreign domination. GNP's popularity soared.

Writing weekly articles on development now being closely scrutinized by development professionals imposed enormous responsibility on Mechai. He had to research his subject matter thoroughly, check his sources meticulously, and make sure that he had his facts correct. A completed article would go to Dr. Ella for final editing. If it passed her scrutiny, it was ready for the press. When he was in college writing for a professor, Mechai could afford to be careless. The only penalty for shoddy work was a lower grade, a consequence Mechai tolerated quite readily at the time. Now he was writing for the public, and the public judges harshly. Mechai may have been an average student at University, but what he missed because of indifference there was being offset by his diligence now. GNP and NEDB were Mechai's real education in development.

Although Mechai was writing anonymously and never publicized it, in time people came to know that he was writing the GNP articles. His standing within the development community was elevated accordingly. He became a regular guest at ambassadorial functions. When foreign notables came to Bangkok, Mechai was on their list of people to meet. He met with Robert McNamara and had breakfast with Henry Kissinger. His development star was rising. As will be seen shortly, he had simultaneously burnished his image as a media personality, building upon his popularity from the Miss Universe incident to become a real celebrity. It was through GNP that he gained his reputation as a respected development economist. That was where his priorities lay.

While Mechai was totally engrossed in his work at NEDB, and devoting ample spare time to studying development and writing his GNP articles, his monthly NEDB salary of 1,600 baht (US$ 80) hardly provided a 25-year-old bachelor with the financial wherewithal required to live in an urban metropolis like Bangkok. The only way he could make ends meet was to take other jobs to supplement his income, a practice that was both legal and common among government employees at the time. Shortly after joining NEDB, Mechai took an evening job as an English teacher at Thammasat University. His classes were always packed with the curious and celebrity watchers who wanted to get a glimpse of the famous Mechai who, as the press purported, was the object of Miss Universe's affections.

Soon afterwards, while on his way home from classes at Thammasat, Mechai was listening to an English language radio program broadcast by Jeff Baker, when it was announced that Baker was leaving the show and the station was looking for a replacement. Only foreigners living in Thailand need apply, it stipulated, as the station wanted to appeal to an English speaking audience. Mechai was intrigued by this opportunity but put off by their preference for a foreigner. He had done some work on radio while in Australia and enjoyed using it as a medium for communication. But he found the station's insinuation that a Thai was not qualified for this position insulting. So he prepared a demo tape, where he played some music and added a bit of humorous chit-chat in his impeccable English, and sent it to the station using the pseudonym "Nicola" so they wouldn't know he was Thai. The station loved the demo and gave him the job. He thoroughly savored the dumbfounded look on the people's face when he showed up for the first taping and they saw who Nicola really was.

The show, which aired at 9:30 P.M. every evening, became very popular, especially among students. He kept the pseudonym "Nicola" so that the show would neither add to nor benefit from the Mechai celebrity. He interspersed popular music with funny or sarcastic comments about life in Bangkok. Then he began adding a little Thai to his commentary to broaden his audience appeal. Listeners were attracted to this "Nicola" who could banter so amusingly in English and Thai. On Sunday evenings he would invite special guests to his show to discuss current events and popular issues, allowing him to dovetail his broadcast with his development work. At the end of each broadcast he would sign off by saying, "It's time for me to go now, and if you are driving please be careful, because the car you hit might be mine."

In 1968, after two years on radio as Nicola, Mechai was invited to perform in an outdoor play at Thammasat University.

The play was called "King Ramkhamhaeng", about the legendary king of 12th century Sukhothai. As the second-ranked general in King Ramkhamhaeng's army, Mechai was the leading supporting actor in the play. Six months of rehearsals were followed by 46 performances, one per night and two performances each on Saturday and Sunday. Before a live audience, Mechai was in his element. He was stimulated by the audience, developed a personal chemistry with them, enjoyed interacting with them, and would tailor his performance to the nuances of each audience. For Mechai, radio was entertaining but acting was electrifying.

Having achieved some critical acclaim for his performance at Thammasat University, soon thereafter Mechai was invited to perform on television. All of Bangkok at the time was engrossed with a television series that offered theatrical presentations of best-selling books. The entire book, which was usually so popular that most people had already read it before it was performed, was presented in sequential episodes televised twice per month over a six-month period. Because the scripts were so faithful to the original book, often using the same dialogue, the audiences liked them as much as the books — sometimes more — and followed the episodes faithfully. When the series was aired on the last Thursday and Friday of each month, the streets of Bangkok were quiet, even deserted, as the people scrambled for the nearest television. It was like watching "Twin Peaks" Thai style.

Mechai was the leading actor in six series, appearing in 12 episodes over a six-month period. He was usually given the script on Tuesday for the Thursday and Friday performance. Since the episodes were performed before a studio audience and aired live, there was little room for error. Mechai always read the book in advance, so he knew the story, the character he played, the emotions being projected, and the milieu in which the story was set. With only two days to memorize the script, he had to learn to ad lib if he forgot his lines, which fortunately didn't happen too often. When it did, he was able to extemporize with an easy self-confidence. Through this experience, Mechai learned to feel at home in front of a camera.

The first series in which he appeared was received well, and Mechai's performance was applauded by the critics and the viewing audience alike. Naturally, he was asked to appear in the next series, based on a book entitled "Koo Kham" (meaning "The Tragic Couple") about an unusually gentle Japanese naval Lieutenant stationed in Bangkok during the Second World War who falls in love with a Thai women. Mechai played the Japanese naval Lieutenant. Koo Kham had already been adapted into a film or television series five times. Most people felt that the version of Koo Kham in which Mechai appeared was the best book adaptation ever performed in the series, not only because of the poignant story but also because of the powerful acting and direction. In the final episode when the hero died, even the camera crew cried.

While his popularity from the Miss Universe episode provided the entrée for Mechai's stage and television career, his talent for acting was the reason for its successful continuation. His was a new and exciting face on the Bangkok theatrical scene. He got to meet Bangkok's leading actors, actresses, and media celebrities, expanding his circle of acquaintances far beyond the development community. Acting taught Mechai how to communicate with his audience, how to sense their mood and react to it, how to customize his message and performance. Through acting, he came to appreciate the power of mass entertainment media, how to utilize and then master it, valuable lessons that would be fruitfully applied when he became an outspoken family planning advocate. He also demonstrated the altruistic side of his personality that Dr. Ella had nurtured for years. He donated his entire salary from television to a fund at Thammasat University to buy dictionaries and learning aides for his English language students.

By 1969, Mechai Viravaidya was one busy young man. A budding development economist in NEDB's Evaluation Division by day, he would transfigure into his various alter personae at night. He continued to teach English to packed classes at Thammasat. Every night, "Nicola" would broadcast his pleasing mix of soft music and light banter, only now he taped a week's worth of shows on a Saturday. Once a week, GNP would produce a major tome on the cogent economic, social, and political issues facing Thailand during this precarious period of rapid development and encroaching war. Almost one year of intensive theatrical work at Thammasat was followed by another year where Mechai appeared twice per month on the most popular television program of the time. Radio, television, stage, and newspaper — Mechai was an active practitioner in all four media at the same time. He was learning to use them. He would soon master them.

From this experience, Mechai also learned how to utilize different media to reach different audiences. Through his GNP articles, he appealed to the educated development elites, both Thai and foreign. Through his radio program, he was reaching youth and middle class audiences. Television was the medium to reach the masses. His message was adapted for each audience. Tailored messages to discrete audience segments using different media as vehicles — this was classic communication theory espoused by McLuhan or Kotler, a guru of social marketing. Mechai, however, didn't learn these lessons from books, or universities, or distinguished professors. He learned by doing, by trial and error, by instinct and intuition, by doing what came naturally and spontaneously. He was a media phenomenon in the making.

It is useful to pause momentarily at this point to reflect on the monumental transformation Mechai had undergone in the space of four years. In 1965, he was just completing an undistinguished university career where card playing and an active social life sometimes took precedence over diligence and scholastic excellence. He had no specific mission driving his life. By 1969 he was a respected development economist and newspaper columnist whose weekly column was required reading for Bangkok's cognoscenti; and a media sensation recognized throughout Thailand. How could someone undergo such a metamorphosis in such a short time?

Gary Hudson was strategically positioned to observe and compare the two Mechais. Gary had known Mechai since Geelong Grammar and Melbourne University days, and maintained close contact with him until Mechai left Australia in December 1965. He had occasion to meet Mechai again in Bangkok in 1968 after a three-year hiatus. Gary was on his way to France with a stopover in Bangkok. He rang up Mechai to let him know he was coming.

"You must stay with me at my parents' compound," Mechai exhorted. Although Gary arrived at Mechai's residence late at night with his wife and daughter, Mechai was still out fulfilling his many commitments. Dr. Samak and Dr. Ella helped Gary and his family to settle in. Mechai didn't return home until 3:00 A.M. that night, considered an early night for him in view of all the acting, writing, broadcasting, and teaching he was doing. For the next three days, Gary hardly saw his "mate", as Mechai scurried around frantically to fulfill the demands of his work and extra-curricular engagements. But he did see Mechai enough to appreciate the extent of his involvement and the magnitude of his achievements in the intervening three years.

That Mechai had become so famous did not surprise Gary at all. In fact, he quite expected it. The outgoing personality, the wit and humor, the interpersonal skills — these were all evident in Australia. That he had honed these attributes back in his own country, where they could be cultivated within a familiar cultural context, and utilize them to launch his media career did not seem unusual to Gary. That Mechai had become a serious student of development and an advocate for the rural poor did not surprise Gary either. His intellectual prowess was never questioned, although his preoccupation with other pursuits while at university may have occasionally camouflaged it. Mechai had always been sensitive toward the plight of others. The influence of Dr. Ella and his education at Geelong Grammar imbued him with social convictions. In Thailand's rural poor, he had found a group whose plight deserved his concern, and to which he was willing to dedicate his copious energy. For Gary Hudson, the Mechai of 1968 was a logical extension of the Mechai of 1965, leavened by his experience and ripened by maturity.

For Mechai, the catalyst in his transformation was NEDB. Not the institution itself but the opportunity it gave him to learn about development and to understand the dilemma of Thailand's rural people. This opened his eyes and widened his horizon like no other experience in life. And what he saw, and impacted him most profoundly, was the enormous number of people that had to be housed, fed, clothed, and employed. Mechai could see that overpopulation was the greatest impediment to Thailand's development. If development was to succeed in Thailand, the population problem must be solved first.

Allan Rosenfield had just finished another late night at his office and was driving home through Bangkok's knotted traffic for a quiet dinner with his wife Clare. Allan had arrived in Bangkok one year before in 1967, as an advisor for the Population Council,[8] a US-based NGO that provided the government of Thailand with technical assistance on population related matters. As he wound his way home from the Ministry of Public Health, where he was advising the Ministry on its embryonic and still experimental family planning activities, Allan would listen to a radio program with a host named Nicola, whose light banter he found amusing and whose command of English and Thai he found quite remarkable.

Once a week, Allan would also read an interesting and informative article in the *Bangkok World* on political and development-oriented issues by an author with the pseudonym GNP. In 1968, GNP wrote an article entitled "The Lonely Advocates of Birth Control" which expressed strong support for the committed individuals who labored in the trenches of various governmental and non-governmental agencies to bring family planning services to the people. As an obstetrician-gynecologist who worked elbow-to-elbow with the anonymous heroes whose virtues GNP extolled in his article, Allan Rosenfield was pleased to see that they had such an articulate supporter in the media. How advantageous it would be, Allan thought, if GNP would write more informed articles on population and family planning. Allan decided he would like to meet GNP.

By coincidence, Allan had a friend at USAID who played poker regularly with GNP.[9] He offered to arrange a meeting. Allan was more than a little surprised to find that GNP was one Mechai Viravaidya, who was also Nicola, and who had also become a quite well-known television personality under his own name. That he also happened to be a prominent official at NEDB added to the mystique. As Allan and Mechai began discussing the GNP column and related population and development issues, they learned that they shared common interests and priorities. They soon became friends. Mechai suggested a series of four or five articles on population and family planning issues. Allan provided the materials and information, Mechai did the writing, and Dr. Ella did the editing. The result was a series of forceful, probing articles on Thailand's population problem and its implications for national development. These were generally acknowledged as the best written articles coming out of Asia about population problems at this time, which educated many senior Thai policy makers at a critical time for Thailand's population program.

They could not have come at a more opportune time. The late 1960s was a turning point in the country's recognition of its population problem. In the 19th century, when birth and death rates were equally high, Thailand's population had stabilized in the range of five to six million people. The first census of 1911 registered a total population of eight million. Soon thereafter, with the introduction of better sanitation and biomedical interventions to control communicable diseases, death rates plummeted but birth rates remained stubbornly high and population growth soared. By the 1960 census, the population had reached 27 million people. More ominously, the population was growing at 3.3% per year. At that rate, Thailand's population would double in 20 years. The Total Fertility Rate (TFR) was 6.5-7.4 children per completed family, which meant that each Thai women would, on average, deliver seven live children during her reproductive lifetime. Only 3-4% of married women of reproductive age (15-49 years) used any kind of contraceptive to limit or space their births. The remainder was caught in the debilitating cycle of pregnancy and childbirth, with increasingly short intervals to recover between them. All of those children Mechai was seeing were not an aberration. A mind-numbing parade of statistics confirmed Mechai's perception that Thailand's population was exploding, with potentially disastrous consequences for the people, the environment, and the economy.[10]

This perception, however, was not shared by everyone. On the one hand, reactionary elements in the Thanom-Prapas Government were averse to any efforts to slow down population growth. With wars raging among Thailand's neighbors, they maintained, they needed a steady supply of military recruits to protect the kingdom's borders against external threats. Then there was the recurring menace of Thailand's Chinese population perceived by politicians. The economically dominant Sino-Thai population served as a convenient scapegoat for a succession of authoritarian rulers in Thailand. The Thanom-Prapas regime contended that the Chinese population would resist any efforts at controlling their fertility while obedient Thai citizens would limit their family size. Hence, their numbers would spiral out of control, amplifying their economic might, while the indigenous Thai population would dwindle. That both of these objections would be proven specious did not deter their proponents, who were powerful forces in the body politic.

On the other hand, there were the lonely advocates of birth control[11] about whom Mechai had written in his article. In 1959, a World Bank assessment of Thailand's economy warned that the rate of increase in Thailand's population threatened economic and social development efforts. Seizing upon this admonition, a small group of Thai leaders from the Ministry of Public Health, Siriraj and Chulalongkorn Medical Schools, and the National Research Council, led by General Netr Khemayodhin, succeeded in staging the First National Population Seminar in 1963. Besides providing a public forum where the diverse sentiments and opinions about the population problem could be debated, one unanimous recommendation emerged from these proceedings: that more information was needed on the attitudes of the Thai people toward the population problem; and specifically, whether they had any interest in practising family planning to control their family size.

In response, a number of pilot projects were introduced which made family planning services more accessible to rural Thai people. These consistently showed that, when safe and effective contraceptive services were made available on a voluntary basis, rural Thai women overwhelmingly chose to space or limit their childbearing. In the Photharam Project, fewer than 5% of married women in their childbearing years in this rural district in Rathaburi Province used a contraceptive method, usually female sterilization. Within 18 months of introducing contraceptive services in the district hospital, 30% of couples used a contraceptive method, usually intra-uterine devices (IUD). When physicians in the district hospitals of Khon Kaen and Roi Et Provinces, two rural agrarian provinces in the Northeast, were trained to insert IUDs, women flocked to the hospitals. By 1965 there were 8,000 new IUD users annually from these two provinces. In Chiang Mai Province in the late 1960s, Dr. Edwin McDaniel at McCormick Hospital pioneered a mobile family planning clinic which offered the injectable contraceptive Depo-Provera. When the McCormick mobile clinic arrived once every three months, long lines of rural women, frequently garbed in colorful tribal attire, could be seen waiting patiently for their next injection of Depo-Provera, which guaranteed them another three pregnancy-free months.

In Bangkok, Dr. Kasetra Snidvongse, one of Thailand's most senior obstetrician-gynecologists, opened a family planning clinic at Chulalongkorn University Hospital in 1965. Within several years, this clinic became one of the largest family planning clinics in the world. Over 60,000 women had IUDs inserted in the clinic's first six years. Women came to the Chulalongkorn clinic from 90% of Thailand's 71 provinces, despite the fact that no public education about family planning was permitted in Thailand then. Its reputation spread by word of mouth alone. So many women descended upon this clinic that commercial opportunities presented themselves to savvy operators. On one particular occasion, Dr. Aree Somboonsouk, one of the distinguished practitioners at the clinic, noticed that a spate of women mentioned the same day, April 1, as the date of their last menstrual period. Since this date conveniently fell within the one-week post-menstrual period, these women were all eligible for immediate IUD insertion. Finding this coincidence somewhat suspicious, Dr. Aree investigated. As it turned out, an entrepreneurial bus driver in the provinces had arranged a package tour for women who wanted to come to Bangkok for an IUD. The package included sightseeing, lunch, and the trip to Chulalongkorn clinic. He told all the women to give April 1 as their last menstrual period to ensure that they departed with their IUDs securely in place.

A Second and Third National Population Seminar followed in 1965 and 1968 respectively. By that time, the voracious demand for family planning services by Thailand's rural women had been amply demonstrated. Despite continued opposition from General Prapas, the Third National Population Seminar strongly recommended that the Cabinet promulgate a National Population Policy aimed at reducing population growth by establishing a National Family Planning Program. Responsibility for drafting the policy was delegated to the Manpower Planning Division of NEDB.

It took two years for NEDB to draft a population policy and course it through the political gauntlet before Thailand's National Population Policy was finally adopted by the Thai cabinet in 1970. General Prapas' two major concerns, that of a burgeoning Chinese population and conscripts for the military, had to be addressed first. Surveys of the Chinese population revealed that their fertility rates were actually lower than the indigenous Thai population; and their desire to limit family size even higher. Demographic studies showed that, even with lowered birth rates projected with a National Family Planning Program, there would still be five times more draft-age men than the military could train. With these concerns assuaged, the Cabinet adopted the policy straight away.

While waiting for the political process to run its course, the Ministry of Public Health took a pro-active approach toward family planning. Assuming that a population policy leading toward a National Family Planning Program was inevitable, it launched its Family Health Research Project in 1967. This program aimed to train one physician and one nurse in each provincial hospital, and all physicians, nurses, and auxiliary midwives at district hospitals and sub-district health centers, on family planning program operations and contraceptive methods. By 1970, 330 physicians, 700 nurses, and 3,000 auxiliary midwives had undergone the one-week training program. When the National Population Policy was passed, the Ministry of Public Health was ready to transform its Family Health Research Project into a National Family Planning Program. Immediately, family planning clinics were opened in every provincial and district hospital. In a landmark study designed and conducted by Allan Rosenfield and his colleagues at the Ministry of Public Health in 1969-70, auxiliary midwives employed by the government were allowed to distribute oral contraceptives in four provinces using a simple checklist of questions to probe for contraindications.[12] When after one year there was an upsurge in pill usage without any perceivable increase in complications or side effects, the Ministry of Public Health authorized all 3,000 auxiliary midwives to distribute oral contraceptives, a milestone in promoting non-physician distribution of contraceptives. Now family planning services were available in every hospital and sub-district health center in Thailand. The stage was set for one of the most successful and innovative family planning programs in the world.

Being in the Evaluation Division of NEDB, Mechai was not directly involved in drafting the National Population Policy. However, as a strong and vocal advocate of the policy and an influential player in the court of public opinion, Mechai was consulted during the drafting and played a role in stirring public opinion in its favor. Mechai had become quite an activist by this time. He found the policy too conservative and the process too slow. He wanted to see action fast.

By 1970 Mechai was becoming increasingly disenchanted with government. He had little patience for bureaucracies and the petty obeisance they demanded from their employees. From his mid-level position in NEDB, where he had become the Acting Division Chief for the Evaluation Division, the path to a senior position would be slow and tortuous, requiring certain obsequious behaviors Mechai found distasteful. Mechai had become frustrated with the glacial pace of change in government, where progress was measured in centimeters. But Mechai wanted to leap ahead in giant steps. For Mechai the shackles government places upon its employees were stifling his enthusiasm, and he longed to be free. But he needed another platform for change from which he could launch his campaign for economic progress and social justice for Thailand's rural poor. Having become a recognized public figure, he now wanted a more visible pulpit from which to deliver his message to effect rapid and even radical change. The decision soon became obvious. He would leave NEDB and run for politics.

*Mechai during a debate at Thammasat University auditorium*

*Mechai with his English students at Thammasat University*

*Mechai as Japanese naval Lieutenant in a TV series "Koo Kham"*

*Mechai (left and below) in the play "King Ramkhamhaeng". The actress is a former Miss Thailand Prapatsorn Panichkul*

*Miss Universe signing Mechai's sleeve, Miss USA (center)*

*Mechai (far right) and Tavatchai Traitongyoo (middle) reviewing development projects while at NEDB*

*Mechai in his NEDB office as Acting Chief of the Development Evaluation Division*

*Mechai and Sunya when Mechai worked at NEDB*

## NOTES:

1 This huge infusion of military aid was not only a boon to the Thai economy. It also enhanced the power and fortunes of the Thai military. Its annual budget of US$ 20 million in 1951 ballooned to US$ 250 million in 1971. Military personnel and materiel increased accordingly. With windfall profits from its expanding budget, military officials became key players in business and commerce. This allowed the Thai military to regain its position of prominence lost after World War II, which it retains in truncated form to this day. For a complete description of the military's role in Thailand during this period, see Pasuk Phongpaichit and Chris Baker, *Thailand: Economy and Politics.*

2 Laos was one of the poorest countries in the world in 1960. Outside its capital, Vientiane, it had no paved roads, few schools, and an illiteracy rate approaching 90%. Its rural agrarian society lived much as it had for centuries — paddy rice farming in the Mekong Valley, subsistence upland agriculture supplemented by hunting in the dense forests of the North, and governed by a King living in the northern royal capital of Luang Prabang. To most outsiders, Laos seemed like a Buddhist kingdom frozen in a time warp. Vietnam had long coveted the extensive territories of Laos to provide more land for its expanding population. By 1960, North Vietnamese troops stationed in Laos were assisting home-grown Communist insurgents, the Pathet Lao, to challenge the right-wing Royalist government in Vientiane. In return, the United States, beginning in 1957, was investing more foreign aid per capita in Laos than it invested in any other country, primarily to prop up the Royalist Lao government against communist Pathet Lao insurgents. Unfortunately, most of this aid was diverted by self-aggrandizing military officers and unscrupulous Royalist politicians to their own coffers.

As a consequence, a corrupt, super-rich elite emerged in Vientiane, but the rest of the country was poorer than ever. The situation was ripe for conflict. In August 1960, a neutralist Captain named Kong Le staged a coup d'état which toppled the Royalist government in Vientiane. In the resultant confusion, the Pathet Lao seized control in their northern Laos stronghold, and Royalist forces under General Phoumi Nosavan, who coincidentally was also Sarit Thanarat's cousin, seized control of the South. Civil war erupted. Chaos ensued. The Laotian Crisis, as it came to be known in the West, caught the US by surprise. Occurring as it did on the eve of the 1960 presidential election, the US government was paralyzed with no clear policy direction. The Communist Pathet Lao quickly allied themselves with the neutralist government. The Soviet Union and North Vietnam provided them with arms and material. As the Royalist forces in the South, with US, Thai and South Vietnamese support, converged on Vientiane for a showdown with the Neutralist-Pathet Lao alliance, with Soviet, Chinese, and North Vietnamese support, the stage seemed set for small, insignificant Laos to be the site of a superpower military confrontation. If Laos fell to communism, the theory went, the other "Dominoes" would fall in turn. The Southeast Asian Treaty Organization (SEATO) provided the institutional basis for a military response in Laos. None was forthcoming. In the end, all sides wanted to avoid military confrontation. In the Geneva Peace Accords signed in 1962, a "neutralist" government was installed in Laos under Prince Souvanna Phouma. All three factions — Neutralist, Royalist, and Pathet Lao — would get seats in the cabinet. All foreign military personnel — Thai, US, North Vietnamese and Soviet — were to leave the officially neutral Laos. All sides then proceeded to disregard the Geneva Accords with impunity while pretending they were inviolate, tacitly ignoring the other sides violations as long as their own violations were ignored in return. It was a convenient solution to an intractable problem for all sides. Thailand felt betrayed when the US abandoned the Royalist government and accepted the Geneva Accords. Only the US commitment to Thailand's defense, combined with ever increasing amounts of military and development aid, assuaged Thailand's grievance. For a complete account of the Laotian Crisis of 1960-62 and its ramifications for Laos during the Vietnam War, see Roger Warner, *Backfire: the CIA's Secret War in Laos and Its Link to the War in Vietnam.*

3 NEDB's name was eventually changed to the National Economic and Social Development Board (NESDB), the title by which the agency is known today.

4 Although agriculture still dominated Thailand's economy in the mid-1960s, its influence was already beginning to wane. Agricultural households as a percentage of total households declined from 73.9% in 1960 to 62.9% in 1970 to 55.6% in 1980. Under the Sarit and Thanom regimes, development policy promoted industrial development at the expense of agriculture. Manufacturing boomed, and soon came to dominate export earnings. In the period from 1959-69, Thailand's GNP increased by an average of 8.6% per year. But the rewards of this growth were not being distributed evenly. In the rush toward economic diversification, the rural Thai farmer was being overlooked, disadvantaged, and left behind. It was this plight that Mechai came to recognize and sought to rectify.

5 See Appendix 1 for a sampling of the diverse range of topics published by Mechai under the GNP pen name.

6 One of Mechai's most popular articles was a three-part series on the "Perils of Prebendalism". A prebend is the subsistence allowance granted by governments to their employees in medieval times. Not enough to live on, the subsistence allowance would be supplemented with bribes and payments for services rendered. Mechai equated the ludicrously low salaries of public servants in developing countries with a prebend, and argued that the corruption which pervaded developing country governments was a natural response of government employees to their low salaries. In effect, the pre-

bend created a fee-for-service civil servant. And corruption was the peril of prebendalism. These articles caught the public eye and made GNP an acknowledged celebrity.

7 Thailand's entanglement with the United States brought short-term benefits, like the massive infusion of military and foreign assistance. However, its long-term implications would have an enduring and destructive effect on Thailand. US military aid embroiled Thailand in the Vietnam conflict. Foreign aid came with intrusive strings attached, as Mechai witnessed at NEDB and criticized as GNP. The economy, perfused with US dollars, had left hundreds of thousands of Thais dependent upon continuing US assistance. All of that money, combined with the Western ideas, values, and fashions that accompanied the 40,000 US servicemen stationed in Thailand and the throng of others passing through on R&R from Vietnam, left corruption, commercialization, and social decay in its wake. Touts, pimps, prostitutes, and honky-tonk bars sprang up in Bangkok and the immediate vicinity of US military installations. Young people flocked to the cities to cash in on the bonanza, abandoning their traditional heritage and values in the process. This pervasive foreign presence, accompanied by the clash of Thai and Western culture that it created, resulted in a political backlash which eventually manifested itself as the anti-government, anti-Western insurgency that would plague Thailand in the 1970s.

8 Unlike much of the foreign assistance coming from the US at this time, The Population Council played an important and much appreciated role in assisting the Thai government from 1963 to mid 1970s. During their formative years it assisted the National Family Planning Program, the Institute of Population Studies, and the NEDB Manpower Planning Unit which developed Thailand's National Population Policy. There was never a Population Council Office in Bangkok. Instead its consultants had offices in the government units where they worked, allowing them to interact directly with their Thai colleagues under the same condi-

tions; and develop the close interpersonal relationships that are essential for effective technical assistance. The young consultants who worked for the Population Council at this time, many of them inexperienced and working on their first overseas assignments, would eventually achieve prominence in the field of Population and Family Planning. Penny Sattersthwaite, Allan Rosenfield, J. Oscar Alers, Nicholas Wright, and Peter Donaldson worked with the Family Health Division of the Ministry of Public Health. Dov Friedlander, Sidney Goldstein, Lincoln Polissar, Ralph Tomlinson, and John Knodel assisted the Chulalongkorn Institute for Population Studies. Gavin Jones and Warren Robinson advised the Manpower Planning Unit of NEDB. Although it provided little direct financial assistance, the Council's consultants were assiduous in cultivating the skills of their Thai counterparts. By the late 1970s, with Thai officials now capable of running their programs independently and the need for foreign technical assistance superfluous, The Population Council withdrew from direct involvement in Thailand's National Family Planning Program.

9 USAID is the United States Agency for International Development, the foreign aid arm of the US government which was channeling substantial foreign assistance to the Thai government at this time. Unsurprisingly, Mechai continued his avid card playing throughout this period despite his busy schedule. When it came to playing cards, Mechai would always find the time.

10 All the demographic data presented in this section and the information on Thailand's National Family Planning Program in the ensuing sections was taken from a paper delivered by Dr. Allan Rosenfield entitled "Thailand: History of the National Family Planning Program" delivered at the 25th anniversary of Thailand's National Family Planning Program on July 11, 1996 in Bangkok.

11 In addition to General Netr Khemayodhin, who was the driving force behind the First National Population Seminar, many distin-

guished Thai officials labored indefatigably to establish Thailand's National Family Planning Program and deserve to be mentioned here. Dr. Sa-Ngad Plengwanich, Dr. Phon Sangsinkeo, and Dr. Manaswi Unhanond from the Ministry of Public Health supported General Netr to organize the first conference. Dr. Sasichan Vimuktanon was the field director of the Potharam Project and a key factor in its success. Dr. Damrong Reinprayoon and Dr. Nikorn Dusitsin joined Dr. Kasetra and Dr. Aree to make the Chulalongkorn clinic program so successful. It was Dr. Sombun Phong-Aksara who, as the Undersecretary for Public Health, decided to proceed so vigorously with the Family Health Research Project while awaiting promulgation of the National Population Policy. Dr. Winich Asavasena was the first of many enthusiastic and competent directors of the National Family Planning Program, followed by Dr. Somsak Vorakamin, who guided the program through its early critical years. Dr. Chitt Hemachudha and Dr. Somboon Vachirothai provided unwavering assistance to the program from their positions as the Director General of the Department of Health in the Ministry of Public Health. Dr. Vira Osathanondh was in charge of the Population Unit in NEDB that drafted the National Population Policy. Senior officials in the Department of Medical Services such as Dr. Vitura Sangsinkeo and Dr. Nibondh Suvatthana assured that family planning services were available in all hospitals. There are many others, too numerous to mention here, whose invaluable unsung efforts contributed to the development and success of Thailand's National Family Planning Program.

12 In this study conducted in 1969, midwives in four provinces who had been trained by the MOPH in contraceptive distribution, were authorized to prescribe oral contraceptives using a simple checklist of symptoms to screen for contraindications. The checklist contained ten questions about symptoms such as "Yellow skin or yellow eyes, severe headaches, severe chest pain, swelling or severe pains in legs, shortness of breath after exertion, excessive or increased frequency of menstrual periods, bleeding after sexual intercourse, a mass in the

breast or discharge from nipple". There was also an examination to check for "yellow skin or eye color, mass in the breast, nipple discharge, blood pressure (above 160 diastolic), pulse, (above 120), and sugar or protein in the urine". If the answer to any of the above were positive, no oral pills were prescribed and the woman was referred to a physician for examination. Midwives in the four provinces were authorized to prescribe oral pills using the checklist. Midwives in 13 other provinces who had received similar training in contraceptive distribution but were not authorized to prescribe oral pills, served as a control. The number of acceptors for the period October 1968-March 1969 prior to introduction of the checklist, and for the period April-September 1969 after introduction of the checklist, were compared in the four study and 13 control provinces. There was a 395% increase in oral pill use in the study provinces, compared to a 29% increase in the control provinces. The 12-month continuation rates for women receiving oral pills from midwives were higher than for women receiving oral pills from physicians. The incidence of side effects in the study provinces was lower than that found in a study of side effects found at a large Bangkok Hospital family planning clinic. This evidence was incontrovertible. On the basis of this study, the MOPH allowed midwives to distribute oral contraceptives in Thailand. See A.G. Rosenfield and C. Limcharoen, "Auxiliary Midwife Prescription of Oral Contraceptives," *American Journal of Obstetrics and Gynecology* (December 1972). It should be noted that this study was designed by Allan Rosenfield and his colleagues in the Family Health Division of the MOPH in one month, and completed in one year. Given the study's impact, this was a remarkable feat. If a similar study were conducted today, with all the checks and constraints placed upon researchers, it would take years to complete. Allan Rosenfield, who went on to become the Director of the Center for Population and Family Health at Columbia University and is now the Dean of the Columbia University School of Public Health, still considers this research as the single most important study in which he has been involved in terms of its national and international implications.

# 5

## CAMPAIGNS AND CONDOMS

*Electoral politics is a dirty and venal business. Influence is peddled, votes are bought and sold, reputations are besmirched, promises are made and broken with impunity, and candidates are routinely threatened and intimidated. Under the benevolent guise of democracy, its main purpose is the acquisition and maintenance of power for one group to subjugate another.*

In Thailand in early 1970, the electoral process was routinely subverted and electoral irregularities had been raised to a fine art. A profusion of small, fractious parties littered the political landscape, their half-life frequently spanning only one election. The principle exception was the Democratic Party, founded in the chaotic aftermath of World War II, which enjoyed a loyal base of support in Bangkok, and which persists to this day. Usually, the dominant party was the "Government Party", formed by the military group holding power, whose main purpose was to wrap the cloak of democracy around the military regime and ensure its dominance in Parliament. The Government Party coerced and threatened, using the full force of the military and the government to achieve its aims. The secular parties were controlled by oligarchs and business elites. Whatever the party, vote buying was a prerequisite to getting elected. Candidates without guns, goons, gold, and strong party support need not waste their time.

It was into this morass that Mechai stepped when he decided to run for electoral office in 1972. During his final year at NEDB, Mechai had been seconded to the Economic Cooperation Center for Asia and the Pacific (ECOCEN), a think tank of bright young professionals from the Foreign Ministry, NEDB, and the Budget Bureau convened by Dr. Amnuay Virawan, the Secretary General of the Board of Investment. Its mission was to propose economic development strategies appropriate for the emerging economies of Southeast Asia. For that final year, each afternoon Mechai would meet with colleagues like Songkran Krachangnetr from the Budget Bureau and M.R.Tongnoy Tongyai from the Ministry of Foreign Affairs. They discussed innovative, even radical ideas, to effect change. If the status quo were to be reformed, they reasoned, it must be done by young people like themselves. Government was too sclerotic. Politics was the venue for change.

In 1972, a Member of Parliament from the Bangkok Metropolitan Region died, and a special by-election was being held to fill the vacant seat. This was Mechai's chance. He consulted with Dr. Amnuay, with trusted friends like Songkran and Tavatchai. They were all enthusiastically supportive and encouraged him to run. Mechai decided to go for it.

This decision, however, was not to be taken frivolously. There were 21 MPs elected at-large from the Bangkok Metropolitan Region, which covered not only urban Bangkok and Thon Buri, but also suburban areas like Don Muang, Nong Chok, and Min Buri. There were millions of people in the electoral area, and a serious campaign would have to reach them all. Besides, the entrenched political parties — the Democrats, the Government Party, the Military Party — would definitely field candidates. For any plausible chance of victory, Mechai's campaign would require money, and lots of it.

Mechai first approached the Democratic Party to see if they might support his candidacy. The Democrats were the dominant party in Bangkok, and had every intention of retaining this seat. After consulting with the Party Chairman, Mechai learned that the Democrats had chosen Khunying Leka Aphaivong, the wife of three time Prime Minister Khuang Aphaivong, as their candidate. With her name recognition and strong party support, Khunying Leka was considered a shoo-in to win.

Next, Mechai consulted with M.R. Kukrit Pramoj, a journalist, intellectual, and political gadfly, whose brother Seni Pramoj had played a critical role in Thailand's post-war political rehabilitation. Kukrit was the proprietor and a political columnist for *Siam Rath,* the most widely read Thai language daily newspaper, which provided a platform for disseminating his progressive, royalist themes. Kukrit knew Mechai as GNP, and as a prominent official in NEDB. Kukrit was also an independent politician,[1] and it was becoming increasingly clear to Mechai that he would be running as an independent as well.

Kukrit warned Mechai that politics was an unsavory affair. "Your campaign will cost you money. Where will you get it?" Kukrit queried. "I will ask the people to support my campaign," Mechai retorted naively. This was a novel idea in Thai politics, where fund-raising usually came from more covert sources of dubious legality. "I will help you, then," Kukrit responded. There ensued a press conference where Kukrit announced Mechai's candidacy, followed by a *Siam Rath* article explaining why Kukrit was supporting him. Kukrit's support for Mechai was solid and emphatic. Mechai had officially thrown his hat into the ring. The race was on.

There was a 28-day period allowed for the campaign. Mechai immediately resigned from NEDB and ECOCEN, and set about establishing a campaign organization. The campaign headquarters were set up in an empty shop house located in Siam Square in central Bangkok which was donated by a supporter. Tavatchai Traitongyoo became his campaign manager. People like Songkran Krachangnetr and Tavatchai Sajakul, now a famous sports promoter, became campaign advisors. Mechai withdrew his entire pension fund accumulated over six years with NEDB, some 30,000 baht, as seed money to finance his campaign. Then, donations were solicited from the people. In his *Siam Rath* article endorsing Mechai, M.R. Kukrit Pramoj had made the first appeal for campaign contributions from the people. Mechai would accept no contributions greater than 1,000 baht, lest political debts be created which were too egregious to repay. He even hired an accounting firm to catalogue and manage his contributions, a level of campaign finance transparency unheard of at the time, indeed even quite rare today. The campaign eventually raised 150,000 baht (about US$ 6,000) in total. His opponents would spend two-three million baht each, much of which was used to buy votes. It was clearly an uphill battle, but Mechai was prepared to begin the ascent.

The campaign had to be carried to the entire Bangkok Metropolitan area. But Mechai had no ward captains or party machinery to disseminate his message or get out the vote. Television and radio were prohibited for campaign purposes. So he did the next best thing — he walked from neighborhood to neighborhood, house to house, from morning to night, all day, every day, distributing campaign leaflets and spreading his message of the politics of change. His campaign slogan was "Young, Honest, and Free", the antithesis of politics as usual.

The entire campaign was a catharsis for Mechai. And a déjà vu. Where NEDB introduced Mechai to rural poverty, his campaign brought him face to face with the urban poor. The parallels were disturbing. He walked through Bangkok's urban slums, where squalor, filth, and poverty were ubiquitous. Despite the cramped housing, there were children everywhere. Like their rural counterparts these children were being brought into an environment where food was scarce, there was no clean water and sanitation, and infectious diseases were uncontrolled. Their chances for survival were equally grim. Sometimes, Mechai could see the towering structure of a modern medical center right from the slums. For the help it provided these people, it might as well have been on the moon. Its geographic distance was small. Its social and economic distance from these people was unbridgeable.

These people had the same presence, dignity, and inner beauty that Mechai saw in Thailand's rural people. Wherever he went in slum areas, the people greeted him warmly and invited him into their homes. Invariably, they would offer him food and refreshment, even though their means were modest. One occasion, a charcoal seller invited Mechai into his home for dinner. In return Mechai gave him a clean handkerchief, not the normal compensation voters expected from Thai politicians but a symbol of the kind of campaign Mechai intended to run. In contrast, when campaigning in affluent neighborhoods where homes were shielded by impenetrable walls, Mechai was chased away by vicious dogs. He developed an affinity for these people, much as he had bonded with the rural poor. They were merely pawns to be sacrificed in the ruling elite's quest for power and wealth.

During the campaign, Mechai honed many of the communication techniques that he would refine as a family planning advocate. T-shirts were printed with his campaign slogan framing a picture of Mechai's recognizable face. He took his campaign to places where the common people congregated. The sight of Mechai or his volunteers standing outside movie theaters or in bus stations distributing campaign flyers and pamphlets would be repeated years later with condoms replacing the flyers. Schools were a focal point of his campaign. Although students couldn't vote, they each had two parents who could. Mechai recognized and capitalized on the influence that children exert on their parents, a novel stratagem in Thai politics.

This indefatigable campaigning was paying off. Two weeks before the election, Mechai was leading in the polls, with especially strong support in Bangkok's urban areas. The Democrats were alarmed. Bangkok was their electoral stronghold, and defeat in a by-election, especially by an independent, would signal political vulnerability certain to be exploited by the Government Party. The Democratic Party's strategists were convened to devise a plan to weaken this political upstart's support. Mudslinging and character assassination, the linchpin of any political strategy, were abandoned because of Mechai's soaring popularity and uncontroversial personal life. In the eyes of the people, Mechai was a golden boy. Trying to run him down, they figured, would probably backfire and burnish his image instead.

Then, they came up with a brilliant idea. One of the candidates in the 14-person field contesting the parliamentary seat was the ex-Lord Mayor of Bangkok and current Director General for Local Administration in the Ministry of Interior, a man representing the Government Party who was feared because of the power he wielded. For many voters, his defeat was more important than who won the election. The Democrats argued that Mechai was taking votes away from Khunying Leka Aphaivong, the only person who could realistically beat the ex-Lord Mayor. "Besides," the Democrats claimed, "Mechai is really one of us. He is supported by Kukrit Pramoj, younger brother of Democratic Party leader Seni Pramoj, so he is really a Democrat anyway. Don't split the Democratic vote by voting for Mechai. Vote for Khunying Leka now and we will get Mechai in at the next election."

The ploy worked, eroding Mechai's support. By election day, however, he still had a fighting chance to win. As the returns came in from the urban areas, Mechai held the early lead. In the suburban areas, the established parties' grassroots organization and vote-buying machine shifted into high gear. When the final vote was tallied, Khunying Leka won the election. Mechai came in fourth, the highest finish for an independent candidate, behind the nominees from the Military and the Government Party. He had garnered substantial numbers of votes, and proved that people who were "Young, Honest, and Free" could compete with established politicians who were old, tainted, and beholden to special interests. He even got enough votes so that his election deposit was returned.

Mechai's foray into politics had been enlightening for him. He saw how hard-ball politics was played, where principle and the issues were subordinated by the overriding pursuit of victory at any price, both literally and metaphorically. Against a well-oiled political machine, an independent, even one with Mechai's popularity, stood little chance of success. He had fought the good fight, given it his best shot, and made his point. Now he was exhausted from 28 days of non-stop campaigning. He decided to take a hard-earned and well-deserved rest. Most important, the recently married Mechai wanted to rejoin his wife Putrie, whom he had virtually abandoned during his campaign, and who was none too happy with this political adventure.

Mom Ratchawongse Putrie Kritakara had known Mechai since they were children on Sukhumvit Soi 39. Their families lived in the same neighborhood. Everyone in the neighborhood knew the Viravaidyas because either Dr. Ella or Dr. Samak had delivered most of their children and provided them with basic medical care. During parties, birthdays, and celebrations at Putrie's home, the Viravaidyas were always invited. Putrie's recollection of Mechai at the time was as a "naughty, raucous boy" who would frolic wildly through the rice paddies, and only slow down when it was time to eat.

Putrie's lineage descends from the Royal Family. Her paternal grandfather was the son of King Rama IV and the first Mon offspring of the Royal Family.[2] Her maternal grandfather was the son of King Rama III. Her father, Mom Chao Jitjanok Kritakara[3] was a cavalry officer working in the Ministry of Defense as a young cadet. Mom Chao Jitjanok was sent to England for military training at Sandhurst. He had learned to speak English from his paternal grandmother, who in turn was taught her English by Anna Leonowens.[4]

His position in the Ministry of Defense required frequent overseas diplomatic service. During the Second World War, Mom Chao Jitjanok was a liaison officer between the Thai Military and the Japanese forces stationed in Thailand under General Nakamura. After the war, he was a member of the diplomatic mission negotiating terms of the peace accord in Colombo, Sri Lanka. In 1947, he was appointed as the Military and Air Attaché to Britain. His entire family joined him for this assignment, including Putrie, who was five years old at the time.

Conditions in Britain were still dire when Putrie arrived in London in 1947. Massive destruction from the relentless German aerial bombing had left London and other major British cities in ruin. Food was rationed and basic necessities were scarce. Putrie was sent to live on a farm outside of London owned by a former nurse to Princess Petcharat, the daughter of King Rama VI. At least there she would get enough to eat and proper discipline. After one year she returned to live with her parents in London, attending the Glendower School near the Thai Embassy, until her father was reassigned to Thailand in 1950.

From 1950 to 1955, Putrie's family lived in cavalry barracks while her father became head of the Cavalry Division and

Military Intelligence. Dr. Samak and Dr. Ella would frequently visit her family while living there. On some weekends, when Mechai was home from Vajiravudh School, they would bring Mechai and his younger brother Sunya along. Putrie was appalled by their behavior. At the Glendower School, she had been taught the refined behaviors which characterized British gentility. To her mind, the Viravaidya boys were wild. From the minute they arrived until the minute they left, they would raise hell in the compound, yelling and screaming as they bounded recklessly across the ditches in the fish pond. She soon learned that when the Viravaidya boys came, she should keep her distance.

In 1955, Putrie's family moved again, this time to Washington DC where her father had been posted as Military Attaché to the United States. For her schooling, she was sent to the National Cathedral Boarding School. Because of her father's position and the many official functions this posting entailed, it was reasoned, it was better for her to attend a boarding school where she could pursue her studies without interruption.

Putrie spent the next 11 years in the United States, temporally concurrent with the period Mechai spent in Australia. She graduated from National Cathedral Boarding School in 1960. From there, she proceeded to get her Bachelor's degree at Hood College in Frederick, Maryland in 1960; then continued on toward her Master's degree at American University from 1964 to 1966, both through scholarships offered by the Thai government. During most of this time, she was separated from her family. Her father was posted as Ambassador to Japan in 1958 for five years, then completed his diplomatic career as Ambassador to Ethiopia in 1965-66. During that 11-year span, Putrie only returned to Thailand once, in 1964, because her family lacked the resources to pay for her travel. Working in the Thai Diplomatic Service was prestigious, but the pay was woefully inadequate.

After six years of education on government scholarships, Putrie returned to Thailand in 1966 to repay the scholarships through service to the government. She was given a teaching assignment at the newly opened Khon Kaen University 400 km. northeast of Bangkok. For her first two years, the assignment was temporary. She would drive up on Sunday and return to Bangkok on Friday. For her final two years, she was stationed full-time in Khon Kaen. In 1970, Putrie was transferred to the National Education Council and stationed in Bangkok doing curriculum development for various universities. It was the first time she had lived in Bangkok since 1955.

When Putrie first returned to Thailand, she met Dr. Samak and Dr. Ella several times at various parties and celebrations, but never met Mechai because he was too busy with his work, acting, and writing. In 1968, they were brought together by an unfortunate event. Mechai's older sister, Sumalee, had married an American named Arthur Stillman, whom she had met while teaching Thai at Yale University. Arthur had come to Thailand in the early 1960s as a Peace Corps volunteer, when he developed an affinity for the country and an affection for its people. After marrying, Arthur and Sumalee came back to Thailand, where he eventually found a job working for International Voluntary Services in Vientiane, Laos. IVS was a private forerunner to the Peace Corps, perhaps a little less tainted by a US government connection, its volunteers possessing more technical skills. While returning to Vientiane from an up-country field trip, Arthur's vehicle was ambushed by Pathet Lao troops, and Arthur was killed.

As a friend of the Viravaidya family, Putrie returned from Khon Kaen to attend the funeral. It was there that she met Mechai. She had neither seen him nor heard any news about him since the 1950s. Living in Khon Kaen, she was isolated from Bangkok's media and gossip, which held little interest for her anyway. They chatted, like two old friends reunited after many years, about shared experiences from their childhood and their exploits in the interim. Putrie was impressed by his transformation from the "naughty, raucous boy" she remembered from her childhood into the sensitive and sympathetic man before her. Mechai found Putrie serene, well-spoken, resolute, and disinterested in external pretensions. They had much in common, not only from their childhood and families, but also from their extended residence abroad and similar circle of acquaintances.

As Putrie recalled many years later, she and Mechai had one paramount characteristic in common. They were both essentially lonely people. Their close, enduring friendships were made during their many years of schooling abroad. They had friends in Thailand, but these were recent friendships that had not yet been ripened by time. It was the solace they found in their mutual loneliness that really drew them together.

Over the next year, Putrie and Mechai kept meeting at funerals, always spending time together afterwards then retreating back into their separate worlds. Admittedly, funerals were not the ideal circumstances under which to cultivate a relationship, but with Putrie living in Khon Kaen, it was the best they could do. For his part, Mechai would route his field trips through Khon Kaen whenever possible to see Putrie. When Putrie returned to Bangkok in 1970, Mechai would invite her over to his family compound, to see the small apartment on top of the garage which he was now converting into a proper house, to get her suggestions for the renovation. One day he said, "Wouldn't it be nice if you could come to live here?" Putrie didn't realize it at first, but Mechai had just proposed marriage to her. The timing seemed right, the circumstances seemed propitious, and Mechai was the right man, so she accepted. They planned to marry on January 22, 1971.

H.M. King Bhumibol Adulyadej had consented to perform the wedding ceremony. After selecting the date, they consulted a monk in the palace to gauge its auspiciousness. The date was deemed unfavorable, hence the monk suggested that, rather than carrying out the wedding in one day, as was the custom, it should be carried out over three days — with the "Blessing of the House" on Day 1, the Marriage Ceremony on Day 2, and the Reception on Day 3. It seemed a reasonable compromise, so both families set about making the myriad preparations.

Putrie almost canceled the wedding on Day 1. Mechai had one bad habit she found particularly irksome. He was always late. Whether it was appointments, engagements, or celebrations, Mechai always came late. Since the "Blessing of the House" would be done at Mechai's residence, Putrie was relieved that, on this occasion at least, he would be on time. When Putrie and her family arrived at Mechai's house on the morning of Day 1, an eerie silence enveloped the compound. They expected the place to be bustling with preparations for the monks' impending arrival. Instead there was only silence. As they made their way into the compound, Putrie had a premonition of disaster. Mechai was nowhere to be found, the house was still locked up, no preparations had been made, and the monks would be arriving shortly. As they tread warily outside the house, harsh guttural snorts could be heard emanating from the rear of the house. It was Mechai snoring away in his bedroom, still in deep REM sleep when he should have been preparing the house for the ceremony. Putrie was furious and threatened to call off the whole wedding. Dr. Samak was summoned to enter the house and awaken the semi-comatose Mechai from his soporific bliss. Mechai was profusely apologetic for his unacceptable behavior as he tried to talk his way out of this dilemma, but Putrie would have none of it. Finally, however, she succumbed to his blandishments of remorse and the ceremonies proceeded. The next three days went off without a hitch, with Mechai arriving promptly for every event. Some lessons are best learned the hard way.

It was not long after their marriage that Mechai decided to run for Parliament. In making this decision, however, Mechai did not consult his wife. Rather, he informed her of his intention to run. Putrie was upset that this decision was made without her involvement. Mechai's life was now her life as well. Decisions with consequences for both of them should be made together, she presumed, yet Mechai had decided to run for politics without consulting with her first. Putrie was pregnant at the time and living at Mechai's house. While he was out campaigning till all hours, she was left home alone to brood. She would receive crank calls threatening Mechai, alleging that he was out with other women, and accusing him of engaging in assorted nefarious behaviors. People would come to the house asking for money, handouts, or favors, figuring this was politics as usual. Putrie bore the brunt of this assault and, not surprisingly, found it exceedingly traumatic. Mechai got none of it. Then one night, as she waited patiently at home for Mechai to finally return, she had a miscarriage. When she started to bleed, Mechai was not there to help her. Her parents had to take her to the hospital. When the doctors told her that she would lose her baby, Mechai was not there to comfort her until the next morning.

As a result of this experience, Putrie did and still does find electoral politics upsetting. In her mind there was no way that Mechai could win with the established parties' campaign apparatus and deep war chests arrayed against him. She could not understand Mechai's desire to make a political statement in the face of such insurmountable odds. Nor could she sympathize with his idealism when she had to field crank calls and deflect would-be political cronies every evening. In defending his decision to run, Mechai would say that Dr. Amnuay said this or his friend said that. "But what about me?" Putrie pleaded. "Doesn't my opinion count for anything?" The bitter distaste that Putrie developed for electoral politics during this campaign is one of the major reasons that it took 28 years before Mechai would throw his hat into the electoral ring again.

Looking back on that campaign in retrospect, however, Putrie can now see that it was one of those defining moments that changed Mechai's life. When he saw how the people lived, how they were being exploited, and that existing public institutions seemed woefully indifferent to their plight, something clicked in his brain. From that moment forward, he would not only write about the tribulations of Thailand's disenfranchised poor; he was committed to doing something about it. That campaign transformed Mechai from a man of words into a man of action.

Following his grueling political campaign, Mechai took some time off to rest. And to reflect. After working in government and then trying his hand at politics, he was convinced that neither sector provided the venue he sought for change. Government was sclerotic, able to install hardware like roads, dams, or bridges but hopelessly inept at making them impact peoples' lives for the better. Politics was just plain corrupt. His passion remained Thailand's economic development, but he had become increasingly convinced that controlling population growth was a prerequisite and logical entry point for economic development. Concepts began to crystallize in his mind, like "fertility-related development" — that Thailand's population growth must be curbed before benefits of development could accrue to the people. And persons who chose to control their own fertility were the bedrock upon which to build.

Having become disenchanted with government and disgusted with politics, Mechai also began considering the potential that other sectors might hold for projecting his development philosophy. Increasingly, he viewed non-governmental organizations and the private sector as more flexible, dynamic, and innovative vehicles for his development ideas.

What became most immediately clear for Mechai was that he needed a full-time job to support his family. He and Putrie wanted to have children. In fact, his daughter was born in 1976. She was given the diminutive Looknoo, which means Little Mouse, and later named Sujima by H.M. the King. After Putrie's first miscarriage, she had to be very careful during this pregnancy, which was a term delivery without problems. However, while in the hospital, Looknoo contracted a Pseudomonas infection and almost died. Fortunately, she survived, and became the cornerstone of the Viravaidya family.

Although he continued to work at ECOCEN part-time, family aspirations made full-time employment his priority. This soon materialized when Mechai was appointed as Senior Economist at the Thai Military Bank. This was a lofty position for a 32-year-old neophyte to the banking industry. Mechai was pleased by his appointment. If the bank's capital could be harnessed as loans for rural agriculture and housing, the prospects were limitless.

What Mechai did not know was that he had been hired as Senior Economist as the Bank President's "Ban Chiang",[5] his trophy that could be displayed to the business community to enhance the bank's image. Mechai's ideas about lending and development were a trivial concern to the Bank President. Inevitably, Mechai and the Thai Military Bank soon clashed. He proposed that the bank provide housing assistance for the poor, even devising a financially sound plan targeted toward poor farmers that had excellent prospects for repayment and profit. The plan was soon scuttled because it competed with a housing company owned by a General on the Bank's Board of Directors, a company with more usurious motives.

After one year as its Senior Economist, Mechai and the Thai Military Bank parted company when Mechai resigned in protest.

There followed another interlude where Mechai considered options for his next career move. Mechai had remained close friends with Allan Rosenfield since 1968, meeting him from time to time to discuss their mutual interest in Thailand's population program. When Allan learned that Mechai was planning to leave Thai Military Bank, he told Mechai about a relatively new affiliate of the International Planned Parenthood Federation (IPPF) in Thailand called the Planned Parenthood Association of Thailand (PPAT). Allan had been assisting PPAT during its developmental stages, and recognized the potential for an energetic non-governmental organization to complement the government's family planning program. PPAT had been established by a prominent and well-intentioned woman named Khunying Suparb Visetsurakarn to replace a small, dysfunctional predecessor with ineffective leadership. PPAT needed someone with vision and creativity to develop a public relations, information, and education program, so Allan suggested that Mechai work as a consultant to PPAT on a part-time basis in that capacity as he wound down his work at Thai Military Bank.

While Mechai's goal and primary interest was (and remains to this day) the economic and social development of Thailand's poor, he always viewed family planning as the logical entry point. This opportunity at PPAT was timely because it would allow Mechai to do something directly about population control rather than just write about it. He decided to give it a try, first part-time then on a full-time basis in charge of the Information, Education, and Communication (IEC) portfolio at PPAT.

Mechai had neither academic training nor specific experience with public relations and family planning education. He did, however, have a genuine appreciation for the awesome power of different communications media to reach selected audiences and affect their behavior; and a profound understanding of the Thai people. During his political hiatus, he had tried different techniques to communicate his message to the electorate, some of them rather unorthodox. He wanted to apply some of these to family planning. PPAT under Khunying Suparb, on the other hand, was a quintessentially conventional organization. Although its mission was to makes contraceptive services widely available so that woman had real choices, its staff seemed reticent to speak freely about contraceptives; and utterly mortified by discussions about sex that contraceptives necessarily precipitated. They were allowing social and cultural taboos about sex and contraceptives to immobilize the organization and impede its effectiveness. "When soldiers are embarrassed by the gun," Mechai observed, "you lose the war."

As PPAT's IEC Director, Mechai launched a frontal assault on those taboos. If family planning was to be successful, he concluded, people must feel comfortable with contraceptives and at ease with the topic of sex. Mechai fashioned an IEC program that would demystify contraceptives, making them socially acceptable and unthreatening. He looked at his arsenal to assess the possibilities. Oral contraceptive pills were innocuous. A packet of twenty eight pills in four rows provoked only indifference. Intra-uterine devices were no better. Most people had no idea what the S-shaped loop with a string at the end was until told. But the condom was a different matter. It never failed to trigger some violent or exaggerated reaction. Just its appearance in packaged form invariably produced shrieks and gasps. When opened and unraveled, it was considered positively obscene. The condom would be the principal weapon in his offensive.

His second weapon was humor. Throughout his travels all over Thailand, Mechai was continuously impressed by the jovial and congenial nature of Thai people. They loved to laugh and joke, just like people everywhere really. People will accept something if you can make them laugh about it. His strategy, then, was quite simple. To challenge the social proscriptions about contraceptives and family planning, take something considered shocking, like a condom, and surround it with humor.

He started by distributing condoms much as one would pass out a name card. At official functions and social occasions, Mechai could be seen passing out condoms. At bus stations, in hotel lobbies, or in front of movie theaters, Mechai would dispense condoms now instead of campaign leaflets. Parking attendants would receive condoms as tips when they parked his car. The reaction was characteristic — and sequential: first surprise, then shock, and ultimately laughter as the condom was covertly pocketed for future strategic reference.

Harking back to his election campaign, he produced stickers, leaflets, posters, and T-shirts, now featuring brightly colored condoms and catchy slogans like "Too Many Children Make You Poor," and "A Condom a Day Keeps the Doctor Away." Familiar with the media, he used it as his ally. Newsworthy public relations events were staged which garnered free publicity on television and newspapers. When a foreign expatriate was vasectomized at a Thai clinic, Mechai would invite the press to publicize it, even to film it, to show that Thai clinics were good enough for westerners; by extension they were also good enough for Thais. Mechai's campaign was not only unconventional, it was a historical landmark in family planning IEC. It was the first time that the controversy surrounding family planning was used as its own advertisement.

Mechai soon found that he was a natural at PR. He felt the pulse and sensed the mood of the public and played to it, as he had done in theater and television. His PR campaign was innovative and unorthodox. Not everyone, however, was amused by the ubiquitous image of Mechai passing out condoms to surprised, incredulous, and usually giggling passersby. After he had been at it for a while and the condom had become his trademark, opponents began to attack and deride him. One detractor in the press referred to him as "Khunying" Mechai, since family planning was traditionally the domain of middle-aged women from high society bearing that honorific appellation. Another wrote a satirical article called "The Mechai Story" which spoofed the movie "Love Story". The author concluded his article by threatening, "if this guy likes condoms so much, let's call a condom a 'Mechai' in the future and see how he likes it." This opportunity to become synonymous with a condom was a public relations windfall too good to be true. The name stuck and Mechai used it to his advantage at every occasion. From then on, to Mechai's great delight, a condom was called a "Mechai" in Thailand.

PPAT offered Mechai a productive path in which to channel his creative energies toward family planning. But under Khunying Suparb's lethargic leadership, he could see that PPAT was going nowhere. Her idea of family planning education was to train the wives of provincial governors about safe sex over afternoon tea. Next to Mechai's condom posters and televised vasectomies, the contrast could not have been more flagrant. Unless there was drastic change in PPAT, Mechai did not see how such contrasting styles could co-exist in one organization.

At about the same time, Khunying Suparb was concerned about PPAT's small membership, and vigorously encouraged friends and colleagues to enroll new members. Mechai was quick to spot this opportunity. He hit the pavement and enrolled large numbers of new members among his friends and associates. At PPAT's annual meeting in 1973, he arranged for two busloads of his supporters to attend the annual meeting, where they proceeded to vote Khunying Suparb out and Mechai in as PPAT's new Secretary General. It was a brilliant coup d'état, covertly planned and swiftly executed within the boundaries of parliamentary procedure. The traditional PPAT under Khunying Suparb was transformed into the unconventional PPAT under Mechai overnight, where norms would be challenged and new approaches would be tried. It was the dawn of a new day at PPAT in particular, but also for family planning in Thailand.

As Secretary General of PPAT, Mechai had much greater latitude with his IEC campaign to desensitize contraception. Despite the tremendous progress that had been made in expanding knowledge and availability of contraceptives in Thailand, however, family planning remained primarily a clinic-based service provided by government health workers. Granted, the government health workers were auxiliary midwives who were now distributing oral contraceptives from their rural, sub-district health posts and directly in surrounding villages, a pioneering innovation by the Ministry of Public Health to expand contraceptive availability, as noted previously. But these were still government health personnel providing services from stationary facilities. Because of geographic and cultural barriers, contraceptives were still not readily accessible to many Thai people. Government clinics and health posts in rural areas were situated in centralized administrative locations not easily reached by people living in remote villages. Rural women requiring their next cycle of oral pills still had to travel great distances to be resupplied. As Mechai had seen during his election campaign, people living in urban areas in sight of large medical centers would not use the clinics, intimidated by the medical mystique these facilities projected. It soon became apparent to Mechai that the "clinic" was the barrier, geographic or cultural, and to really make family planning accessible, it had to be taken out of the clinic. Couples seeking to control their fertility were not sick, so why should they have to go to a medical clinic for contraceptives.

Under the auspices of PPAT, Mechai pilot-tested a scheme for non-clinical distribution of contraceptives by village volunteers. In a slum area close to Siriraj Hospital in Bangkok, he organized a team of doctors to examine women in the community who wanted to use oral contraceptives. For subsequent cycles, he trained community volunteers who lived and worked in the slum areas to resupply them. The peoples' response was enthusiastic; large numbers of new acceptors were recruited. By simply taking services to the people, geographic and cultural barriers disappeared. As he marveled at the program's appeal and its unmitigated success, he noticed one remaining superfluous element. "Why don't we take this experiment one step further, eliminate the doctors, and have community members distribute oral contraceptives to new and continuing users?" The requirement that physicians prescribe oral contraceptives was another example of medical imperialism that was gradually, and necessarily, becoming obsolete. It had already been conclusively shown that non-physicians could safely and effectively distribute oral contraceptives.[6] The next logical step was to train community members to distribute them.

Although he didn't know it at the time, Mechai had stumbled upon a community-based oral contraceptive distribution program, a concept gaining considerable cachet around the world as a strategy to overcome geographic and cultural barriers to contraceptive availability. Embryonic programs in Colombia had demonstrated the concept's potential. Now Mechai was demonstrating its effectiveness in Thailand.

Back in London, meanwhile, the doyen of IPPF were watching events at their affiliate in Thailand with a mixture of apprehension and eagerness. Don Lubin, IPPF's Deputy Secretary General, immediately called Allan Rosenfield in Bangkok after Mechai's coup to replace Khunying Suparb, asking for his assessment of the situation and whether any action was necessary from headquarters. This whole episode had placed Allan in an awkward position. Allan was a close friend of Khunying Suparb and General Netr. When Mechai informed Allan of his planned coup, he was in a quandary. However, Allan honestly believed that Mechai could potentially turn PPAT into a much more dynamic organization. With a great deal of discomfort, he refrained from mentioning Mechai's plans to Khunying Suparb. In response to Don Lubin's queries, Allan wisely advised him to sit tight, let the dust settle, and that Mechai just might become the most exciting IPPF affiliate director in the world.

Malcolm Potts, IPPF's Medical Director, was much more interested in Mechai's bold experiment with non-physician oral contraceptive distribution. An unwavering advocate of family planning programs worldwide, Malcolm had taken a keen interest in community-based distribution programs and was attracted by any strategy that would expand family planning choices, however unconventional. A bit of a non-conformist himself, Malcolm was eager to challenge existing norms and upset the status quo if the end result was greater family planning practice. As a physician he knew that the alternatives, closely spaced or unwanted pregnancies and high parity births, were infinitely greater risks to women's health. As reports trickled back to IPPF's London headquarters about the new Secretary General of it's Thai affiliate, with his ornate T-shirts, catchy slogans, and pioneering community-based distribution program, Malcolm was intrigued. He wanted to visit Thailand, meet this unconventional character named Mechai, and observe his programs first hand.

While traveling to a scientific meeting in Sydney, Malcolm had made arrangements to visit Thailand on his return trip, and notified Mechai accordingly. While in Sydney, however, Malcolm learned that the sale of oral contraceptives without a physician's prescription, an issue of great significance to him, had just been legalized in Fiji, so he arranged to return to the UK via Fiji rather than Thailand. He canceled the Thai trip, telegraphing profuse apologies to Mechai while expressing his sincere wishes to meet him another time. When Malcolm returned to IPPF headquarters in London, he was met by agitated inquiries.

"Whatever did you do in Thailand?" his colleagues asked.

"What do you mean? I didn't even go to Thailand." Malcolm responded, perplexed.

"Then where did these press clippings come from?" In due order they produced a sheaf of press clippings from the *Bangkok Post* describing the press conference Mechai had arranged for Malcolm where he proceeded to blast Malcolm for canceling his trip.

"This is so typical of the foreign experts," Mechai impugned in the clippings. "They come here to tell us what to do, then they don't even show up for their own press conference." The article continued with Mechai heaping all sorts of scorn upon Malcolm and IPPF, much of it justified. As it turned out, Mechai had arranged a press conference to protest USAID's unilateral decision to switch the oral pills it supplied to Thailand's National Family Planning Program from low dose to high dose pills. Having heard that Malcolm Potts was something of a family planning renegade likely to support him on this issue, Mechai had scheduled Malcolm to appear at the same press conference. When Malcolm canceled the visit, Mechai went ahead with the press conference, feigning dismay at Malcolm's absence, complaining about the shabby practices of international experts and donor agencies, then pounding USAID and IPPF for imposing their policies on Thailand's family planning program.

Mechai had learned never to forego a media opportunity. For good measure, he added a little donor-bashing to keep them honest and generate domestic support for his program.

Far from being offended by this episode, Malcolm found the whole thing quite amusing. "This Mechai is not only a nonconformist," Malcolm thought, "he has chutzpah, too." Now Malcolm was more eager than ever to meet Mechai.

By the time Malcolm Potts finally did meet Mechai Viravaidya, Mechai had resigned as Secretary General and was no longer associated with PPAT. Mechai's dissociation from PPAT was inevitable from the minute he joined the organization. His unconventional style and disdain for the status quo were incompatible with PPAT's staid and conservative image. Their divorce was only awaiting the incident that would trigger it.

Upon becoming Secretary General, Mechai had reorganized PPAT to reflect the public relations and community-based directions he intended the organization to take. This naturally created a fissure in the organization. Some staff saw Mechai as a visionary leader who was re-engineering PPAT's identity and mission. Others hated him, seeing Mechai and his flamboyant and sometimes confrontational style as PPAT's ruination.

Mechai brought in a new management team to run the reorganized PPAT. Tavatchai Traitongyoo joined as a consultant to the Secretary General. Two other junior officers joined as Chief of Finance and Chief of Operations respectively. These two had a hidden agenda, to take over PPAT, and worked furtively to undermine Mechai. Tavatchai, who knew these two newcomers when they were students at Thammasat University, learned of their duplicity, and warned Mechai of their impending betrayal. Together, Mechai and Tavatchai devised a plan to preempt both by reassigning one to a regional position in the North and the other to Northeast Thailand. Unfortunately, the plan was leaked to the plotters, who marshaled support among PPAT's disaffected staff and took their case to the Chairman of PPAT's Board of Directors, a respected benefactor of Thailand's Family Planning Program.

The Chairman was a man of integrity and good intentions, but a family planning traditionalist at heart. He thought Mechai was moving PPAT too fast in a questionable direction. When the two young instigators came to him with trumped up allegations of corruption against Mechai, with some PPAT staff buttressing the charges, the Chairman supported them. The next day, when Mechai arrived at his office, there was a sign on the blackboard listing all of PPAT's divisions, with an announcement that half would now report directly to one of the plotters and the other half directly to the other; and both officers now reported directly to the Chairman. For the moment, Mechai had been outflanked. Round One went to the opposition.

As Mechai pondered this predicament, his thoughts wandered back to an incident he remembered as a boy, when Dr. Samak was removed as Director of the Thai Tobacco Monopoly Hospital but was too much of a gentleman to contest the charges of his accusers. Mechai had vowed then that, if he was in the same position, he would resist vigorously. Now was his chance to show his mettle. He rolled up his sleeves and fought back. The allegations against him were brought to PPAT's Board of Directors, who investigated them thoroughly. The charges were petty and inconsequential. In all instances, he produced the appropriate receipts, even for trivial items like cigarettes and paper pads. The investigation found that Mechai had been wrongly accused. All charges against him were dropped and he was absolved of any wrongdoing. All those who had plotted against him were summarily dismissed. Mechai was reinstated as PPAT's Secretary General.

This whole incident had left Mechai with a bitter taste in his mouth. He could see that PPAT was too resistant to the kinds of innovation he wanted to introduce. Besides, Mechai now wanted to devote his entire energy to developing the community-based oral contraceptive distribution program, free of the shackles an organization like PPAT would place on him. Since his two-year term as Secretary General was almost finished, Mechai resigned from PPAT to work on the community-based distribution program full-time.

Mechai now realized that if he wanted to do things his way, he would have to establish his own non-governmental organization (NGO) to do it. But this would require money and support from a donor agency. He consulted with Allan Rosenfield, who was preparing to leave Thailand to direct an international Maternal Child Health/Family Planning Program for the Population Council in New York City. "Malcolm Potts at IPPF is the person who is supporting community-based distribution programs most energetically," Allan informed Mechai. "Despite what you said about Malcolm at the press conference, I suggest you take your proposal to him."

When they finally did meet, Mechai and Malcolm hit it off immediately, igniting a life-long friendship that persists to this day. They were both kindred spirits, non-conformists who disdained the status quo, family planning rebels ready to push the edge of the envelope. They were both dissatisfied with the torpid pace of family planning expansion. They both knew instinctively that clinic-based family planning could never bring real contraceptive choices to the people. And they both saw community-based non-physician distribution of oral contraceptives as the wave of the future. Malcolm was the physician and scientist who would cloak community-based distribution in the appropriate medical context and provide medical credibility. Mechai was the development economist who had been to the villages and seen population growth erode all the economic benefits of development. They would pool their energy and enthusiasm to find the resources required for Mechai to launch the most successful community-based distribution program in the world.

There was one small problem to overcome first. IPPF has a policy that it can only support one affiliate in each country, in this case PPAT, regardless of its efficacy. Malcolm had always considered this policy IPPF's greatest weakness. If the affiliate was sluggish or moribund, as PPAT had become after Mechai's departure, they were stuck with it. No longer associated with PPAT, Mechai was theoretically ineligible to receive IPPF assistance. Malcolm was so impressed by Mechai's ebullience and the prospects for effecting radical change that Mechai's proposal embodied, that he decided that, if the IPPF policy were ever to be stretched, this was the time to do it. He was ready to go to the wall to help Mechai secure IPPF funding.

Julia Henderson, IPPF's Secretary General in late 1973 when these events transpired, had ardently supported Malcolm's notions of community-based distribution of oral contraceptives, to the point where a special Community Based Distribution Department with a budget had been created in IPPF to support promising community-based programs. Malcolm brought Mechai's proposal to Julia and asked her to consider IPPF funding for it.[7] Malcolm had seen non-clinical distribution work in other settings, specifically in Colombia where Fernando Tamayo had created Profamilia to bring family planning services to women. If it succeeded in Colombia, he was convinced that a similar program spearheaded by someone with Mechai's personality and charisma might be revolutionary. Malcolm was way out on a limb here, because he was breaking IPPF's long-standing policy of only supporting its affiliate.

In reality, Julia Henderson needed no convincing. She was one of IPPF's more adventurous Secretary Generals, a person who recognized the pivotal role that the organization could play in expanding family planning worldwide. In her view, if IPPF did not encourage risk-takers like Mechai, it was failing in its mission to catalyze change. If Mechai would develop a proposal for his community-based distribution of contraceptives, Julia would assure that it would be taken to the IPPF Board of Directors to consider funding. Malcolm and Julia found small bridging grants to support Mechai while developing his proposal and testing some strategies.

When the good news reached Mechai, he immediately rented a house on Soi 14 Sukhumvit Road in Bangkok's Sukhumvit area and recruited staff to help him. Tavatchai Traitongyoo came over from NEDB to help develop the proposal. People like Somchit Tippayaprapha, Sophon Suriwoong, Vilas Lohitkul, Sunida Chattanont, Praween Payathviphapong, Thanothai Sukdis, and Vilas Techo all joined Mechai to help with his grand experiment, paid just 35 baht/day on a daily basis because there was no guarantee they would get the IPPF grant. Their gamble paid off. Twenty-six years later, they are all still with Mechai in senior positions in his organization.

By early 1974 the proposal was complete. It proposed the formation of Community Based Family Planning Services (CBFPS), which would start a community-based distribution program in Vietnam, Laos, Cambodia and Thailand. In Thailand, the program planned to reach 76 districts over five years. Village volunteers would be trained to distribute oral contraceptives and condoms, and sell them to fellow villagers. A portion of the sale would be retained by the volunteer as their incentive. The balance would be used to make CBFPS self-sufficient, and independent of external donor support, except for contraceptives, in five years. The proposal was accompanied by cash flow projections and break-even points worthy of the two economists who prepared it. Funding was requested for Year 1 only, US$ 250,000 to reach 24 districts. Subsequent funding would be contingent upon an evaluation after Year 1 to assess the programs' impact.

Mechai flew to New York in spring 1974 to defend the proposal before IPPF's Board. He had thoroughly digested every projection, assumption, target, and budget figure contained in the proposal. The Board was impressed with Mechai's presentation, especially with his command of the proposal's substance. One member, George Cadbury of Cadbury Chocolate fame, remained skeptical. Cadbury was one of those prominent people who supported worldwide family planning efforts, full of good will and totally committed, but cynical toward new ideas and people. Exasperated with Mechai's mastery of the subject, Cadbury blurted out:

"Mr. Mechai, you seem to know everything about this project." Mechai was unfazed and responded,

"Hardly, Mr. Cadbury. You only asked me questions I know. Why don't you try asking some questions that I don't know?" Laughter rippled through the chamber at Mechai's ingenuous reply. More frustrated than ever, Cadbury persisted with his questioning.

"This whole project looks like a one-man show. Everything depends upon Mechai. What happens if you get run down by a bus?"

"What kind of bus did you have in mind, Mr. Cadbury?" The suppressed laughter from the previous exchange erupted into full-bodied guffaws. The Board of Directors proceeded to award the Grant for US$ 250,000 to Mechai. CBFPS was born.

*Mechai with M.R. Kukrit Pramoj campaigning for Parliament*

*Mechai speaking at a campaign rally at Sanam Luang*

*Monk blessing the newly formed CBFPS, 1974*

*Mechai as candidate No. 6*
*on the campaign trail*

*Mechai and Putri receiving a gift from Their Majesties the King and Queen of Thailand at their wedding*

*Putri and Mechai in their wedding picture with parents and close relatives*

## NOTES:

1 As head of the Progressive Party in 1946, Kukrit was instrumental in getting Khuang Aphaivong appointed Prime Minister in 1946. When the Phibunsongkram, Sarit, and Thanom-Praphas regimes dominated politics from 1947 to 1973, Kukrit became a journalist, actor, novelist, and political commentator. After Thanom was toppled in 1973, Kukrit formed the Social Action Party and eventually became Prime Minister for a year in 1975. When Mechai was running for election, however, Kukrit was a distinctly independent politician.

2 The Mon are an ethnic group of Burmese origin that settled in Central Thailand in the 18th century. In 19th century Siam, alliances with the Royal Family were established by presenting children to the Court. If the daughters' were favored, they became a Royal Concubine. If they had children they became a Royal Mother. When Putrie's grandfather was born, there was great rejoicing in the Mon community because he symbolized the first Mon connection to the Royal Family.

3 Mom Chao literally means "His Serene Royal Highness" or grandchild of a King. In practical terms, a Mom Chao is considered a Prince in the hierarchy of the Royal Family. Mom Chao Jitjanok was the younger brother of Prince Boworadet, who led the aborted rebellion against Phibunsongkhram in 1933.

4 In 1862, Somdetch Phra Paramendr Maha Mongkut, King Rama IV, sent to Singapore searching for an English lady to undertake the education of his children. He selected Anna H. Leonowens, an English Governess living in Singapore with her son. Upon meeting Anna Leonowens, King Mongkut commissioned her with these words,

"I have 67 children. You shall educate them, and as many of my wives likewise, who may wish to learn English. And I have much correspondence in which you may assist me. And moreover, I have much difficulty for reading and translating French letters for the French are fond of using gloomily deceiving terms. You must undertake, and you shall make all their murky sentences and gloomily deceiving propositions clear to me. And furthermore, I have by every mail foreign letters whose writing is not easily read by me. You shall copy by roundhand, for my readily perusal thereof." Thus did she embark upon her six-year assignment as Governess in the Court of Siam, which would become the basis for the play "The King and I". Putrie's paternal grandmother was one of Anna Leonowens' students.

5 Ban Chiang is an archaeological site discovered in Udon Thani Province in the 1970s that revealed an advanced agricultural society dating back almost 5,000 years known for its early bronze metallurgy and clay pottery. Ban Chiang artifacts such as steel implements and clay pots from the site are highly prized by collectors as primitive art pieces. Mechai used this metaphor to describe his position at Thai Military Bank because the owner displayed him there as a collector would display Ban Chiang artifacts.

6 See A.G. Rosenfield and C. Limcharoen, "Auxiliary Midwife Prescription of Oral Contraceptives," *American Journal of Obstetrics and Gynecology* (December 1972).

7 It should be noted that Mechai's community-based distribution ideas had been developed while he was Secretary General of PPAT. Preliminary discussions about IPPF support for a pilot project were first broached under the aegis of PPAT. Julia Henderson knew that Mechai was the heart and soul of this project. When he left PPAT, it was obvious that PPAT was neither interested nor capable of implementing this pilot project. If IPPF really wanted to pursue community-based distribution in Thailand, Mechai was their only viable alternative.

# 6

## THE CONDOM KING

*Starting an organization is one thing. Making it successful is another challenge altogether, as Mechai would soon learn. Mechai faced two significant hurdles. First, community-based distribution of contraceptives by village volunteers had to be tested on a wider scale to see if the concept was workable. Then, he still needed the Ministry of Public Health's (MOPH) approval of his proposal before IPPF could fund it. Since non-physician distribution of contraceptives by non-Ministry of Public Health personnel was still illegal in Thailand in 1974, neither of these obstacles was inconsequential.*

In the period between January and May 1974, while awaiting formal approval of the proposal, IPPF had provided Mechai with a small grant to pilot test community-based distribution in one district before scaling up further. Finding a sympathetic District Health Officer who shared Mechai's vision and ideals, and who was willing to take a chance with this experiment, was crucial to the success of the pilot test.

This Mechai found in Bang Lamung District of Chon Buri Province situated about two hours south of Bangkok, where Dr. Kom Pongkham was the District Health Officer. Today Chon Buri Province is better known for its Pattaya Beach, where a combination of beautiful beaches lined with Go-Go Bars was making it the Times Square of Southeast Asia. But in Chon Buri's Bang Lamung District, Dr. Kom was quietly looking for a way to bring contraceptives to his constituents. When he learned that Mechai was looking for a district to test his Community Based Distribution (CBD) Program, Dr. Kom volunteered Bang Lamung and offered to provide the medical cover. It was the perfect partnership.

Arrangements were immediately set in motion to conduct the pilot test in Bang Lamung. Twenty-four villages, one third of all villages in the district, were chosen for the pilot test. The strategy was to train ordinary village people to distribute oral contraceptives and condoms directly in the villages. In short order, contraceptives were procured, training materials prepared, and consultations held with select government, community, and religious leaders to explain the program and obtain their support. With input and concurrence from the community, a volunteer was selected from each village to become the CBFPS village contraceptive distributor. Mechai had not, however, sought the Ministry of Public Health's official seal of approval for this endeavor. Since IPPF's decision to fund the pilot project, Malcolm Potts remained closely involved with the program, endowing it with both the professional credibility and controversy that usually accompanied him. On the day before training was scheduled to begin for the first group of village distributors, Dr. Kom received a cable from the Permanent Secretary of the Ministry of Public Health telling him that he was prohibited from proceeding with training family planning volunteers because it was illegal to distribute contraceptives without a physician's prescription; and that he should cease and desist from all further involvement with Mechai and Potts. A crisis ensued.

Dr. Kom, Mechai, and Malcolm conferred to discuss the crisis. "We can't stop this now," Mechai implored. "We are ready to go and there is too much at stake. I say we proceed as planned, but we'll call the village distributors 'health volunteers' rather than 'family planning volunteers' to appease the Permanent Secretary." Malcolm, of course, agreed wholeheartedly.

Dr. Kom needed little convincing. "Telegrams take several days to arrive. As far as I'm concerned, this one hasn't arrived yet. Perhaps it will arrive tomorrow," Dr. Kom explained calmly. "Let's proceed." At the end of the one-day training, each volunteer returned to their villages with a box of oral contraceptives. As a precaution, each box had Dr. Kom's name on it, asserting his ownership. The volunteers were just keeping the contraceptives in their homes for Dr. Kom. Under these conditions, they decided to proceed.

When contraceptives became accessible to the residents of these 24 villages, the community's response was emphatic. Community-based distribution was greeted with the people's unqualified approval, proving once again that when contraceptives are made readily available to women by someone they know and trust, they do not hesitate to use them, even if they have to pay for them. The payment scheme was simple. Each cycle of pills cost five baht (the equivalent of 25 cents US), and five condoms cost three baht. The village distributor kept one baht for each sale as an incentive. The remainder was remitted to the project to defray the costs of training and administration. A district supervisor visited each village distributor once per month on a motorbike to examine records, answer questions, resupply contraceptives, and collect funds. The system worked because it was so simple.

In view of the community's enthusiastic response, the Ministry of Public Health was loath to interfere with the Bang Lamung experiment. For his part, Mechai realized that further expansion of this program beyond Bang Lamung could only be done with the acquiescence and blessing of the Ministry of Public Health. He had gone this far without it, but now things had to be done correctly.

Besides, IPPF funding was contingent upon Ministry of Public Health approval. He would now proceed to the second hurdle.

IPPF procedures required that PPAT endorse the proposal to the Ministry of Public Health for its approval. Relations between Mechai and PPAT were still uneasy after his departure as Secretary General. The new President of PPAT was opposed to Mechai and his community-based ideas. He viewed them as competition to PPAT, which he did not welcome; hence his endorsement appeared unlikely. To circumvent this impediment, Mechai arranged for the President to go to a meeting at IPPF regional headquarters in Kuala Lumpur, which he gladly accepted because of the opportunity for international travel. While he was away, Mechai personally drafted the covering letter for PPAT endorsement of the CBFPS proposal, which was willingly signed by the Vice-President of PPAT, a Mechai supporter who was sympathetic to his ideals. PPAT endorsement was obtained forthwith.

To further complicate matters, protocol required that PPAT defend the proposal before the Ministry of Public Health review committee. Unfortunately, the PPAT representative sent to defend the proposal was an ally of the PPAT President, hence not supportive of Mechai and his organization nor sympathetic to their proposal and unlikely to defend it with much enthusiasm. Under these circumstances, Ministry of Public Health approval seemed unlikely. Anticipating this problem, Mechai rang up the Secretary to the Minister of Public Health the night before the meeting. He asked permission to explain his proposal because he was afraid the PPAT representative was not well acquainted with the project would not be able to defend it. Since the Minister would be chairing the meeting and wanted to give Mechai a chance to explain his proposal, he agreed.

The day of the meeting, Mechai waited outside while other business was being conducted. When his proposal was about to be discussed, the Secretary to the Minister of Public Health summoned Mechai. He explained the entire proposal to the Ministry of Public Health Review Committee, every detail.

"But you have no doctors working on this project," a senior health official objected.

"My mother and father are doctors. They will be assisting us."

Mechai was getting worried. Again he was being stymied by the medical nemesis. Sitting next to him was Dr. Choed Tonavanik, Director General of the Department of Medical and Health Services, and probably the most powerful and influential physician in the Ministry of Public Health. Seeing that Mechai was getting agitated, Dr. Choed patted him on the back and whispered, "Jai yen yen, (stay cool). I'll take care of this."

Dr. Choed assured his colleagues that "the Department of Medical and Health Services will provide all medical backup for the first phase of the CBFPS experiment in 24 districts." That was the clincher. Even the Permanent Secretary found himself unable to oppose Dr. Choed. With Dr. Choed's support, approval was immediately forthcoming. Ironically, on the agenda for the same meeting was a Ministry of Public Health proposal for community-based distribution with support from USAID. Much to Mechai's surprise, the Ministry of Public Health/USAID proposal was rejected. The consensus coming from the meeting was "We don't need this. We have already approved a similar proposal from a Thai organization. Let Mechai do it."

In another country at another time, Mechai's experiment might never have worked. But in Thailand in 1974, with a Government and Ministry of Public Health strongly committed to family planning, and with an audacious non-conformist like Mechai ready to push the edge of the envelope with creative, even controversial approaches, anything seemed possible.

Mechai also learned a valuable lesson, which would be confirmed continuously in the future. Most successful things in family planning are controversial when first introduced. If you ask for too many permissions in advance, your efforts will invariably be stymied before they get started. The experience in Bang Lamung taught Mechai "In launching any new development endeavor, it is easier to ask for forgiveness than to ask for permission."

Following Ministry of Public Health approval, IPPF gave Mechai the go-ahead to proceed with the entire project. Actually, the IPPF-funded project had three components. The first component, and by far the largest, was the Village Program that was piloted in Bang Lamung and planned to expand to 76 districts in five years. The second was the Private Sector Program, a condom social-marketing project where Gold-, Silver-, and Rainbow-brand condoms were marketed at subsidized prices through retail outlets throughout the country. The third component was the Institutional Program, where Mechai's organization trained teachers about population and family planning and brought family planning services to teachers, parents of school children, and factory workers. The IPPF grant was allocated annually, with each subsequent year's funding contingent upon an external evaluation of the previous year's results. The grant would terminate after five years, at which time the pr oject was to be self-sufficient through the sale of contraceptives. The first grant of US$ 250,000 for Year 1 came in 1974.

The requirement for self-sufficiency was a blessing in disguise. Since working at NEDB, Mechai had been skeptical about the sustainability of foreign aid. In the long term, it was unreliable and dependent upon the whim and policies of foreign governments or international agencies. Incorporating mechanisms for cost recovery and self-sufficiency would guarantee a project's sustainability, and make it independent of the vagaries of foreign assistance. In the future, Mechai would make self-sufficiency an inherent feature in all his projects because, as he remarked to a US Congressional delegation in 1976, "Foreign assistance is like an erection. It's nice while you have it, but it doesn't last forever."

The Institutional Program actually started while Mechai was awaiting final IPPF approval of his proposal. The Teacher's Council, a union of teachers to which all primary and secondary schoolteachers working for the government belonged, would bring teachers together each summer for special courses to upgrade their qualifications and skills. Dr. Pongsak Witayakhom, Director of the Teacher's Council Medical Center, suggested that family planning training be incorporated into the summer courses, an idea which Mechai included in his proposal to IPPF and which was funded first. In five years, his organization trained 320,000 schoolteachers, all of whom could order contraceptives by mail for themselves or for resale to others in their villages and pass useful family planning information on to their students. Starting in Bangkok, the training was eventually expanded to 24 locations around Thailand. CBFPS had one half day during the training to transmit family planning messages.

Prior to launching this program, Mechai commissioned survey research to identify the most influential and respected leaders in the community. First were the Buddhist monks. Then came the schoolteachers. If these were the two most respected informal leaders, he wanted to assure that Buddhist monks would not oppose him; and to enlist the active support of the teachers, because each teacher could reach many children — and children had always been a crucial component of Mechai's strategy.

The teachers were taught new rhymes and songs to be introduced into the classroom. First was the family planning ABCs, in which A was for Abstinence, B was for Birth spacing, C was for Condoms, D was for Delayed marriage, S was for Sterilization,

V was for Vasectomy etc. Then there was a popular Thai jingle, perhaps as familiar as "Jingle Bells" in English, in which the words were changed so that every contraceptive method was mentioned, and demographic messages explaining overpopulation were explained. Teachers were encouraged to have students take an oath to "try to marry as late as possible after 20 and try to have no more than two children."

Mechai became personally involved as a trainer, a role he maintained until his staff could replicate his techniques. On one particularly sultry morning in Bangkok, he walked into an auditorium where 2,000 teachers were gathered for the training. With fans whirring overhead to dissipate the heat, Mechai was introduced to the expectant audience. Most of them had heard of Mechai from his stint in television and family planning, hence his reception was warm and spirited. With a presentation honed over several performances, he began by explaining Thailand's population problem, and that now the means were available to delay pregnancy.

Next came the explanation of the different contraceptive methods. To explain the methods, Mechai used a colorful analogy. "The female reproductive system is like a Mercedes Benz," he explained. "The male reproductive system is like a bicycle. There are many places where a woman's fertility can be adjusted because it is such a brilliant machine. But the male apparatus, being simple and mundane, has only one intervention point — to block the emission of sperm using either a condom or vasectomy."

The teachers sat and listened politely, somewhat bemused by the whole thing. But the mood was somber, like a lecture hall during a philosophy class. There was no stir of excitement or fun in the air. From his experience, Mechai knew that where there is no fun, no excitement, and no humor, learning will not take place and attitudes would not change. As he fingered the ubiquitous condom in his hand, a thought occurred to him. As a child on Soi 39, he had once found some of Dr. Samak's condoms and blew them up. The stunt never failed to get attention, even some laughs. "Why don't I try it now?" he thought.

In short order the condom was unfurled to its full length. Holding it up before the audience, he said, "The condom is actually a very versatile implement. It can be a tourniquet, for snakebites and deep cuts. It can cover the barrel of a gun, and the lubrication can be used for skin cream. It can even carry water, coffee, or Coca Cola. It is also a balloon." He then put the condom to his lips and started blowing it up. "It was like magic," Mechai remembered. One minute the audience was just sitting there, quite moribund, looking self-conscious, and the next minute they were roaring with laughter." Now he knew he was on to something. Why not get the audience to participate in the fun?

Soon his staff had distributed condoms throughout the audience. As the teachers played with the condoms now flooding the auditorium, Mechai intoned, "Don't be afraid of them, it's just a piece of rubber. There's more rubber in a tennis ball. The availability or possession of a product doesn't govern one's behavior. We have knives in our kitchens, but we are not all killers. The condom is really clean if your mind isn't dirty. If you have a dirty mind, please don't take one." Everybody took one.

"Let's see how clean your mind is. Why don't those with the cleanest minds join me in blowing up these condoms," Mechai encouraged the teachers. Bashful at first, the audience demurred. Then one person marshaled enough courage to try it, then another, and another. The sight of their fellow teachers with condoms at their mouths blowing them up like balloons sent the audience into hysterics. It was a wild scene. Then Mechai had another brilliant idea. "Let's have a condom-blowing contest."

Mechai's assistants fanned into the audience and ushered dozens of reluctant but curious volunteers to the front stage. Each was given a condom. "On the count of three, I want all of you to start blowing up your condoms. The one to blow up the largest condom in one minute will win a year's supply." This group of quite ordinary teachers started frantically blowing up their condoms on the count of three. Some were quite adept, slowly but surely inflating the condom like a giant balloon. Others were clumsy, unable to express exhaled air into the condom. All of them were hysterically funny. The occasion was hilarious, as 2,000 people laughed uncontrollably at their colleagues blowing up condoms, with Mechai at the microphone providing a humorous play by play of the action. Mechai's announcement of the winner of the contest elicited wild approbation and applause from the audience. They loved the entire experience.

On that day in that hall, a social phenomenon took place. The condom — and by extension, all contraceptives — was desensitized. In the hands of those teachers, it was just a balloon. Not something to be shunned, or shirked, or shrieked at. It was just a balloon. The condom-blowing contest soon became Mechai's trademark. It was repeated in classrooms, at political rallies, on television, at bars and nightclubs, even at mosques — just about anywhere, in fact, where it was likely to lighten the mood by making people laugh.[1] Mechai had blown up a condom and started a social revolution.

As the Director of his own private, non-profit organization, Mechai could now let his imagination roam in his campaign to demystify contraception and break down social barriers to their acceptance. There was no government to rein him in, no PPAT to criticize his ideas as outlandish or distasteful and stifle his resourcefulness. Now Mechai would set the parameters for his creativity; and he was ready to widen the goal posts.

Between 1974 and 1980, there ensued one of the most dynamic, energetic, and imaginative campaigns to bring contraceptives to the Thai people, clearly unparalleled in the annals of family planning either before or since.[2] In addition to the community-based family planning program, which brought contraceptives to the people by the people, Mechai proceeded to effect one of the most remarkable attitudinal metamorphoses about contraception and family planning ever experienced in a traditional society. Not a paroxysm, nor an upheaval, but a gradual transformation of attitudes as Mechai introduced Thai society to the "facts of life", and family planning came out of the closet. And out of the closet with it came family planning supermarkets, vasectomy tour buses, fertility restaurants, condom key chains, a family planning stud pig, and T-shirts depicting "Proud Pete", the anthropomorphic penis, slipping a condom over his head and beaming, "I'm Safe Now."

His strategy was simple. He combined showmanship and imagination with his innate understanding of the Thai people, always interwoven with humor and fun, to desensitize contraception in Thai society. Mechai essentially transported Madison Avenue panache to rural Thailand. "I want to take the seriousness and embarrassment out of birth control and make it a clean, fun thing," Mechai explained. "I want people to accept contraceptives the same way they do soap and toothpaste. Sometimes I shock people. Sometimes I make them laugh. The important thing is to make them think and react." He merchandised family planning like any commercial product. If gimmicks and publicity could sell soap and toothpaste, they could sell family planning.

First came the business cards for Mechai and his staff — a brightly colored condom glued to a mail order form with information on family planning methods and population statistics. Next came the condom key chain, containing a condom encased in plastic with the warning, "In Case of Emergency, Break Glass." Then he established family planning supermarkets in Bangkok's three major up-country bus terminals, where passengers could asks questions about family planning, purchase contraceptives, get pregnancy tests, or buy T-shirts, pillow cases, and lace panties bearing the motto, "Too Many Children Make You Poor."[3] In one of his more memorable stunts, Mechai dispatched pretty Thai girls all over Bangkok to hand out condoms to traffic policemen on New Years Eve. The next day their pictures appeared in all the newspapers under the headline "Cops and Rubbers".

He enlisted taxi cab drivers to distribute condoms. Buddhist monks blessed them and vendors passed them out in the streets. Each New Years Eve, helium filled condoms with prize tickets inside for a free vasectomy or a years supply of oral pills would waft over Bangkok courtesy of Mechai. A family planning jingle based on a popular children's song was introduced at rural schools. Family planning messages were inserted into Northeastern folk songs and popular Southern folk puppet plays performed by over 300 troupes around the country. Some sports teams wore jerseys emblazoned with the motto "A Condom a Day Keeps the Doctor Away." Christmas cards with the message "We wish you much happiness and subdued fertility in the New Year," were sent to heads of state, even the Pope. The Good Humor Man of Thailand could integrate family planning into anything and make it fun.

Mechai would go to any extreme to get his message across. To mark the International Women's Year, he invited women in Bangkok to "vasectomize the man of your choice." On Labor Day and H.M. the King's birthday, he set up a clinic near the Grand Palace and offered free vasectomies to any interested customer. Television crews from around the world, there to film H.M. the King's birthday celebration, beamed Mechai's brightly colored mobile vasectomy van around the world. In 1979, the first year the mobile vasectomy clinics appeared, 146 men walked in off the street for vasectomies at the various sites Mechai had set up around Bangkok. In 1984, a total of 129 vasectomies were performed on H.M. the King's Birthday in one site, believed to be a world record at the time, although the Guinness Book of World Records was too stodgy to acknowledge it.

After his family planning organization had been operating for one year, the condom had become Mechai's visual trademark. It had become synonymous with family planning. In practice, however, the trademark was proving none too reliable. The organization was receiving a growing number of complaints from men that their condoms were falling off or disappearing during intercourse. Some men even reported that they had to tie the condoms to their waists to secure them in place. This was a troubling problem — not only for the product's credibility but also because of potential contraceptive failure. Mechai could only assume that the condoms being supplied to CBFPS, which actually came from USAID, were too big. But what was the right size and how could he find out?

To answer this question, Mechai turned to his cousin, Dr. Debhanom Muangman, who was the Dean of the Faculty of Public Health at Mahidol University and a graduate of Harvard University School of Public Health, to design a reliable research study that could provide a definitive answer to this question.

Dr. Debhanom used the Chao Phraya Massage Parlor, Bangkok's largest and most ostentatious, as the field site for the study. He enlisted five massage girls who were willing to participate in the study. When the clients came in for a massage the girls explained that they were research assistants in a study to find out the average length and circumference of the penis of Thai men, so that condoms could be manufactured to fit securely. When a Thai customer came in for a massage, each was classified according to their height (tall, medium, or short) and their weight (thin, medium, or heavy). The girls had a piece of paper that was torn off to measure the length of their client's penis, and another to measure the circumference. They were asked to measure the client's penis in its flaccid and erect state. Unfortunately, the occasion for the former never arose. By the time the girls got around to measuring it, they had to settle for measurement of the erect penis only.

Dr. Debhanom found that the average penis of Thai men, when erect at salute, was 5.4 inches long and 49 mm. in diameter. The condoms provided by USAID were 52 mm. in diameter, explaining why so many of them were coming off. When this information was provided to USAID, it led to the production of the Asian-size condom, specially designed for the circumference of the Asian penis. This was practical research providing answers to real problems.

While most of his methods delighted and entertained people, sometimes Mechai's methods shocked people. This never deterred Mechai, who would use any occasion to advance the cause of family planning. He approached his work with missionary zeal. In 1975, months after the end of the Vietnam War, the first official North Vietnamese delegation was visiting Thailand. Because of Thailand's alliance with the US during the war, relations between the two countries were icy, yet Thai officials, acknowledging the post-war Realpolitik, knew that some sort of modus vivendi must be established with their powerful neighbor. They were understandably tense during the visit and wanted to make a good impression on their Vietnamese colleagues.

The first state dinner for the North Vietnamese delegation, led by Deputy Foreign Minister Phou Hien, was held at the Ambassador Hotel. Coincidentally, Mechai was dining at the Ambassador Hotel that evening with Provincial Health Officers from the 24 districts where his family planning program would be launched. After a while, the waiter came up to Mechai and asked "Aren't you attending the dinner reception upstairs for the Vietnamese delegation?" Since Mechai was something of a celebrity, the waiter just assumed that he should be attending the reception.

"This could be an opportunity for us," Mechai thought. He sent his staff to get some T-shirts and condoms, a supply of which he always kept close at hand. There were police guarding the lift up to the reception room. When they saw Mechai coming and recognized him, they assumed that he had been invited to the reception and waved him on to the elevator. When he got upstairs, the Army officers guarding the reception assumed that Mechai had been invited by the Foreign Ministry and welcomed him. When he got into the reception, even Thai Foreign Minister Chatichai Choonhavan, who happened to know Mechai personally, assumed that Mechai had been invited by the Army and welcomed him cordially.

"I have gifts for your visitors," Mechai told the Foreign Minister.

"Good. Why don't you hand them out," the Foreign Minister replied.

As Mechai withdrew the condoms, Khun Chatichai was taken aback and put his hand over the bag as if to stop him. When the Vietnamese delegation eagerly grabbed the condoms from Mechai, Khun Chatichai relented and said, "You may as well give them to everyone."

Mechai proceeded to pass out condoms and traditional Thai peasant shirts with family planning messages to the assembled Vietnamese delegation. Like everyone else, they assumed he was passing out official gifts from the Thai government, and dutifully donned their colorful shirts. The press was there to capture the whole thing.

The next day pictures of Mechai handing out condoms and senior Vietnamese officials wearing their new shirts over their formal suits appeared on the front page of every newspaper. The Thai press loved it, praising Mechai for his bravado. The English language *Bangkok Post* had the same reaction. Only the *Nation*, the other English language daily, criticized him. Seeing that they were the odd man out on this issue, the *Nation* rang up Mechai to interview him about the incident.

"Don't you think that you went too far last night? Don't you think that an official state dinner is too formal an occasion, too high a place, for promoting family planning?" they asked him.

"No occasion is too formal, no place is too high, for family planning," he responded sternly. The *Nation* got the message.

The very next day Mechai's secretary told him that the Foreign Ministry had rung him up and wanted to speak with him. He was slightly perplexed, even a little nervous, that perhaps there had been some diplomatic fallout from his visit with the Vietnamese. "Why was everyone so upset?" he wondered.

As it turned out, no one was upset at all. The Vietnamese had been so impressed with his performance that the Vietnamese Deputy Foreign Minister wanted to invite Mechai and his staff for afternoon tea, in order to speak with him further.

Mechai took a team of 12 staff with him, equal to the number of Vietnamese in the delegation. They also brought along some Eugynon pills produced by the Germans to complement the American-made condoms he had given them the previous evening, to show them that family planning was a truly international endeavor. Upon meeting Mechai, the Deputy Foreign Minister told him, "We Vietnamese don't know much about family planning, but we know more about war."

Not knowing what he meant, Mechai eventually responded, "You may have won the last war, but you will surely lose the next."

Somewhat perplexed by Mechai's response, the Deputy Foreign Minister asked, "What next war?"

"The population war," Mechai answered.

The Deputy Foreign Minister reflected upon Mechai's statement. "You are right. Despite the war and all the destruction, we still have so many children. There should be some world organization that can assist us with this problem."

"There is one, called IPPF," Mechai noted, plugging the donor for his family planning project. "I am sure they could help you."

After distributing more shirts and oral contraceptives, Mechai and the Vietnamese Deputy Foreign Minister parted company. Six months later, the Vietnamese requested, and were supplied by the French government with, one million cycles of Eugynon for their family planning program. When Dr. Krasae Chanawong, the Thai Deputy Foreign Minister, made a return visit to Vietnam a year later, one of the first things his Vietnamese counterpart asked was "How is Mr. Mechai?"

For all the publicity and showmanship, all the unconventional antics and humorous behavior, the real core of Mechai's family planning program was its novel grassroots approach to contraceptive distribution. From long experience, Mechai knew intuitively that any solution to Thailand's population problem had to rest with Thailand's people. Unlike traditional family planning programs, conceived centrally and administered vertically, this program began at the village level and was run by the people. As Mechai repeated so often it became his mantra, "The people must have a sense of participation. They must be enlisted as partners. They must ultimately assume responsibility for the program's success."

The backbone of the program was the village distributor. Most were married women, many of them shopkeepers with a place of business frequented by the villagers. The distributors were chosen carefully, in consultation with each community, on the basis of their community standing, support for family planning, and their ability to keep accurate records. "The village people know our distributors. They trust and confide in them. And the distributor is right there in the village. The villagers don't have to take a long, expensive bus trip whenever they want contraceptives. Our distributors offer the convenience of round the clock, on the spot service."

Ostensibly a volunteer, the village distributors received a small commission for the sale of each cycle of pills or package of condoms. They came in all sizes and shapes — school teachers, rice farmers, shopkeepers, village elders, silk weavers, taxi drivers, golf caddies, floating-market boat vendors, and at least one undertaker. The distributors received the initial supply of pills and condoms on consignment at their one-day training program, where they were taught to distribute pills using a simple checklist, reminiscent of the one Allan Rosenfield developed for auxiliary midwives, to screen for complications. They returned to their villages with a depot sign even bigger than Coca Cola's, announcing that that they were now official village contraceptive distributors. Mechai's organization retained a paid supervisor in each district who visited each distributor monthly to check records, resupply contraceptives, and answer questions about side effects.

From its humble beginnings in Bang Lamung District in 1974, much of which is now Pattaya City, the program expanded first to 76 districts with IPPF support, then an additional 80 districts through a grant provided by USAID in 1976. By 1980, the program had 10,800 village distributors covering a population of 18 million people operating in 16,000 villages, one third of all villages and districts in Thailand. In this short span, 320,000 new family planning acceptors had been recruited, and 250,000 couples relied on CBFPS for their contraceptives.

Reflecting upon this remarkable period, Malcolm Potts summed it up most succinctly. "Most of Mechai's contemporaries, either in Thailand or other countries, said family planning was difficult, embarrassing, even shameful. The people don't want it. The only way they will accept it is if you package it as a maternal and child health service, as if the population issue is not important. Because he empathized with poor people and understood them, Mechai grasped the fact that poor people wanted to space pregnancies and limit the number of children they had, just like everyone else. Unlike his contemporaries, Mechai felt like he was giving the people what they needed and wanted as a human right — contraceptives — and he let the people do the rest; finding boundless ways to amuse them in the process."

This period also saw Thailand experience one of the most dramatic and rapid declines in fertility ever recorded. By 1981, Thailand's Total Fertility Rate had fallen to 3.9 from its peak of 7.4 in the 1960s. Its Crude Birth Rate of 46.6 live births per 1,000 population had fallen to 28.6 by 1984. The Population Growth Rate had plummeted from the 3.3% in 1960 to 2% by 1980 and 1.6% by 1984; or in more tangible terms, rather than doubling every 21 years, Thailand's population was doubling every 44 years by 1984, still high but no longer economically debilitating in view of the sustained trend of declining fertility. Most impressively, 65% of eligible Thai couples were practising some method of contraception by 1984, up from 3% in the 1960s.[4] Some observers called this performance a miracle. Most attributed it to plain hard work.

That Thailand's rapid decline in fertility rates coincided with the inauguration of Mechai's community-based family planning program and its well-publicized success should not, however, be construed to mean that Mechai was solving Thailand's population problem on his own. Mechai sincerely believed that the critical ingredient in Thailand's fertility decline in the 1970s was the Thai government's commitment to a population policy and its enthusiastic support for the National Family Planning Program, a fact that Mechai was quick to remind people of. It was the Ministry of Public Health that first integrated family planning into its national health service. It was the Ministry of Public Health that pioneered non-physician distribution of contraceptives; and that maintained the nationwide clinic-based system where his village distributors could refer couples for more reliable contraceptive methods like IUDs, injectables, or sterilization. It was the Ministry of Public Health that encouraged private, non-profit organizations like Mechai's to play such an active role in the National Family Planning Program.

In return, his organization provided services to large segments of the population in remote rural areas at no cost to the government. In fact, Mechai's program developed a symbiotic relationship with the government. Its operational districts were chosen in conjunction with the government to prevent duplication; and local government officials were consulted prior to launching any activities in their jurisdictions. All achievements were credited to the National Family Planning Program. Mechai used a simple analogy to explain his synergistic partnership with the government. "The government is like the whiskey and we are like the soda. To make a good drink for large numbers of people requires good whiskey and a lot of soda."

Amid all the hoopla surrounding the introduction of his village-based program, Mechai always kept his priorities straight. His principal objective was socio-economic development for Thailand's people. Family planning and population management were a means to an end. Since his days in the Evaluation Division at NEDB, Mechai recognized that reducing population growth required immediate intervention. But family planning is an abstraction, a non-event. Rural people don't live in an abstract world. Women take the pill and don't get pregnant, but they have no concrete symbol of the benefit. By linking family planning with development, income generation, and poverty alleviation, he could demonstrate that not getting pregnant produced tangible results. Conversely, family planning was a logical entry point and vehicle for introducing other development programs. By using contraceptives, family planning acceptors were demonstrating their responsibility for their own fertility and their commitment to make their lives better. Why not give them first priority for other development services?

"Rural development is my first love and primary goal," Mechai explained. "Family planning is the linkage. Once the community's credibility as family planning acceptors is established, we are able to move into a series of health and development programs. We regard family planning as the first step in a long war. It teaches people that if they participate, it works to their benefit."

He called this strategy "Fertility-Related Development", introducing livelihood opportunities through family planning acceptors first. As fertility declines and their lives improve, you add other things. Mechai had always wanted to combine family planning and development. Since the family planning donors had been more responsive to his requests for funding, he started with family planning first. As the program became more successful, he began to integrate community development activities.

Mechai started slowly, but with characteristic flair. Farmers practising family planning could rent a team of buffalo to plow their fields at half price while others paid full price; or could use the services of a Family Planning Stud Pig at concessionary rates. He arranged low-interest loans for family planning acceptors. Families using contraceptives were assisted to buy livestock. In a program called the "Non-Pregnancy Agricultural Credit", his organization would provide concessionary interest rate loans to farmers practising family planning to pay for fertilizer, seed, and insecticide.

Following this assistance on the production side, the next logical step was the "Better Marketing Program". In this scheme his organization, using its existing network of offices, functioned as a marketing agent helping family planning acceptors to sell products like onions, potatoes, pumpkins, silk, and handicrafts, essentially cutting out the middleman. Mechai's organization would find the markets and arrange the transportation. The villagers would get 30% more for their products, at the middleman's expense.[5]

Next, the incentives were expanded to benefit entire communities. Entire villages were provided with a Village Development Fund, the size of which was determined by the extent to which the community practised family planning. Mechai contributed 1,500 baht for each village member who had a vasectomy, 1,000 baht for female sterilization, 800 baht for an IUD user, 600 baht for injectable contraceptive users, 400 baht for oral pill acceptors, and 200 baht for condom users. An additional contribution of 200 baht was made for every woman who did not get pregnant during the calendar year, demonstrating that women could bring resources to the village through their fertility behavior. Elderly women and young girls were credited 20 baht for every pregnancy free month.

This program was carried out for two years. In one village, family planning acceptance was so high that the fund reached US$15,000. A committee was selected to screen requests and loan money. Loans were made for income-generating activities. The villagers received shares in the fund that determined the extent of their credit. A vasectomy qualified the villager for 80 shares, female sterilization got 40 shares, IUD users got 20 shares, and oral contraceptive users got ten. Villagers who did not practise family planning could also borrow from the fund, but family planning acceptors, especially women, received preference.

In villages where this program was introduced, contraceptive use soared from 30% to 70% of eligible couples because now the benefits were tangible, not only for individuals but for entire communities, including those who didn't practise family planning. Some critics complained that these incentive programs might be seen as a quid-pro-quo for family planning practice, raising the specter of coercion, a practice that Mechai inherently abhorred and consciously avoided. Mechai dismissed his critics with a sensible homily. "Anything involving force between the navel and the knee has never worked in the history of mankind. So keep it joyful, voluntary, relevant, and fun."

As his program spread around the country and the desensitization campaign achieved wider publicity, Mechai became a visible symbol of Thailand's successful family planning program. The Thai people began to equate family planning with Mechai and his programs, even when their actual contribution in terms of contraceptive users was still negligible. The brightly colored logo at Mechai's office on Soi 12 Sukhumvit Road in Bangkok became a beacon for couples with all kinds of fertility-related problems.

One of the most frequent questions asked by women ending up on his doorstep was, "What do I do about unwanted pregnancies? Can you help us?" Thailand's law was ambivalent on the issue of abortion. De jure, the Thai penal code stated that "if a woman causes herself to abort, or if another causes her to abort with her consent, they may be liable to imprisonment, or a fine, or both." The law goes on to state, however, that "if an abortion is carried out by a medical practitioner and is (1) necessary for a women's health or (2) the woman is pregnant under certain conditions, such as rape, is less than 13 years old, or if she is abducted, then there is no offense." De facto, in the 1970s safe, sterile abortion was unavailable to the overwhelming majority of Thai women seeking to terminate an unwanted pregnancy,[6] being relegated instead to the sleazy domain of the stereotype back-alley quack who inserted a foreign object into a woman's uterus to induce a miscarriage. When confronted with that alternative, poor Thai women really had no choice.

Yet even in the absence of a safe alternative, there was ample evidence that abortions were taking place on a massive scale in Thailand. An authoritative study published by the Population Council of New York, which questioned rural abortionists about their annual caseload, concluded that nearly 300,000 induced abortions took place in 1978, a rate of 37 abortions for every 1,000 Thai women aged 15-44.[7] The primary cause of so many abortions was ignorance about contraceptive availability and contraceptive failure. Other anecdotal evidence confirmed this conclusion. Data collected by Dr. Suporn Koetsawang in the early 1970s at Siriraj Hospital in Bangkok showed that women suffering from uterine infection and hemorrhaging, the short term complications of septic abortions performed by unqualified practitioners, filled 25% of beds in Siriraj Hospital's Obstetrics/ Gynecology Ward. Death from these complications was not uncommon. In addition to the huge costs the medical system was incurring to treat the complications of septic abortion, women were dying because they had no choice.

The methods employed by traditional abortionists and quacks to induce abortion were barbaric by any yardstick. Massage abortion was by far the most common technique. The abortionist would massage or knead the uterus using the heel of their foot, causing intense pain, sometimes over several visits. If that was unsuccessful, they would literally kneel on the uterus and jump up and down until bleeding ensued. Objects like bamboo sticks or coat hangers were inserted into the uterus. Chemical and herbal abortifacients were taken orally to induce abortion. In some cases non-physicians of dubious skill who used non-sterile instruments and faulty technique did the abortions. If the contents of the uterus were not totally evacuated, hemorrhage and infection ensued. The lucky ones made it to a hospital. The unlucky ones died.

Why did so many Thai women resort to this barbaric alternative? It is a demographic fact of life that replacement fertility cannot be achieved without abortions. When a society experiences a rapid fertility decline from a Total Fertility Rate (TFR) of 6-7 down to 2-3, as Thailand was undergoing in the 1970s, women will have on average two abortions per fertile lifetime. As family planning became more popular and couples decided to space births or limit childbearing, more pregnancies were unwanted. In Thailand in 1974, unless they had a lot of money, quacks and traditional abortionists were the only recourse for women with unwanted pregnancies. Now they were hoping Mechai could help.

Since his program was not clinic-based, there was not much Mechai could do. At first he would refer them to a government hospital, which was a non-starter because abortions were not performed there. So these women ended up going to quacks anyway, and eventually ended up in Siriraj Hospital's emergency room as another one of Dr. Suporn's statistics. As Mechai saw this scene repeated over and over, he began to feel that "there must be something we can do to help. We can't just turn our backs on these women and, in effect, tell them, 'I'm sorry. You'll have to go to a quack and risk your life.' We can't just deny responsibility and say we are a non-clinical distribution program. We have to help these people."

Mechai consulted with Malcolm Potts about this problem. Malcolm had been instrumental in having the abortion law liberalized in the United Kingdom in the 1960s, hence was extremely sympathetic to the plight of these women. He firmly believed that you couldn't just give women contraceptives and then tell them they are on their own. Only when a contraceptive distribution program provides reliable information, advice, and education for women who want to practise family planning; and was backed up by a safe, sterile abortions for unwanted pregnancies, did women have real choice. Malcolm urged Mechai to establish a comprehensive clinical facility which could provide women with a full range of services — ambulatory care, clinical family planning methods like IUDs and sterilization, and pregnancy termination for contraceptive failure.

There were two problems that Mechai wanted addressed satisfactorily before he proceeded. The first was legal. In fact, abortion was legal in Thailand if continued pregnancy was detrimental to a woman's health. If "health" was interpreted as physical and emotional well-being, an unwanted pregnancy was detrimental to a women's mental health. The World Health Organization (WHO) further buttressed this interpretation when it defined health as "not only the absence of disease, but a complete state of physical and emotional well being" in its declaration of "Health for All by the Year 2000" made in 1978. Since Thailand was a member of WHO, its acceptance of this definition was clearly implied. The law, though narrow, was on Mechai's side. Plus, Thai society was sympathetic to the plight of women who had been put into this painful predicament. Concerned physicians, none of whom had ever been prosecuted under Thai law for terminating a pregnancy, had helped many women. It seemed inescapable that Mechai should help these women with what was essentially a legal and socially acceptable clinical service.

The second obstacle was financial. Setting up a modern clinic with proper equipment, supplies, and trained physicians would require capital and competent management. Malcolm Potts had an idea where Mechai could access capital. An organization called International Pregnancy Advisory Services (IPAS) had been set up with funds from the Scaife Foundation to loan money to multi-purpose clinics such as the one Mechai was contemplating. Malcolm knew the IPAS management and Board of Directors. Upon submission of a proper proposal accompanied by a business plan that forecast repayment of the loan and eventual self-reliance, a one-million-baht loan was soon secured. The venture had passed the second litmus test. Mechai was ready to proceed.

Mechai chose the Patpong area off Silom Road in Bangkok's most popular entertainment district, known to Thais and foreigners alike, to set up the clinic because it provided anonymity. In the general chaos that prevailed there, no one would notice the couples entering the clinic for pregnancy termination and other services, thus their privacy was assured. He soon found a sympathetic building owner who rented him space. Next he needed a clinic manager, someone who could not only run the clinic as a business but who would also be available at the odd hours such a clinic would require. By this time, Tavatchai Traitongyoo had left NEDB and was working full-time with Mechai as Manager of the Operations Division and Finance/ Admin. Division. Tavatchai had a close friend, Sudha Chatchavalvong, who was intrigued by the CBFPS experiment and frequently came to see Tavatchai there. Like Mechai and Tavatchai, Sudha was an economist and currently an employee of NEDB. He saw how happy Tavatchai was working in the organization; and how stimulated he seemed working so closely with Mechai. During one of his visits to see Tavatchai, Mechai asked him if he was interested in managing the new clinic. Sudha knew nothing about clinic management, but Mechai convinced him he could learn on the job.

It didn't take Sudha long to decide. He respected Mechai and recognized the importance of his work. To work with Tavatchai and Mechai on this new venture was the opportunity of a lifetime. He was bored at NEDB, stifled by its bureaucracy, and looking for a new challenge. Most important, Sudha liked the hours. The clinic would be open from 12 noon to 12 midnight. He was a night person who abhorred waking up early. This was the clincher. "I accept your offer," Sudha told Mechai. "I will resign from NEDB tomorrow."

The triumvirate of Mechai, Tavatchai, and Sudha that would successfully lead the organization for the next 25 years, had now been formed as a team.

The clinic opened on July 1, 1975 as a separate legal entity from CBFPS, Mechai's family planning organization. Physicians from the Ministry of Public Health, Bangkok Municipality, and the Teacher's Medical Council worked part-time at the clinic. Dr. Ella worked there as a volunteer. Some of the physicians provided only routine outpatient care and family planning services. Specialists performed pregnancy termination procedures using strict protocols for sterility and safety. The clinic had an umbrella policy which covered any procedure performed there — it must be within legal and safety limits, the couples must be thoroughly counseled and willingly consent to the procedure, couples were advised on subsequent use of safe and effective contraceptives, and the clinic would take complete medical and financial responsibility for complications resulting from any procedure performed there. Women seeking assistance with unwanted pregnancies now had a safe and legal alternative to quacks and traditional abortionists. They now had a choice.

Counseling was an integral component of the clinic's service. Mechai encouraged the man and woman to attend the counseling together to impress upon them that this was a difficult situation for both partners, not just the woman. He wanted couples seeking termination of an unwanted pregnancy to fully understand the ramifications of the procedure and its potential consequences. He wanted the couples to understand that unwanted pregnancy was preventable if modern contraceptives were used properly. If medical evaluation deemed that a pregnancy had gone beyond the first trimester, clinic staff would counsel couples to deal with a full-term birth. Sometimes they referred them for adoption, sometimes they intervened with the girl's father, and sometimes they even found them a job.

To repay the IPAS loan, a nominal fee was charged for all medical procedures. Mechai preferred to view this fee as a donation. However, Mechai did not want the fee to deter women from seeking care. When it came to pregnancy termination, clients were encouraged to donate on a sliding scale. If counselors considered a donation too burdensome for their clients, it could be adjusted downward. Some clients not only didn't pay, they were given taxi fare to go home.

Mechai's Patpong clinic was a welcome alternative for Thai women. As the word spread that pregnancy terminations performed by medically qualified clinicians, all of whom were Board Certified as well, could be obtained there at affordable prices, the clients came. Conversely, the numbers of women going to quacks dropped dramatically. With the surplus generated from the clinic, Mechai could repay the loan to IPAS. This came as a surprise to IPAS, because it had already converted loans made in other countries into grants because the ventures were not financially viable. Once half the principal had been repaid, IPAS agreed to forego the balance as a gesture acknowledging the professional management of this venture. For Mechai, Tavatchai, and Sudha, they learned to operate efficiently in an environment where everything was done to ensure that failure was not an alternative. Not only did they operate in this environment, they were successful and thrived.

There were many reasons for the clinic's success, not least of which was the management acumen of its three principals. It provided an essential service for which there was great demand.

It provided a high quality service at an affordable price, unlike what was available previously. Timing was also a critical element in its success. Abortion, though theoretically legal in 1975, still existed in a judicial gray area. Because of this ambiguity, most clinicians avoided it. When Mechai offered a safe and affordable alternative, women embraced it and the medical/legal establishment allowed it to exist, recognizing that the Patpong clinic was providing an essential service. For similar reasons, most people in Bangkok knew about Mechai's clinic but did not want to disturb it. For his part, Mechai never broadcast or publicized the Patpong clinic, preferring to quietly fill the vacuum for pregnancy termination services while being careful not to offend sensibilities. Although abortion in Thailand in 1975 was not the wrenchingly divisive political and emotional issue it has become in the West, it still had opponents who could make trouble for Mechai. By maintaining a low profile, he mostly avoided controversy and trouble.

With a multi-purpose clinic now providing pregnancy termination services in Bangkok, Mechai felt the time was right to expand up-country in areas where his village contraceptive program was operating and his organization had an administrative presence. First, however, he moved the clinic in the Patpong area to the premises of his offices at Soi 12 off Sukhumvit Road in 1977. The Patpong area was getting too seedy, and with the clinic at Soi 12, there was more privacy and it could be better supervised. In 1982, a new clinic was opened in Chiang Rai, the first in Thailand's provinces. In 1985 two more clinics were opened in Bangkok. Then, in 1987, a clinic was opened in Chiang Mai followed by another in Nakhon Ratchasima in 1989.

Mechai's success and the respectability that followed him emboldened other organizations and practitioners to provide sterile abortions in their family planning clinics. Even PPAT, not renowned for its audacity, began performing pregnancy terminations. Some physicians would use the term "community" in their clinic names, identifying themselves with Mechai in the people's eyes and benefiting from his credibility. As other organizations and private physicians came to the forefront, this obviated the need for Mechai to expand services. He was more pleased to see others take up the mantel. From the sleazy realm of the quack, Mechai had elevated abortion into a service of kindness, compassion, and generosity for women in trouble.

As this entire episode is reviewed in retrospect, several exceptional achievements stand out. Clearly the most significant was providing safe alternatives for women with no choice, thereby eliminating the medical exploitation that quacks relied on. Mechai also demonstrated to other practitioners that safe abortion could be provided at an affordable price and still be economically viable. Rather than expanding himself, Mechai got others to open clinics where pregnancy termination was provided. In this way, services expanded around the country. He even trained physicians to perform pregnancy termination procedures and brought equipment into Thailand for them. Equally important, Mechai provided an affordable alternative for poor people seeking pregnancy termination, something never available to them before.

It should be noted that the Patpong clinic was established first and foremost to provide a desperately needed service for women in need. It was not done to make money, only to generate enough revenue to repay the IPAS loan and make the clinic self-sufficient. The physicians were paid on an hourly basis rather than by procedure. Any surplus was used as a reserve for clinic expansion or some other charitable cause. Some was used for scholarships, some for low-interest loans to farmers, and some to maintain family planning stud pigs. All was used for a humanitarian purpose.

Many years later, Mechai received the UN Population Award for his many contributions to population and family planning.

In his acceptance speech before ambassadors and UN officials, he made special reference to this episode: "I am especially proud that I was able to help unfortunate women to terminate unwanted pregnancies. In doing this, I am supported by my wife and my daughter. It has given women a real choice."

By 1977, Mechai's family planning organization had grown in both size and scope. To accommodate that expansion, Mechai recognized that it was time for CBFPS to be converted from a project into a proper legal entity. He wanted to use his family planning network to expand beyond family planning. For this he would need a broad-based development organization. The Japanese Organization for International Cooperation in Family Planning (JOICFP) had provided money for an integrated family planning and parasite control program. He was negotiating with a Dutch NGO about a rural-development project.[8] With so many opportunities presenting themselves, Mechai could see the advantages of greater organizational flexibility than CBFPS could provide.

In 1976, steps were taken to achieve that flexibility. The Population and Community Development Association (PDA) was established as an umbrella organization for Mechai's various endeavors. CBFPS was one agency within PDA. There could and would be others to accommodate the rapidly expanding initiatives in health and development. In 1977, all profit-making activities from clinics to paraphernalia were subsumed under the Population and Development Company (PDC). PDC was a private, for-profit company independent of PDA. Tavatchai was its Chairman and Sudha was the Managing Director, providing the glue binding PDC with PDA. Mechai held no position within PDC, functioning more as its patron. By its charter, PDC could only use its profits for charitable purposes. To this day, PDC remains the only profit-making entity in Thailand with this proviso. It was this ingenious arrangement that allowed the rapid growth that PDA would see in the next five years. Previously, Mechai had been synonymous with CBFPS. In the future he would become synonymous with PDA.

The first opportunity for PDA to expand beyond family planning came in 1978. An agency called Appropriate Technology International (ATI) had funds to develop appropriate technologies and transfer them to rural people in Asia. ATI had done some small-scale technology development with integrated farming, biogas generation, simple well construction, and water pumping. It was developing linkages in Asia through a network of appropriate technology agencies in Bangladesh, Sri Lanka, Indonesia, Philippines, Thailand, and India. Knowing his interests in development, members of that network had directed ATI to Mechai. After hearing Mechai expound upon his fertility-related development strategy and seeing the enormous potential of his 10,000 volunteers in 16,000 villages as agents of change, ATI gladly provided PDA with a grant to establish the Community Based Appropriate Technology Development Services (CBATDS pronounced "see-bats"). Like CBFPS, CBATDS became an agency within PDA, but its mission was community development. Using the infrastructure established by CBFPS, it could seek independent funding to go beyond family planning and introduce community development inputs to family planning acceptors. Programmatically and organizationally, PDA was poised to pursue Mechai's dream of community development for Thailand's people.

But an event occurred in 1979 that propelled PDA into the thick of an international crisis, and expedited its transition into a community development organization exponentially.

*Monk blessing family planning paraphernalia with holy water*

*A CBFPS poster with the inscription "Too Many Children Make You Poor" at a TV interview*

*Condom package for the condom social marketing project*

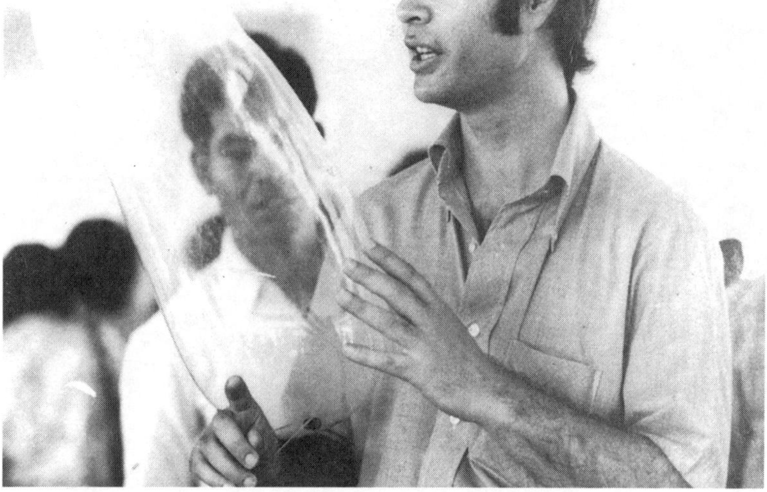

*Mechai blowing up condoms*

*Family planning buffalo*

*Family planning distributor plying her wares*

*Birth control poster on a bus stop in Bangkok*

*Family planning volunteer distributor explaining about birth control pills from a boat, 1974*

# NOTES:

1 Incidentally, as Mechai held condom-blowing contests in other settings, he began to notice that the blue and black condoms always seemed to burst first. He reported this to the manufacturer, who found that the carbon from the color was reacting with the latex to make the condoms more brittle. This led to a change in the manufacturing process that made them less brittle and prevented breakage, and probably prevented untold numbers of contraceptive failures.

2 Coincidentally, Indonesia was introducing a community-based, family planning program using the non-physician village distributor concept in 1974 under the auspices of its National Family Planning Coordination Board, better known by the abbreviation BKKBN for its Indonesian name, Badan Kordinasi Keluarga Berencana Nasional. BKKBN used the exact same checklist developed in Thailand for midwife distribution of oral contraceptives. Allan Rosenfield even assisted with its adaptation. Under its charismatic leader, Dr. Haryono Suyono, BKKBN's village based program would eventually reach every village in the Indonesian archipelago. Being a government program, BKKBN lacked the flexibility that Mechai could apply to his desensitization campaign. Although its communication program lacked the pizzazz and showmanship that Mechai's exhibited, BKKBN pursued a sound nuts-and-bolts approach to management that accounted for the program's success. Also, BKKBN was operating within a conservative Muslim society less tolerant than the more laissez-faire Thai society. Nevertheless, Haryono Suyono was a master communicator, manager, and leader who understood the idiosyncrasies of Indonesian culture much as Mechai understood Thai culture; and who could fashion his communications messages within a cultural context understandable to

the Indonesian people. Indeed, Haryono Suyono and Mechai Viravaidya shared many personal characteristics that were intrinsic to the success of family planning in their countries. Each is recognized worldwide for their contributions to Population and Family Planning.

3 The origin of this motto demonstrates how Mechai used his profound understanding of Thai society to fashion his messages. In Buddhist scripture, there is a saying, "Too Many Children Cause Suffering." To make it more meaningful to the Thai people in the modern context, and to connect rampant population growth with its deleterious impact upon the Thai economy, he simply modified it to "Too Many Children Make You Poor."

4 These data are taken from the *Statistical Handbook of Thailand*, National Statistics Office, Office of the Prime Minister.

5 Middlemen have not been famous for their tolerance of competition, especially when increased profits to farmers are achieved at their expense. In the late 1970s, when Mechai introduced the "Better Marketing Program", middlemen were not concerned because the marketing was done on a small scale and focused on nonperishable products. And with Mechai having become such an icon for the rural farmer, it was best, they decided, to just leave him alone. As will be seen later, this situation would change in the early 1980s when Mechai's "Small Farmers' Fair Price Program" expanded rapidly into perishable produce, making him a force that middlemen could no longer ignore.

6 As in most countries where abortion is either illegal or an ambiguous law makes it generally unavailable, safe, sterile abortion services were available to better-educated Thai women with money. They could always obtain the services of highly skilled and ethical medical practitioners to terminate unwanted pregnancies but at exorbitant cost. This option was simply not available to women

from middle and lower socio-economic groups. It is probably more accurate to say that safe, sterile abortion services were available in Thailand in the 1970s, but they were tightly rationed by price.

7 Tongplaew Narkavonnakit, "Rural Abortion in Thailand: A National Survey of Practitioners," *Studies in Family Planning* 10 no. 8/9 (August-September 1979).

8 Mechai was negotiating with a Dutch NGO called NOVIB in 1977 to support an integrated family planning and community development project. NOVIB maintained that you can't mix family planning and community development, a hypothesis that Mechai would empirically and emphatically disprove with his Community Based Integrated Rural Development Project (CBIRD) in 1982, that would become one of his most innovative and successful projects (see Chapter 8). Mechai even flew to the Netherlands to defend his proposal before the NOVIB Board, but they rejected his proposal. In hindsight, NOVIB missed a golden opportunity for a donor agency to pioneer a community development phenomenon.

# 7

## CABBAGES AND CONDOMS

*Between 1973 and 1977, all of Southeast Asia was in turmoil. The Vietnam War came to its inevitable but cataclysmic conclusion when Communist regimes came to power in Vietnam, Cambodia, and Laos. The old order was turned upside down, and scores were brutally settled following years of intractable civil war. Thailand traversed one of the most unsettling periods in its tumultuous history, as it navigated its way from a military dictatorship to representative democracy then back to military dictatorship, all while trying to achieve some political accommodation with its hostile Communist neighbors.*[1]

Of the Communist regimes that displaced Indochinese governments in 1975, the Khmer Rouge in Cambodia was easily the most extreme and brutishly oppressive. Prior to 1970, the clandestine Communist Party of Kampuchea[2] (CPK) was subservient to the North Vietnamese Communist Party, which in turn restrained the CPK so as not to jeopardize its furtive alliance with the Government of Cambodia under Prince Norodom Sihanouk. Only in 1968 did the CPK launch an armed struggle against the government, which was inconsequential at best. That changed in 1970. First General Lon Nol, Sihanouk's Prime Minister, ousted the Prince in a coup d'état. Left with few options, Sihanouk emerged in China and North Vietnam to head a united opposition front against Lon Nol. The forces of the CPK, better known as the Khmer Rouge, would be the front's foot soldiers.

In May 1970, the United States invaded Cambodia to flush North Vietnamese forces from the Parrot's Beak region of eastern Cambodia. This not only drove the North Vietnamese deeper into Cambodia, it also freed the Khmer Rouge from direct North Vietnamese restraint to pursue its military and political goals. The corrupt and inept Lon Nol Government, propped up by massive infusions of US military aid, was no match for the Khmer Rouge and their North Vietnamese patrons. Though the war in Cambodia dragged on for another five years, the outcome was inevitable. On April 17, 1975, two weeks before the fall of Saigon, the Khmer Rouge forces overcame final government resistance and converged upon the capital of Phnom Penh to install the Democratic Government of Kampuchea.

The four-year reign of Democratic Kampuchea would usher in one of the most repressive, genocidal "People's Revolutions" of the 21th century. Within weeks of April 17, more than 3.5 million people, including the entire populations of Phnom Penh and Battambang, Cambodia's two largest cities, were physically uprooted and forced into the countryside, ostensibly to grow enough food to survive, but all part of a grand Khmer Rouge strategy to launch the Khmer people on a forced march into socialism.

The evacuation took an enormous toll in lives. It is estimated that 1.5 million people were killed by the Khmer Rouge between 1975 and 1979. Many of them were the forced evacuees, who succumbed to disease, starvation, and overwork. Others were the "petit bourgeois", the middle class pr ofessionals and urban elites who were not only deemed dispensable but socially unredeemable under Khmer Rouge doctrine; and were systematically executed.

During the final stages of Democratic Kampuchea, as the regime grew increasingly insecure, the Khmer Rouge began intramural purges to murder their own comrades, whom the paranoid leadership saw as internal threats to the revolution.

As the revolution faltered, the Khmer Rouge leader Pol Pot looked for scapegoats. The domestic ones he methodically killed. Internationally, the Vietnamese provided a convenient antagonist. The alliance between the Vietnamese and Cambodian communists fractured immediately after their respective victories in 1975. Looking to consolidate territorial gains, the Khmer Rouge and Vietnamese scuffled over disputed islands in the Gulf of Thailand in April 1975. Cross-border incidents fueled by incendiary rhetoric increased the tenor of their traditional animosities. Superpower rivalries led to a final, permanent cleft between the former allies. Democratic Kampuchea allied itself with China, Vietnam with the Soviet Union. Each saw the other alliance as a provocation. They embarked on a course that must inevitably lead to war.

The prelude came in December 1977 when the Vietnamese mounted a military offensive against Democratic Kampuchea that penetrated 32 km. into Cambodia. The Vietnamese withdrew after teaching the Khmer Rouge a lesson. On December 25, 1978 they delivered the coup de grâce. Over 100,000 Vietnamese soldiers invaded Cambodia. Encountering perfunctory opposition, the Vietnamese were in Phnom Penh within two weeks. After Pol Pot's four-year reign of terror, the Khmer people welcomed the Vietnamese as liberators. But Pol Pot and his Khmer Rouge forces managed to escape, bringing thousands of peasants with them. In the ensuing confusion, hundreds of thousands of Khmer took the chance to flee. En masse they headed in the only direction with a gateway to freedom — westward toward Thailand. As the Vietnamese army pursued the Khmer Rouge, a huge exodus of Khmer criss-crossed the country in their vanguard. The chaos following the Vietnamese invasion destroyed the rice crop. A famine confronted the survivors.

After Vietnam occupied Phnom Penh, a puppet regime under Heng Samrin was quickly installed to provide a facade of respectability. Reporters and aid agencies were invited to enter Cambodia to witness firsthand the terror and destruction that Pol Pot and the Khmer Rouge had wrought — the mass graves, the Killing Fields, the Tuol Sleng torture prison, the massed deportations, the indiscriminate slaughter — all barbarous examples of man's inhumanity to man. There was an international outpouring of grief for the tragedy that had occurred — and guilt for having let it happen.

Meanwhile, over 500,000 Khmer refugees amassed on the Thai border north of Aranyaprathet District in Prachin Buri Province by December 1979, sandwiched between the Vietnamese Army to the west and the Khmer Rouge ensconced in their strongholds to the North. Frightened, starving, and with dwindling options to escape, they crossed the border and entered Thailand. It was a heart-wrenching sight. Men, women and children, all dressed in rags, all their earthly belongings either carried on their backs or piled into makeshift push carts, faces expressionless from the horror from which they had escaped. The refugees inundated Thailand — 15,000 the first day, 25,000 the next, and the next, and the next. Within two weeks, 200,000 Cambodian refugees had fled to Thailand. Another 300,000 remained perched on the Thai-Cambodian border. It was the largest refugee crisis in the world until that time. All of these people would need food, clothing, water, sanitation, shelter and medical care. And it would be Thailand, with copious assistance from the international community that would be left to deal with the crisis.

Back at PDA, Mechai was following the evolving refugee situation closely. The refugees would undoubtedly place a huge burden upon Thailand's fragile resources; and their presence in Thailand would fray the frail political coalition that propped up the Kriangsak Government. The Cambodian Refugee Crisis, as it came to be known, elicited an immediate and magnanimous response from the international community. Donors were searching for appropriate ways to provide humanitarian relief. Although Mechai and PDA knew nothing about refugee relief, he was willing to help if the need arose.

In mid-December 1979, Mechai was sitting in his office at PDA when he received a telephone call from the Director of the German Volunteer Service (GVS) in Bangkok. PDA had an affiliation with GVS, using German volunteers to assist its small-scale, community development projects. The Director of GVS, Dr. Wolfgang Behrens, informed Mechai that there was a German NGO called Deutche Welthungerhilfe (Agro-Action) that wanted to assist Cambodian refugees on the Thai border. Agro-Action had a substantial amount of money to donate, but needed a counterpart agency to work with in Thailand. Dr. Behrens wanted to know if Mechai could help. There was one catch. Agro-Action needed a proposal by 3:00 P.M. the same afternoon — only six hours away — or the money would have to be sent to Phnom Penh.

"No Problem. We are prepared," Mechai responded without a moment's hesitation. "Agro-Action will have a proposal by 3:00 P.M. today." The fact that neither Mechai nor anyone else in PDA had any experience with refugee relief didn't faze him for an instant. Mechai viewed refugee relief as community development with an abbreviated time frame. Agro-Action would have a proposal by 3:00 P.M.

Mechai gathered the troops — Tavatchai, Sudha, and other senior PDA staff like Tanothai Suktit, Somjit Tippayaprapha, and Sophon Siriwong. Logically, they assumed that food and medicine were the most obvious immediate needs during the emergency surrounding the refugees' arrival and settlement in the camps. Agro-Action required that all commodities had to be procured before December 31, meaning they had less than two weeks to get organized. In short order a proposal was crafted, and sent to Agro-Action that same afternoon.

Since he might soon be involved in refugee relief, Mechai decided to visit the camps inside Thailand and on the border to see the situation firsthand. There were five camps housing about 200,000 Cambodia refugees inside Thailand: Khao-I-Dang, the largest with about 140,000 people, and Sa Kaeo with 35,000 people, both in Prachin Buri Province; Kamput in Chanthaburi Province; and Mairut in Trat Province. Later on, a refugee holding center would be established at Phanat Nikhom in Chon Buri Province where refugees awaiting relocation to third countries would be accommodated temporarily for processing. On the Thai-Cambodian border, an indeterminate number of refugees estimated at 300,000-500,000 lived in makeshift camps like Ban Mak Moon, Ban Nong Samet, and Ban Nong Chan, named for the Thai villages to which they were adjacent.

The border camps were like a no-man's land. Nominally united under the Khmer Seri (Free Khmer) resistance, these were actually independent enclaves ruled by warlords and bandits who were too preoccupied fighting among themselves for control of the lucrative black market into Cambodia to offer much resistance to the Vietnamese. There was an aura of random chaos and lawlessness about these camps. Armed militiamen carrying loaded M-16 or AK 47 assault rifles swaggered through the camps. Each had a thriving market where consumer goods from Bangkok would find their way to Phnom Penh, Saigon, and even Hanoi. Each had a gold exchange where the price of gold in London was quoted every hour, and where the refugees could exchange their gold for the Thai baht or US dollars they would now need to survive. Each camp could degenerate into a battleground at a moments notice when disputes between warring factions erupted into violence, or if the Vietnamese chose to liquidate a site.

Though relatively more secure due to the protection provided by the Thai military, the refugee camps inside Thailand were equally chaotic when Mechai arrived in December 1979. Khao-I-Dang, with its 140,000 refugees located just ten kilometers from the border, was a shambles. Under the administrative control of UNHCR, the camp was constructed on a dusty, barren plain at the foot of the mountain that bore its name. Food and water had to be trucked in daily. Crude bamboo shelters with thatched roofs spread as far as the eye could see. Shallow, open trenches served as latrines. The overwhelming stench emanating from the open latrines was Khao-I-Dang's distinctive trademark. Flies breeding in the latrines enveloped the camp. The haggard refugees, exhausted by their year-long exodus following four years in Khmer Rouge-imposed hell, seemed to have the same blank look of despair on their faces. There was a lot of work to be done here, Mechai concluded. He instructed his staff to get started.

As Mechai toured the camps, he also noticed all the western emergency relief workers now ministering to the refugees. In addition to UNHCR, the Cambodian Refugee Crisis had attracted a host of international Voluntary Agencies, which collectively identified themselves as "Volags". CARE, American Refugee Committee, International Rescue Committee, Project Concern, Medecins Sans Frontier, ICRC — the "Volags" descended upon the refugee camps with near missionary fervor to save the unfortunate Cambodians. What puzzled Mechai was that there were no Thai agencies among the Volags. Here was an international crisis being played out on Thai territory with foreign relief agencies running the entire show. There was something inherently juxtaposed here, which Mechai intended to rectify.

Agro-Action was extremely pleased, not only with PDA's hastily prepared proposal, but also with the efficient manner in which supplies were subsequently delivered to the camps. "If you have any other ideas to help the refugees," they queried Mechai, "we would like to provide you with more support." Little did they know that asking Mechai if he had more ideas was like asking Beethoven if he had more symphonies. He had ideas in spades. Rather than giving the refugees more handouts, which encouraged greater dependence on the giver, Mechai preferred to use the same strategies he used in Thai villages — building on local resources, stressing self-help, and relying on community input for program development. His ultimate objective was to provide assistance to Khmer people through programs designed and implemented by Khmer people that would prepare them for their eventual return to Cambodia or resettlement to third countries. He viewed the Khmer as partners with common interests. It worked in Thai villages, he figured. It should work in the camps too.

Neither CBFPS nor CBATDS was well situated to provide refugee relief, so Mechai proposed that another bureau be created under the PDA umbrella. Agro-Action liked all of Mechai's ideas and provided the core support to establish the Community Based Emergency Relief Services (CBERS, pronounced "see-bers"). It was the third bureau established under the PDA umbrella. It was the first Thai agency to actively provide emergency relief to Cambodian refugees, except for the Thai Red Cross, which was assisting under the auspices of the International Committee of the Red Cross. In a matter of weeks CBERS was a functional entity. Senior staff were seconded from CBFPS. New staff were hired. By January 1980, CBERS had offices in

Khao-I-Dang and Sa Kaeo camps in Prachin Buri Province and was providing services.

With Agro-Action's support, CBERS initially got involved in food for work programs, skills training, and some sanitation and vector control. Slowly but surely, the open-pit latrines were closed with special Ferro cement covers designed by CBATDS. The latrines were liberally sprinkled with lime each day to kill the flies and suppress the odors. Khmer workers employed by CBERS earning ten baht per day did all the work.

While establishing the CBERS beachhead in Khao-I-Dang and Sa Kaeo, Mechai observed the healthcare being provided to the refugees. The camps were divided into housing sections containing about 7,000 people each. A different Volag provided medical care for each section. Invariably, each had an outpatient clinic and hospital staffed with nurses and physicians from Germany, Switzerland, France, or the US. The place was swarming with foreign medical personnel. Some would stay for as little as two or three weeks, most for two or three months, attracted as much by voyeurism as by humanitarianism, but all motivated by a noble altruism. By February 1980, there was one physician for 1,400 people in Khao-I-Dang, and one percent of the total population was hospitalized. In contrast, there was only one physician for 80,000 people in rural Thailand outside municipal areas.

These doctors and nurses brought the medical technologies and treatment biases from their home countries with them, hence the predilection for medical care and the absence of good preventive medicine and public healthcare. The Cambodian refugees suffered from diseases like cholera, typhoid, malaria, giardia, amoebas, liver fluke, and intestinal parasites. You don't see many cases of these in places like Paris, Hamburg, London, Rome, or Chicago from whence the medical missionaries came. One had to wonder what special qualifications they brought to their task. But if qualifications could be measured by their ardor and Albert Schweitzer-like commitment to help the refugees, you couldn't ask for better people.

Good intentions, however, do not equate with good healthcare. During the first few months in the camps, following the privations of the past four years, many of the Khmer refugees were acutely ill and required intensive medical care. After several months in the camps, however, the refugees began to resemble normal rural population groups in developing countries. Food intake had stabilized, clothing and shelter were provided, security was no longer an issue, and most of the refugees settled into a more routine existence. Now they needed good public healthcare and preventive medicine — clean water, proper sanitation, sanitary waste disposal, immunizations for their children, infectious disease control, ante-natal and post-natal care, Vitamin A for children and pregnant women, and family planning. The Volags were neither organized for nor disposed toward preventive medicine and public health. And when it came to family planning, the Volags, many of which represented religious or sectarian organizations, were vehemently opposed.

It was this situation that Mechai confronted when CBERS began working in the camps in January 1980. The sanitation and vector control were proceeding apace. But Mechai was concerned about the refugees' healthcare. Was the western model practised in the camps, emphasizing hospitals and curative care, sustainable in the long run? What about the Khmer people themselves? Couldn't they be trained to provide their own medical care? What about the near total absence of maternal/child health and family planning services in the camps? When it came to family planning, Mechai was consistently egalitarian. He viewed the right to plan a pregnancy and control their fertility as a basic right of all women regardless of race, ethnicity, social class, or circumstances.

Moreover, the Cambodian women desperately needed access to family planning. Women who were previously amennorheic during the hardships of the Pol Pot years were regaining their fecundity under the more secure conditions prevailing in the camps. Pregnancy rates were soaring. Evidence began to surface that unwanted pregnancies were being handled in the customary way — traditional practitioners in the camps performed septic abortions that put women's lives at risk. For obvious reasons, the camps were not ideal environs to become pregnant, deliver babies, and raise children. Delaying pregnancies and spacing births was not only good preventive medicine. It was common sense.

The medical Volags didn't quite see things this way. Not understanding demographic realities, they felt that the Khmer people should be encouraged to propagate in order to replace the populations decimated during the genocidal Pol Pot years rather than practising family planning. In spite of the hazard of closely spaced, high-risk pregnancies and the impracticality of raising children in the camps, the Volags encouraged Khmer women to go forth and multiply with almost religious conviction.

So when Mechai proposed that a voluntary family planning program be introduced in the Cambodian refugee camps, there was an understandable uproar of protest from the western Volags. When he proposed that non-physicians using a simple checklist of contraindications distribute oral contraceptives, as they were in Thailand, there was a further uproar of protest from the same group. They insisted that only physicians be allowed to distribute oral contraceptives, like in their own countries. When Mechai proposed that the injectable contraceptive Depo-Provera — which had been approved by the Thai Food and Drug Administration (FDA), had been included in Thailand's National Family Planning Program for years, and was being used in 67 countries around the world — be made available through the program, the most vociferous furor ensued. The US Food and Drug Administration had not yet approved Depo-Provera for use as a contraceptive, the Volags righteously proclaimed, so it shouldn't be used for the Cambodian refugees.

This was a classic example of medical imperialism. The western Volags were trying to impose the standards of France, Germany, and the United States upon Cambodian refugees living in camps in Thailand. Fortunately, the Thai government and its Ministry of Public Health demanded that Cambodian women should have the same access to contraceptives as Thai women for the same reasons — to prevent unwanted pregnancy and delay pregnancy until optimum child-bearing years. There was no ambiguity or double standard about this position. In February 1980, the Royal Thai government and UNHCR invited CBERS to offer family planning services to the 150,000 Cambodian people living in the Khao-I-Dang and Sa Kaeo refugee camps.

For Mechai, the critical word was "voluntary". He would spare no effort to assure that Cambodian women knew their options and had real choices. He would offer only temporary methods to avoid any misunderstandings. The process he used to introduce the program was fairly standard by this time. First, influential Khmer leaders were consulted about the impending program and their support was enlisted. Then, a general education program was launched using Mechai's familiar education and communication approaches. The program's climax came when Mechai brought a mobile movie van into the camps to screen Thai movies, interspersed with family planning messages and information about the upcoming introduction of contraceptive services during intermissions. In Khao-I-Dang, 40,000 people attended each screening, jockeying for a place to see their first movie in five years. Just like audiences in Thailand, the Cambodians shrieked at the sight of the unfurled condom and laughed uproariously during the condom-blowing contest. Regardless of the culture, it never failed to get a laugh.[3]

On the first morning services were offered, women began queuing up early outside the CBERS thatched-roof clinic. Each was interviewed by a Khmer volunteer prior to choosing a method, screened with a checklist, and asked to sign a consent form. Mechai invited all the foreign Volags to observe how the family planning services were being provided. They were amazed to see Thai and Khmer people providing all the services.

More than 6,000 couples in Khao-I-Dang chose to practise family planning in the next five days. When the program was repeated in Sa Kaeo, the response was equally enthusiastic, with over 2,000 acceptors. Within a month of introducing contraceptives, 52% of the married women of reproductive age in the camps were contracepting. The overwhelming majority chose the injectable contraceptive Depo-Provera. Cultural acceptability and convenience explained this compelling predisposition for Depo-Provera. It is a well-known fact that Asian people prefer medicines administered by injection. When the injection is accompanied by three guaranteed pregnancy-free months, the high rate of Depo-Provera use was understandable.

In 1980, the USFDA's non-approval of Depo-Provera made it one of the most controversial pharmaceuticals in the world.[4] Opponents used unsubstantiated allegations and groundless accusations about its safety and effectiveness to undermine its credibility as a contraceptive. Its use in the refugee camps provided another stage in which the Depo-Provera controversy could be played out. The western Volags actively tried to discourage Cambodian women from practising family planning. Leaflets were circulated in the Khmer language exaggerating the dangers of Depo-Provera use. Cases presented at Volags clinics with complications from incomplete abortions were attributed to Depo-Provera.[5] Scurrilous articles based upon misinformation supplied by the Volags appeared in the western press, raising an international furor over the issue.

Having been through all of this before, Mechai knew how to handle the situation. Plus, he had one distinct advantage. He was doing the right thing and was convinced of it. Mechai had learned long ago to trust his instincts and act on his convictions. So CBERS continued to provide voluntary family planning services to Cambodian women in exactly the same way that CBFPS offered them to Thai women. Mechai did not allow CBERS to get swept up in the controversy. He would not respond to unsubstantiated allegations, realizing that even acknowledging them bestowed an element of credibility they did not deserve. He just made sure that family planning services remained available to Cambodian women, and let the women decide for themselves. Despite all the misinformation, the women chose to practise.

The controversy eventually waned as more experienced medical professionals replaced the volunteers who responded to the original crisis. Committed for longer periods of service, experienced working in developing countries, and more sensitive to the prevailing conditions in the host country, the post-emergency medical Volags recognized family planning as the essential maternal child health service that it was. By September 1980, the western medical Volags in Khao-I-Dang and Sa Kaeo camps asked CBERS to integrate family planning into their outpatient clinics and hospitals. The controversy had been deflated. CBERS and the Volags replaced confrontation with cooperation. The real winners were the Khmer women in the camps.

Mechai's perseverance with the family planning program established CBERS reputation as an emergency relief organization, not only among the Volags but also with UNHCR, which administered the camps. In May 1980, UNHCR delegated full responsibility for all sanitation, vector control, and waste disposal in Khao-I-Dang to CBERS. With its burgeoning population of 120,000 people, Khao-I-Dang was the third largest city in Thailand. And CBERS, which did not even exist six months before, was providing all its basic public health services.

Mechai approached this monumental challenge using the same principles he applied to community development in Thailand. Consultations were held with the Khmer leaders in the camps, strategies were devised to organize and implement sanitation and waste disposal, and responsibility for implementation was turned over to Khmer leaders within each of the camp's housing sections. Mechai also saw an opportunity here. Many of the bench technologies being developed by CBATDS could be scaled up in the experimental crucible of the refugee camps. The camps would provide the laboratory for developing appropriate technologies to be used in Thai villages.

CBERS introduced these technologies immediately. Organic wastes were deposited in specially constructed landfills. After four months of composting, the fertilizer was used to enrich home vegetable gardens. Human wastes were pumped from pit latrines into an oxidation pond system, where they were detoxified and the purified water was recycled for crop irrigation. Where positive synergies could be found between the refugee camps and the Thai people, Mechai wanted to exploit them.

Vector control, however, posed a unique problem. Fly and rat populations were reaching epidemic proportions in the camps. A Swedish Volag was spending 50,000 baht (US$ 2,000) per month spraying the camps with DDT, which was not only expensive but also a health hazard. Because of the crowded conditions, widespread pesticide use was impractical and even dangerous. Besides, these would have limited impact unless the cause of the problem, garbage accumulating in and around the refugees' homes, was eliminated. Mechai realized that, unless the refugees could be motivated to take responsibility for the problem, it would persist despite CBERS' most energetic efforts. He needed an innovative campaign, very public in nature, which would catch the refugee's attention, raise their awareness of the problem, and motivate them to take collective action.

So he organized fly-catching and rat-catching contests. A reward of 100 baht or five US dollars was offered for each kilogram of flies caught, one baht for each rat, regardless of size, and five baht for a pregnant rat. There were special prizes for the most original rat-catching devices. An intensive education and motivation campaign accompanied the media event surrounding these contests. This was Mechai in his element doing what he did best.

Children fanned through the camps in search of their prey. Rats with a bounty on their heads can quickly become an endangered species. During the 14 days of the campaign, no fewer than 24,000 rats were caught. Lines of children holding bags of flies to collect their rewards were visible symbols of the magnitude of the fly problem. Ingenious contraptions to catch rats, built with Rube Goldberg-like complexity, were displayed at the contest and prizes awarded. A campaign was launched to clean up refuse around homes and prizes were given for the cleanest housing sections, a practice which continued beyond the intensive campaign. The Thai press was there to capture the whole thing. Articles appeared in Bangkok newspapers with pictures of children holding rat traps and bags of flies, visible proof of Khmer refugees helping themselves. These were tried and true approaches. No one had ever thought to use them in refugee relief.

The Cambodian refugee camps became a focus for smuggling and black market profiteering within weeks of their establishment. Khao-I-Dang, with 120,000 inhabitants located close to the Cambodian border, was the most egregious offender. Electronic equipment, textiles, jewelry, and consumer items could be found in the central market in Khao-I-Dang in abundant supply. Most of it was headed for Cambodia and Vietnam. However, there was considerable consumer demand building among the refugees residing in Khao-I-Dang. Many had exchanged their gold for Thai baht or US dollars and could purchase consumer items to supplement services provided by UNHCR. There was also a growing middle class in the camps working for CBERS, UNHCR, and other Volags who received ten baht per day for their labor. They now had disposable income to purchase on the black market as well.

This situation concerned the Thai military. Not only was smuggling illegal, but as the black market grew, syndicates and gangsters came to control it. A climate ripe for crime and lawlessness was soon created as the syndicates fought over their turf. The refugee camps existed in a zone of political and military instability. The crime associated with the black markets and smuggling exacerbated it.

The Thai military decided to eliminate the black market by placing a cordon sanitaire around Khao-I-Dang that would prevent smuggling in and out of the camp. There was one problem, however. There were thousands of Khmer workers receiving a daily salary of ten baht for working in the camps. If there were no consumer items for them to purchase, it would undermine their incentive to work. The Thai military had a solution, which they asked Mechai to help them implement.

They proposed to replace the workers' daily salary with a chit that would entitle them to purchase ten baht worth of consumer items to be sold at fixed prices at centralized stores in Khao-I-Dang. The chit would, in effect, become an alternate currency to the Thai baht. To make this system work, three conditions had to be met. First, consumer items had to be brought in to the centralized stores daily at a value equivalent to the total daily wages of all Khmer workers receiving ten baht per day in chits. For example, if there were 5,000 workers receiving a daily wage, then 50,000 baht worth of consumer items had to be brought in to Khao-I-Dang every day. Second, these consumers items had to be desirable to the consumers, something they wanted to spend their chits for. Finally, the black market had to be totally subdued so that the centralized stores were the only market that provided consumers with goods.[6] What was being proposed, in effect, was to create a centralized, planned economy for 120,000 people. And the Thai military asked Mechai and CBERS to administer it.

Mechai was none too enthusiastic about this proposal. As an economist, he knew the inherent weaknesses of centralized, planned economies and the difficulty of intervening in markets. He was also highly skeptical that the three conditions could be completely met. Most importantly, neither he nor CBERS had the expertise to become the central bank for a planned economy. The Thai military was insistent, however, so with some reluctance he accepted this new challenge.

In April 1980, the Thai military and CBERS embarked on a grand experiment in microeconomics in Khao-I-Dang refugee camp when the black market was suppressed, and the Thai baht was removed from circulation, replaced by a new currency called a "CBER". The exchange rate was one CBER for one Thai baht. All workers in Khao-I-Dang would now receive ten CBERs per day for their labor, and could purchase consumer items available at centralized storehouses in Khao-I-Dang with their CBER notes. Mechai printed brightly-colored notes, bearing a distinct resemblance to Monopoly money, as the CBER notes. The CBER notes came in denominations of 1, 10, 20, 50, and 100 CBERs. Mechai and CBERS were charged with bringing consumer items into the camps in daily amounts equal to the Thai baht equivalent of the daily wages of the Khao-I-Dang workforce. In addition to an emergency relief organization, CBERS was now a central bank for 120,000 people.

History has shown that centralized planning is contrary to human nature. The experience in Khao-I-Dang in April 1980 supported what history eventually demonstrated. While Mechai was busy printing CBER notes and his staff were busy making sure that sufficient goods were brought into the camps each day, the Khmer workers were not particularly pleased when they received their 10 CBER notes as salary in lieu of Thai baht. But they were willing to give this new system a try.

Two fatal errors undermined the scheme. Black markets have traditionally proved remarkably resilient in the face of forced suppression, and Khao-I-Dang's was no exception. The Thai military was not able to totally eliminate the black market. Other goods were still getting into the camps, and these could only be purchased with Thai baht or US dollars, undermining the value of the new CBER currency. Most fatal to the scheme was the decision by the Thai military to limit the consumer items that could be brought into the camps and purchased with CBER notes. In a righteous effort to positively influence the consumption patterns of the refugees, the Thai military only allowed a circumscribed list of essential items for personal hygiene, sanitation, clothing, and food to be brought into the camps and sold for CBER notes at the centralized stores. Unfortunately, these did not match the consumer preferences of the refugees. The result was predictable.

With prices fixed, demand for consumer items in the centralized stores plummeted. Consumers took their CBER notes and exchanged them on the black market for Thai baht to purchase more desirable consumer items available there. In turn, the black marketeers took the devalued CBER notes and purchased essential items at the centralized stores at a steep discount, reselling them on the black market in Thai baht at a fraction of the original price. Consequently, the exchange rate of the CBER notes collapsed. The black market exchange rate reached ten CBERs for one Thai baht and hyperinflation threatened. Worker unrest followed when the value of their daily wage was depleted by the devalued currency. To forestall further unrest, Mechai asked the Thai military to reinstate the Thai baht as payment for workers in the camps, which they did. It was a noble experiment with an inevitable outcome. It lasted about one month.

To deal with the boredom and sense of hopelessness inherent in a refugee camp situation, CBERS introduced agriculture and skill-development programs for the refugees. Vegetable seeds were distributed to all families in Sa Kaeo and Khao-I-Dang. Within weeks, the bleak landscape in the camps erupted in a verdant green. Home vegetable gardens became ubiquitous, and crawling vines infiltrated trellises in front of bamboo houses, as people supplemented the still meager camp diets with fresh vegetables. CBERS trained people in simple agricultural techniques that could be used if and when they returned to Cambodia. An integrated farm, another technology being developed by CBATDS that used the simultaneous production of food, fuel, and fertilizer to increase productivity, was built in Khao-I-Dang as a training site. The skill-development program taught simple skills like fishnet weaving, pottery, mat weaving, soap making, and construction of rainwater collection systems, which could be used to generate income when they returned to Cambodia.

Refugee relief had traditionally been viewed as charitable emergency assistance. CBERS approached it as community development, which viewed the recipient as a partner with common interests. Mechai wanted to restore the refugees' self-respect and self-esteem and prepare them to return to their country. It was a novel approach but it was working among the Khmer, evidenced now by the large CBERS presence in the camps where it was the largest NGO and getting larger. If there were complementarities in refugee relief that could also help the Thai people, as Mechai was now finding, so much the better.

This final objective was reasonable in view of the significant burden the refugees were placing on Thailand. They created a zone of instability along Thailand's entire eastern border with Cambodia. Vietnam's army, with 200,000 troops poised along the Thai-Cambodian border, would make cross-border incursions into Thailand chasing elusive Khmer resistance groups, forcing Thailand into an unprecedented military buildup that diverted resources from national development. Unable to deal with both a worsening economy and the deteriorating security along its border with Cambodia, the Kriangsak Government was forced to resign in 1980, to be replaced by a broader coalition headed by General Prem Tinsulanonda.

For Thai villagers in the immediate vicinity of the camps, the burden was more direct. Over 80,000 Thai villagers were uprooted from their villages and traditional occupations by the fighting, massive human migrations, and the teeming refugee camps encroaching on their living space. As the caravans of food, water, and medicine destined for the camps bypassed these destitute Thai villagers, an understandable resentment began to surface. Mechai was very sensitive to these sentiments and sought ways to ameliorate the resentment.

As Mechai studied the situation, he discovered even more sinister ways in which the refugees were impacting Thai villagers. Despite CBERS' best efforts to help refugees grow supplementary food in home gardens, UNHCR still had to provide a basic diet of rice, protein, and vegetables for 150,000 refugees. It procured the food directly from middlemen, who in turn purchased it from Thai farmers at disadvantageous prices. In effect, the food requirements of the refugees were reinforcing the unbalanced relationship between middlemen and farmers that Mechai was trying to rectify with his "Better Marketing Program". Wouldn't it be nice, Mechai reflected, if food for the refugees could be purchased directly from Thai farmers, bypassing the middlemen and passing their cut on to Thai farmers as higher prices for their produce. Then the refugees would be seen as directly helping Thai farmers while breaking the back of the middlemen. The idea was utopian and fraught with danger. Mechai decided to pursue it nonetheless.

Mechai brought his proposal to the Royal Thai government and UNHCR in mid-1980. Neither could argue with its sensibility nor with the benefits for Thai farmers. They did question its practicality. "Who will identify the Thai farmers? Who will convince them to abandon the middlemen, with its resultant consequences? Who will purchase the food and deliver it to the camps? Who will deal with the inevitable wrath of the middlemen?"

Mechai's response, made without a moment's hesitation, required only two words. "We will," he said. Lack of confidence was never one of Mechai's weaknesses. He didn't lack confidence when Agro-Action requested a proposal by 3:00 P.M. the same day. He didn't lack confidence when he started CBERS from scratch. He never lacked confidence during the controversy surrounding family planning in the camps, nor when CBERS took over sanitation and waste disposal for 120,000 people. He wasn't about to get cold feet now in what was possibly his greatest challenge. "We will do it," he responded calmly. Incredulous but willing to give it a try, the Thai government and UNHCR agreed. Subconsciously, they may have thought they were giving Mechai just enough rope to hang himself, but they agreed. In the future, PDA would be responsible for purchasing and delivering all the basic foodstuffs required for all 150,000 Cambodian refugees living in camps in Thailand.

Mechai's proposal was actually just a logical extension of his "Better Marketing Program", only on a grander, more systematic, and more visible scale. He gave the job to CBATDS. They would identify farmers using the CBFPS network in 16,000 Thai villages. Building upon Mechai's fertility-related development strategy, preference would be given to family planning acceptors and villages where contraceptive prevalence was highest. All the pieces were coming together. CBATDS would arrange all logistics for transport and delivery. PDC would rent vehicles and provide transport. CBERS would see that food was distributed in the camps. The whole operation would require synchrony among the four PDA agencies. Mechai would handle the middlemen himself.

The next six months were among the most hectic in PDA's history — and in Mechai's life. Purchasing food for 150,000 people[7] on a daily basis is a mammoth task. Trying to buy it directly from individual farmers is logistically insurmountable — unless you have a network in 16,000 villages where your credibility has been established, your motives are genuine, and your reliability unquestioned. CBFPS began identifying suppliers for unmilled rice, cabbage, kale, cauliflower, onions, garlic, pumpkins, eggs, and Chinese broccoli. Each farmer selling their produce to CBATDS was given a card addressed to the Central Command of the Royal Thai Army, which stated what had been sold, and at what price. The Thai military would spot check to assure that farmers were receiving fair prices. The price offered to the farmers was several baht above the middleman's price. The price CBATDS charged to UNHCR was several baht below the middleman's. Except for the middlemen, this was a win-win situation.

Within a month, the CBATDS "Small Farmers' Fair Price Program" was in full swing. Produce purchased in rural Thailand would be transported to Bangkok, consolidated by type of produce, and then shipped to the camps. Excess shipments usually ended up on the premises of PDA's residential Bangkok office site on Soi 12 Sukhumvit Road for want of other storage space. Among the brightly-colored vasectomy vans, the urbane PDA office staff, and couples being counseled prior to their menstrual regulations, could now be found heaps of garlic, onions, pumpkins, and cabbages.

Mechai even had a rice mill installed on the premises just in case brown rice needed to be milled before being shipped to the camps. When they milled rice for the first time, a mushroom cloud of rice bran dust spewed into the atmosphere and descended on PDA's Soi 12 neighbors. Complaints from the Darling Massage Parlor right next to PDA were the most strident. It seemed that rice bran didn't do much to enhance the sensuality of a body massage. Even Mechai had to admit that Soi 12 Sukhumvit Road was not the ideal place for a rice-milling operation. The mill was soon dismantled and moved directly to the refugee camps, where brown rice was now milled on the premises. The site that the rice mill formerly occupied on Soi 12 was converted into a daycare center for construction workers. Even Mechai agreed that this was a better use for the space.

With all those fresh vegetables hanging around, local residents of Soi 12 began to ask whether they could buy some. Always the entrepreneur, Mechai never missed an opportunity to generate some revenue for PDA. In short order, a small vegetable stand was opened on the PDA office premises where the vegetables, along with lace panties, T-shirts, key chains, condoms, and oral contraceptives were sold to the local residents. Mechai called the shop "Cabbages and Condoms", a catchy sobriquet that never failed to elicit chuckles from passersby; and was extraordinarily successful at drawing the curious into the shop. Soon Mechai added a small outdoor restaurant where the "Som Tam" (Green Papaya Salad) and "Larb Gai" (Spicy Chicken Salad) were among the best in Bangkok. At first, PDA staff would gather there after work for drinks and snacks. As the cuisine gained a reputation, outsiders began showing up. Today, the "Cabbages and Condoms" Restaurant is acknowledged as one of the finest Thai restaurants in Bangkok. The hundreds of people who eat there every day are a testament to its excellence.

The Small Farmers' Fair Price Program was an unqualified success. The Thai government and UNHCR were happy with the excellent fresh produce being delivered to the camps regularly at lower prices. They soon asked CBERS to take over the preparation of meals at the Panat Nikhom holding center, where about 10,000 refugees at any one time congregated prior to resettlement in third countries. CBERS was given the contract one day and providing meals for 10,000 people by 10:00 A.M. the next day. The Thai farmers were happy because of the higher prices they received from CBATDS. For the first time, Thai farmers were experiencing tangible benefits from the presence of Cambodian refugees in their countries. It was a public-relations coup. Favorable articles began appearing in the press, leavening Thai public opinion toward their guests from Cambodia.

Everyone was happy except the middlemen. When Mechai first started his Better Marketing Program, the middlemen dismissed it as novel but negligible. Now he had a market for 150,000 people, still small in a country of 45 million, but visible and dangerous precedents were being set. If Mechai continued to popularize the advantages of bypassing the middlemen, others might try it. He was becoming a troublesome thorn in their collective derrières.

The threats that Mechai soon received were inescapable sequelae of his better marketing strategy. As the most vocal proponent, he was the most likely target. For his part, Mechai was amazingly unperturbed. He had resigned himself to threats as an occupational hazard. If push came to shove, he would take his chances.

There was something else working to Mechai's advantage during this latest crisis. By late 1981, he had been working indefatigably for the Thai people for 15 years. He had a proven track record of commitment and dedication to the people's welfare. Here was a popular celebrity who had taken up their cause. They knew him and trusted him. In the process, he had become the people's icon. Not an icon in the sense of a religious image, but as a unifying symbol with whom Thailand's people could identify. He was the underdog fighting for their interests against the entrenched establishment. If the icon were harmed pursuing his crusade for the people, it would only enhance his ideals and make the people cling to them even more. The middlemen knew this. They could make their threats, but in the end they could only be empty ones.

*Cambodian refugee encampment on the Thai-Cambodia border, 1979*

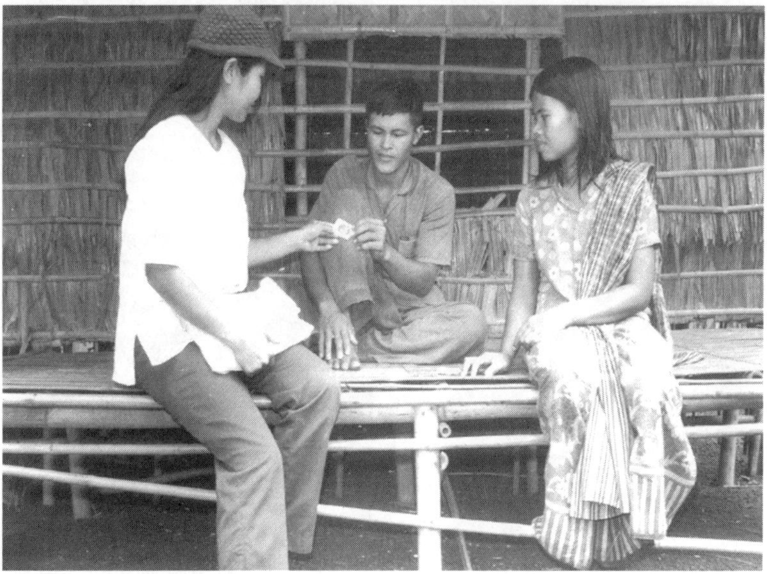

*Family planning volunteer in the refugee camp at Khao-I-Dang, 1980*

*A family planning session for refugees*

*Cambodian women registering for family planning services*

*Movies being shown in the refugee camps prior to family planning campaigns*

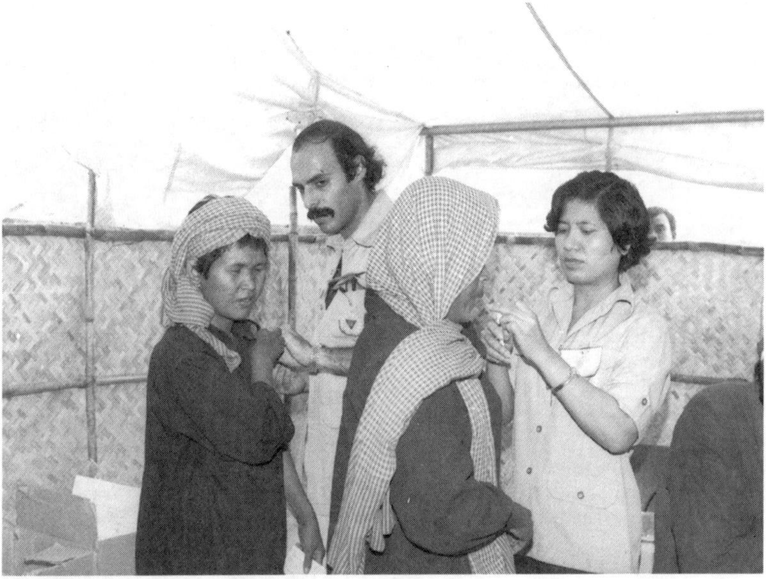

*Cambodian women receiving Depo-Provera injections.*
*The author is at left with Chief Nurse Vallee, 1980*

*Introducing agriculture into the refugee camp at Khao-I-Dang, 1980*

*Mechai in front of the first Cabbages and Condoms vegetable stall, 1981*

*The PDA old guard — from left Tavatchai, Sudha, Mechai, Nikom, Somjit, Praween, Songnam, 1980*

## NOTES:

1 Even by Thailand's standard, the period between 1973 and 1977 had degenerated into political chaos. The Thanom-Praphas Government, which had inherited the authoritarian mantel of the Sarit-Thanom Government, was expressing its final hypoxic gasps before expiring in 1973. A growing Communist insurgency, loosely aligned with fraternal brethren in China, Vietnam, and Laos, was exerting military pressure on the government from strongholds in the North and Northeast. Students and workers demonstrated against the government's close alliance with the United States, and were increasingly impatient with a regime representing partisan military interests only. Massive demonstrations against the government erupted in October 1973. When even the military refused to support the regime, Thanom and Praphas were forced into exile, making way for a civilian democratic government for the first time since the post-World War II period. From 1973 to 1976, Thailand experienced democracy of the most chaotic and frenetic variety. A civilian government under Dr. Sanya Dharmasakti as Prime Minister prepared the country for elections, scheduled for January 1975. Freedom of speech was given a wide birth. Political parties were allowed to organize. Farmers and students demonstrated. Workers went on strike. Essays by Thai leftist intellectuals were published and circulated. Marxist-Socialist tracts were distributed, while the writings of Mao, Lenin, Ho Chi Minh, and Stalin were freely available. Political philosophies from the far left to the far right were openly debated in preparation for the elections. Results of the 1975 election, however, were inconclusive. First Seni Pramoj of the Democratic Party tried to rule with a weak coalition, which collapsed in two weeks. Then his brother Kukrit Pramoj, head of the Social Action Party, stitched together an equally fragile coalition government that miraculously survived until January 1976, steering Thailand through

the turbulent events of 1975. Facing a no-confidence motion, Kukrit resigned. The Democrats returned to power under Seni Pramoj in April 1976, hoping to usher in a period of stable civilian democratic government. Thailand's experiment with democracy could not have come at a more inauspicious time. Victories by Communist forces in Vietnam and Cambodia in April 1975 were followed by a consolidation of power under the Pathet Lao Communist regime in Laos in December 1975. By year's end, Thailand was surrounded by Indochinese neighbors ruled by Communist regimes that it had vigorously opposed in alliance with the United States. Following the ignominious US withdrawal from Indochina in 1975, Thailand was left to face these potentially hostile neighbors alone. The domestic situation soon degenerated into chaos. The Communist victory in Indochina emboldened left-wing radicals, creating a backlash of mistrust and fear. Newly organized right-wing organizations such as the Village Scouts and Red Gaurs resorted to force as a means of political expression. This hostility erupted in an orgy of violence on 6 October 1976, when Village Scouts, Red Gaurs, and right-wing extremists attacked students at Thammasat University, protesting against Thanom's return from exile. Students were beaten, lynched, burned alive, and summarily executed. Thailand's brief experiment with democracy was over. As happened in the past when civilian governments had failed to achieve stability and domestic politics eroded into pandemonium, the military stepped into the breach. Thanin Kraivichien, a former high court justice, was installed as Prime Minister and immediately embarked on a program to suppress the left. The Thanin Government was even more repressive than its military predecessors in its enthusiasm to purge suspected radicals. He rescinded freedom to speak freely and congregate. Rigid censorship was introduced. Leftists were expelled from the civilian bureaucracy. Student leaders fled to the countryside to contribute their intellectual vigor to the Communist Party of Thailand's growing insurgency. Alienation ensued. The Thanin Government lasted one year, just long enough to discredit itself and allow the military to re-exert its control. In

October 1977, General Kriangsak Chamanand forged some limited reconciliation between left and right on the Thai political spectrum. The deteriorating situation in Thailand's Indochinese neighbors would eventually cause his downfall.

2 In this section, the terms "Kampuchea", "Cambodia," and "Khmer" will be used frequently. It is useful to clarify these terms here. The country is called Cambodia. Cambodia is inhabited by the ethnic Khmer people. Kampuchea was the name given to Cambodia during the period 1975-1979, when it was ruled by the Khmer Rouge as Democratic Kampuchea. Once the Khmer Rouge were driven from power in 1979, the name of the country reverted back to Cambodia.

3 Malcolm Potts, who borrowed liberally from Mechai's repertoire when speaking in other countries, was always amazed at how Mechai's methods transferred culturally. "You could draw a map of the world with 'laughter isobars' on it to gauge how quickly different cultures responded," Malcolm recalled. If you blew up condoms in the Philippines, the laughter response time was almost as quick as in Thailand. Once, in post-revolutionary Iran, I blew up a condom, tore off its elastic ring, and used it as a hair tie for a woman in the first row. There was icy silence for 30 seconds before the first smile broke out on someone's face, followed by the typical response of uncontrolled laughter. The only thing that really separates cultures is how long it takes them to start laughing."

4 Next to abortion, the controversy over Depo-Provera use in developing countries in the 1970s and 1980s evoked one of the most strident, fractious, and ideological debates in the public health community. By 1980, Depo-Medroxy Progesterone Acetate or DMPA, the generic name for the contraceptive marketed by the Upjohn Company as Depo-Provera, was being used by 1.2 million women in 76 countries. It had already been used in Thailand for 15 years, and officially included in its National Family Planning Program in

1974. The World Health Organization's Toxicology Review Panel concluded that there were no toxicological reasons why DMPA should not be used for contraceptive purposes. Why all the controversy? Opponents of DMPA objected because Depo-Provera had not been approved for use in the United States by the USFDA, which westerners patronizingly considered the final arbiter of pharmaceutical safety. In fact, the USFDA Medical Committee on Obstetrics and Gynecology had twice recommended Depo-Provera for contraceptive use to the FDA Commissioner. The USFDA even announced its final approval of Depo-Provera in 1974. But political pressure from special interest groups delayed any action until 1978, when the FDA Commissioner decided not to approve Depo-Provera for contraceptive use for women in the United States based upon a complex assessment of the risk/benefit ratio for this drug solely applicable to the US population. The risk of Depo-Provera rested solely upon a single study in which two of 16 beagle dogs developed mammary carcinoma when given 25 times the human contraceptive dose of DMPA. This finding was disputed and eventually discredited because evidence suggested that all progestogens, including naturally occurring progesterone, can promote mammary tumors in beagle dogs, hence the species was not an appropriate animal model. When similar studies with mice, rats, and monkeys could not replicate the beagle dog findings, the issue should have been closed. Once the Pandora's box had been opened, however, other dangerous side effects to Depo-Provera use were alleged. It increases the chance of birth defects, it causes miscarriages in pregnant women, it delays return to fertility after discontinuation, it causes blood clots and liver disease — these and other side effects were attributed to Depo-Provera without even a pretense of convincing scientific evidence. Credible clinicians and researchers like Dr. Edwin McDaniel and Dr. Tien Pardthaisong, using data from their 15 years of experience using Depo-Provera in Chiang Mai Province, refuted these allegations with hard scientific data. No sooner were they refuted than even more spurious and unsubstantiated allegations were made. This controversy had practical ramifications.

Because Depo-Provera was not approved for use in the Unites States, the US Agency for International Development could not supply it to the many countries that received contraceptives through its very successful population assistance programs, despite its popularity and safety. The number of women who were denied access to this effective and safe contraceptive was immense. This controversy raged on for the next 12 years, but eventually became moot when the USFDA approved Depo-Provera for use in the United States in 1993.

5 Peter Fajans, a young physician doing his Preventive Medicine Residency, was in Khao-I-Dang from June to August 1980 during the family planning controversy in the camps. When the Volags made multiple reports of incomplete abortion resulting from Depo-Provera use, he decided to investigate. Depo-Provera was not known as an abortifacient. In fact, it had been used in the United States to prevent spontaneous miscarriage in the first trimester of pregnancy. Following an examination of charts, he found that, in many of the cases attributed to Depo-Provera, the women had no record of ever using Depo-Provera. In all cases, there were other symptoms that may have explained the abortions, such as malaria or sepsis secondary to induced abortion. These epidemiologic investigations were followed by anthropologic investigations, where Peter discovered that there were indeed traditional abortion practitioners in the camps, and they were doing a booming business. In his interviews with several of them, he learned that the method of choice was the insertion of bamboo slivers through the cervix and into the uterus, aborting the fetus but likely to result in sepsis, hemorrhage, or tetanus. Further investigations disclosed that Khmer medical staff working in the Volag clinics and hospitals were performing dilatation and curettage abortions after hours in the clinics without the knowledge of their self-righteous employers. The practice had arisen to provide women with a safer alternative to the induced abortions performed by traditional practitioners. Even in a refugee camp where contraceptives were available, women would resort to induced abortions to terminate unwanted pregnancies. Peter Fajans eventually

went on to become a faculty member at the University of Michigan School of Public Health and now works for the Division of Reproductive Health and Research of the World Health Organization.

6 There was one other factor at work that would also undermine this scheme. Even if these three conditions were met, it didn't take into account the Thai baht and US dollars that were already in circulation in the camps. Theoretically, if the system proposed by the Thai military were implemented perfectly, and only chits could be used to purchase consumer items in the camps, the Thai baht and US dollars in circulation would lose their value vis-à-vis the new currency. It was unlikely that any system could be implemented that perfectly.

7 The number of refugees in the camps was constantly changing over time. Some were resettled to third countries: others were voluntarily repatriated. The four camps in Thailand fluctuated from 200,000 inhabitants when they first arrived to about 120,000 three years later. The numbers of refugees quoted at various stages in this chapter vary according to the fluctuating refugee populations.

# 8

## GOVERNMENT SERVICE

*Between 1974 and 1981, PDA experienced meteoric growth. From its origin as a community-based, family planning organization, it had now expanded into community development and refugee relief. The original coterie of 30 staff who helped Mechai launch the organization had expanded to 700 by 1981. Its annual budget had increased from US$ one million in 1974 to US$ 12 million in 1981, albeit a sizable portion of that was devoted to refugee relief work. It was now the largest private, non-profit, community development organization in Thailand.*

From Mechai's perspective, further expansion into health and community development was now PDA's strategic priority. Using PDA's two greatest assets — its grassroots network of 10,800 village contraceptive distributors in one third of all districts in Thailand; and the villagers they served who knew and trusted PDA — Mechai prepared to go "Beyond Family Planning" more systematically. Health services could be vertically integrated with family planning; then community development programs could be horizontally integrated into the entire system.

Health services were integrated first. Ministry of Public Health surveys had shown that 60% of Thailand's population harbored intestinal parasites. In 1976, with assistance from the Japanese Organization for International Cooperation in Family Planning (JOICFP), PDA launched the Family Planning and Parasite Control Program (FPPC) to treat villagers for parasites in the districts in which it operated.[1] In 1977, the Integrated Family Planning, Health, and Hygiene Project was introduced with financial support from USAID. In addition to the one-day training on family planning, village distributors in 80 districts received an additional day of training on health and hygiene. In addition to contraceptives, the distributors were provided with household drugs to treat villagers for minor ailments.

Within the scope of the new integrated program, PDA began building latrines, household water jars, and village water supplies. If you asked Thai villagers to prioritize their felt needs, clean water would rank near the top of the list. Thailand has monsoon weather patterns — a rainy season from June to October followed by a dry season from November to May when almost no rain falls. Depending upon the dry season's severity, ground water supplies may evaporate by March, leaving potable water in short supply.

Water shortages are most acute in Thailand's Northeast, which is coincidentally its poorest and most populous region. During an average year, northeastern Thailand receives 100 days of rain and 120 cm. of rainfall. Traditionally, water for personal and domestic use was obtained from unsealed wells and village ponds. During the dry season, when ponds dry up, villagers may travel as much as five kilometers to obtain even contaminated water.

Lack of clean water is a serious impediment to improving health and quality of life in Thailand's rural villages. Providing reliable village water supplies, however, is a particularly difficult task. The three technologies being used by government were expensive, unreliable, and suitable for selected situations only.

Gravity-fed water systems are costly and difficult to build. Bore wells require expensive drilling equipment. Dug wells are suitable only where shallow ground water is available. Bore wells and dug wells frequently dry up during the dry season. All are communal water systems and difficult to maintain.

Rainwater catchment systems, on the other hand, have many attractive features which make them ideally suited for household water supplies. Sufficient water is available everywhere — it is collected from corrugated roofing, which is ubiquitous in rural Thailand, during the rainy season. Rainwater catchment can be built for individual households requiring minimal investment. They are affordable and easily constructed. Even more important, Thai villagers liked them and wanted them.

Mechai seized upon this inexpensive and appropriate alternative to expand PDA's clean water program. His challenge was to devise a way to build large numbers of rainwater catchment systems while recovering costs from villagers. The hardware was easy. A rainwater catchment system consisted of a cylindrical reinforced concrete water tank 3.6 meters high and two meters in diameter for each house with a capacity of 11.3 cubic meters (11,300 liters) of water, enough for the drinking, cooking, and household requirements of a family of five for the seven-month dry season. Gutters channeled water collected from corrugated roofs into the concrete water tank.

Designing the software — where and how to build the tanks, and how to recover costs from the villagers to make it sustainable — was the real challenge. For this Mechai relied upon his understanding of rural Thai communities and his Fertility-Related Development strategy — provide the rainwater catchment systems to family planning acceptors first using community-based participatory methods to build them and a revolving fund mechanism to finance them.

The result was the Tung Nam Project. "Tung Nam" literally means "water tank" in Thai. Capital to build the tanks was provided by the German foundation Agro-Action,[2] which had previously assisted PDA with refugee relief and was now expanding its grant assistance for community development projects. A water catchment system for one family cost about 4,100 baht (US$ 164) for the raw materials required to build it. The payment could be made in one lump sum or interest-free installments — 500 baht down and 200 baht per month for 18 months. Payments were made to a village water committee, which collected money and "revolved" the capital to build more water catchment systems in their village. With this multiplier effect, capital for one water catchment system would ultimately build seven.

To build tanks, villagers provided labor and PDA provided tools, equipment, raw materials, and technical supervision. Each family having a tank constructed contributed one laborer to a construction crew of 15, which could build one tank in one day. One or two workers in each village were specially trained as technicians assigned to each construction crew.

The Tung Nam Project was successful because it provided villagers with a commodity they considered desirable, affordable, and essential — clean water for personal and domestic use in the dry season. Between January 1980 and July 1985, PDA built nearly 9,000 rainwater catchment systems providing clean drinking water to 201,000 people during the dry season, more than all other agencies combined providing village water supplies, including the government. Since resources were limited, it was targeted to villages with severe water shortages in poverty-stricken areas where family planning acceptance was high to assure that the investment had maximum return.

Encouraged by the success of the Tung Nam Project, Mechai decided that the timing was right to make his biggest and most concerted foray into community development. For years, Mechai had been developing ideas for integrated rural development that combined family planning, health, clean water, environmental sanitation, agriculture, skill development, income generation, and better marketing. As isolated projects, they had all been tried in one setting or another. In the crucible of the refugee camps, several were combined to explore synergies. In some projects, services like clean water and parasite control had been integrated with family planning.

In 1979, PDA tried a small scale, integrated rural development project in Wiang Pa Pao District of Chiang Rai Province and Phutthaisong District of Buri Ram Province. Both districts had high family planning acceptance and had participated in the parasite control program. A small, integrated farm was built as a training and demonstration site in each district where food, fuel and fertilizer were produced simultaneously. To these were added animal husbandry, income-generating activities, and assistance with marketing. PDA evaluated the results.

They found that introducing a full package of community development activities at one time was overload — too much too soon for the villagers, the village volunteers, and the PDA infrastructure. A sequential approach was considered far more effective.

Armed with this information and with the experience in the refugee camps, Mechai embarked upon his most ambitious project yet — the Community Based Integrated Rural Development Project, or CBIRD (pronounced "sea-bird"). CBIRD was the culmination of Mechai's 16 years of family planning and community development experience — a district-wide project aimed at improving the livelihood of village people. For assistance, he turned to Agro-Action, the German organization that had become PDA's most reliable and consistent donor.

The result was a US$ one-million grant to implement the CBIRD project in Ban Phai District of Khon Kaen Province in northeastern Thailand. The funds were for investment only. Like other PDA projects, it was designed to be self-sufficient over time. Its objective was to increase farmers' average household income by 30%, while simultaneously improving nutrition and health status. The real innovation introduced under CBIRD was the credit it made available to rural Thai farmers at non-usurious interest rates. The CBIRD project had three models: Intensive, providing US$ 300 investment per household; Moderate, providing US$ 200 per household: and Light, with investment of US$ 150 per household.

The basic activities in the CBIRD project, after family planning and parasite control were: 1) village water-resource development; 2) animal- and crop-raising schemes;[3] 3) credit to farmers to purchase feed, fertilizers, seeds etc., repayable after livestock or produce was marketed; 4) home and cottage industries like silk/cotton weaving, brick making, and food processing to improve non-farm dry season incomes; 5) revolving loan funds for latrines, water resources, or bio-gas digestors; 6) assistance to establish village cooperatives; and 7) better marketing for livestock and agricultural produce. The linchpin holding these inputs together was credit at affordable rates. Inputs were introduced sequentially based upon perceived absorptive capacity.

An integrated farm was constructed in each district. It demonstrated the appropriate technologies being introduced through CBIRD; functioned as a training center for animal husbandry, agriculture, and skills needed for home and cottage industries; and served as the CBIRD headquarters in the district.

The combination of credit, technical assistance, and better marketing that the CBIRD project embodied was a powerful stimulus to the district economy. It freed villagers from the cyclical hold of middlemen, the primary market and source of credit for rural farmers, usually at usurious rates. It turned small farmers into small business people. Most important, it started villagers on the path to a better life through their own efforts. The program was so successful that, in short order, Agro-Action funded additional CBIRD projects in Muang District of Maha Sarakham Province and Putthaisong District of Buri Ram Province. Soon after, the Canadian International Development Agency (CIDA) provided funds for CBIRD projects in Nang Rong District of Buri Ram Province and Pak Chong District of Nakhon Ratchasima Province; and GTZ, the German foreign aid agency, supported a CBIRD project in Chakkarat District of Nakhon Ratchasima Province.

Today there are 14 CBIRD projects operating primarily in north and northeastern Thailand,[4] many of them self-sufficient,[5] all of them generating employment and income opportunities for rural farmers, and some of them spun off as independent companies generating profits. CBIRD is generally acknowledged as one of PDA's most effective programs.

By the end of 1982, PDA's many programs were gaining worldwide attention. Organizations in other countries wanted to see PDA's community-based, family planning program for themselves; how health and parasite control were integrated with family planning; how PDA financed and built rainwater catchment systems; and now how it managed this ground-breaking integrated community development project. Mechai was inundated with requests from other countries for study tours and personal visits to observe PDA's diverse projects.

Rather than deal with these in an ad hoc fashion, Mechai established the Asian Center for Population and Community Development. Started in 1978 with assistance from the Center for Population and Family Health at Columbia University, where Allan Rosenfield was now its resident Director, and the International Fertility Research Program, where Malcolm Potts was now the Director, plus additional assistance from the Pathfinder Fund and JOICFP, the Asian Center held regularly scheduled training programs for people from other countries interested in PDA's activities. The first group of trainees came from Kenya. Others followed from Indonesia, China, India, Nepal, and Sri Lanka. By 1983, the Asian Center had hosted 650 trainees from 34 countries. The numbers and diversity of trainees would continue to swell.

Other countries were not only clamoring for training. They wanted to try Mechai's community-based initiatives in their own countries, and access Mechai's expertise to do it. Eager to help fledgling NGOs in other countries, Mechai agreed. However, obtaining grants from US foundations for PDA to implement projects in other countries would incur the onerous oversight regulations required for making grants to organizations abroad. To solve this problem, Mechai turned to his friend Henry David. Henry was President of the Transnational Family Research Institute in Bethesda, Maryland and had done pioneering work on abortion and incentives for family planning. They met in Bangkok in 1974, subsequently collaborated on the Community Based Incentives Program, and co-authored articles and papers.

Together they formed Population and Development International (PDI) in 1983, a non-profit, non-governmental organization incorporated in Maryland. Mechai is PDI's Chairman and Henry is the Secretary/Treasurer. Allan Rosenfield serves on PDI's Board. PDI can receive US Foundation grants using the less restrictive oversight standards required for approved domestic organizations. As an international affiliate of PDA, PDI operates primarily outside Thailand, building on PDA experience in community-based development and conservation projects. Currently, its most active programs are in Vietnam and Laos. PDI has also had programs in Cambodia and China.

CBFPS, CBATDS, CBERS, CBIRD, PDC, PDI, the Asian Center — PDA was like a multi-headed hydra with tentacles penetrating every aspect of family planning, health, and community development. Mechai was at the apex of it all, watching as his vision for helping Thailand's rural poor was inexorably becoming reality. PDA's management was sound, revenues were solid, and the organization was heading in new and exciting directions. What better time then, for Mechai to step away from it all and try something completely different.

In December 1982, Mechai received a call from his good friend Songkran Krachangnetr, now the Director of the Evaluation Division in the Budget Bureau, informing him that the Ministry of Interior was recruiting a new Chief Executive Officer (the position title was referred to as the "Governor") for the Provincial Water Works Authority, and would Mechai like to be considered for this position. Before responding, Mechai decided to familiarize himself with this ne w and relatively obscure organization.

The Provincial Water Works Authority was a state enterprise with 5,300 employees incorporated under the Ministry of Interior in 1979 to provide piped water to municipalities outside of Bangkok. It was an amalgamation of the water divisions from two Ministries, Health and Interior, the employees from each possessing disparate technical disciplines. The water quality experts from the Ministry of Public Health and the water engineers from the Ministry of Interior had never been melded into a functional entity, leaving the organization fragmented and torn by factional infighting. It was no surprise that staff morale was dismal.

Its physical facilities were equally grim. The Provincial Water Works Authority had no offices, renting space instead from the Police Department. Because of the premium on space, there were two office sites located six kilometers apart. In Bangkok's prodigious traffic, getting from one office site to the other was no small task. On one of the sites, numerous tubes of chlorine were being stored without adequate safety precautions. If there were a leak or an explosion, millions of people were at risk if the wind were blowing in the wrong direction.

To complicate matters, the organization was deeply in the red with few prospects for reversal. Rural water was a sensitive political issue in Thailand. In the early 1960s, the government decided to subsidize rural water supplies, setting the water tariff at two baht per cubic meter. By 1983 the tariff was still two baht per cubic meter, and the Provincial Water Works Authority was hemorrhaging money. It had an operating loss the previous year of 111 million baht (US$ 4.4 million),[6] with nothing but more deficits on the horizon.

What Mechai found, in effect, was a sick organization riven by internal conflict that was losing money and in desperate need of someone to turn it around. This challenge appealed to Mechai. After creating and leading one of Thailand's most successful non-governmental organizations, the opportunity to take an executive position in a large parastatal, especially one with the Provincial Water Works Authority's myriad problems, was attractive. Besides, PDA was poised to launch more community development projects, and in the capable hands of Tavatchai Traitongyoo, Mechai had a competent manager who could lead the organization in his absence. There was one additional attraction. PDA had always been criticized as a one-man show. Without Mechai, it was alleged, the organization would crumble. "Do I have to die to prove that this isn't a one-man show?" Mechai would ask the critics. Here was an opportunity to disprove them without resorting to such a draconian measure.

Mechai rang up Songkran and asked that he be considered for the position of Governor of the Provincial Water Works Authority.[7] His was one of nine names submitted to the search committee. In December 1982, he was offered the position and confirmed by the Cabinet. Mechai accepted the position with one proviso

— he would accept a three-year appointment only. At the end of three years, he would resign automatically.

When Mechai's appointment was announced on National Radio, staff at the Provincial Water Works Authority were shocked. They had heard of Mechai, of course, but associated him with condoms and family planning. What did he know about piped rural water supplies? Previous Governors had been engineers and PhDs. None had lasted very long. Mechai was a development economist. Some people liked the idea. Here was an energetic outsider with charisma who might be able to shake up the organization. Some were opposed. This energetic outsider with charisma might also upset the status quo that operated to their benefit. Most were skeptical that anyone could reform such a moribund organization.

Once installed as Governor, Mechai undertook a thorough organizational analysis of the Provincial Water Works Authority. Its abbreviation was PWWA, which he found difficult to pronounce. In the future, he called it PWA, a simple and less imposing appellation that persists to this day. During this period, his approach was simple: he listened to everyone but believed no one. His analysis uncovered a hornet's nest of problems even greater than he had anticipated. The entire organizational culture was stricken with mistrust, melancholy, and aimlessness. Factionalism between the Health and Interior groups had cleaved the organization. There was no formal channel for internal communications. Instead, there was a "black market network for internal communications that distorted the message for its own ulterior motives and thrived on hearsay and innuendo." There was a powerful labor union being manipulated by people opposed to change. Staff morale was abysmally poor. In general, employees had neither a sense of their mission nor pride in their work. Working in cramped facilities that were dilapidated even by government standards, PWA's staff had little reason to feel good about their work.

The organizational structure was inefficient and redundant. PWA had 15 regions operating 180 piped water systems. Some of the regions overlapped. Others were run by their Regional Directors as personal fiefdoms. The result was inefficiency and low productivity. PWA had 17 staff per 1,000 connections. The worldwide standard recommended by the World Bank was 12 staff per 1,000 connections.

Finally, there were the inevitable allegations of corruption. Cozy deals with suppliers resulted in overpriced and substandard equipment. Bidding procedures were often neither transparent nor equitable for all suppliers. Preferred users tapped into the water systems illegally without fear of fine or retribution.

The challenge facing Mechai was daunting. PWA was a demoralized organization needing management and organizational reform. It had labor problems compounded by a recalcitrant union. The specter of corruption haunted the organization. Its services were inefficient and it was losing money.

As Mechai prepared to assume his position as Governor, friends advised him to bring in an outside management team to revamp the organization. Mechai viewed things differently. "I am already a foreign body being transplanted into the Provincial Water Works Authority. There is always the possibility of rejection. If other organs are transplanted simultaneously, the chance for rejection will be infinitely greater." Mechai went in alone. His philosophy was that if the organization were to be improved, it would have to be done by the employees themselves.

Because of the corruption and the campaign he would have to mount against it, he had to be viewed as squeaky clean and avoid even the appearance of impropriety. Rather than use a government car, he used a car and driver borrowed from PDA. Rather than traveling with an entourage, as was the custom of previous Governors, he would travel alone or with minimal staff. He would not accept per diem for travel for fear of breaking some arcane rules. He would not accept gifts or favors. On one occasion, he was having lunch at a seaside restaurant in Pattaya with colleagues from PWA. After a nice meal of fresh seafood, he asked for the bill. The waiter told him that the bill would be paid by "friends of PWA" sitting at another table, a euphemism for contractors seeking special treatment. Mechai told the waiter, "No. I will pay for our bill and their bill." Then Mechai walked up to the contractors and said "We have paid our bill and we have paid your bill as well because PWA has more money than you. PWA has a multi-billion baht budget. We can afford to pay for our own meals. And we can pay for your meals too." This sent a powerful message to his staff. Mechai would set the standard he expected others to follow.

Mechai had a five-pronged strategy for turning PWA around: improve staff morale, reduce corruption, increase efficiency, improve relations between the unions and management, and institute management and organizational reforms. With so much skepticism surrounding his appointment as Governor, he would certainly be tested by his enemies. He vowed that, regardless of the provocation, he would never lose his temper. In Thai culture, if you lose your temper, your credibility is compromised. Once your credibility is compromised, your effectiveness is nullified.

Within months of his appointment, Mechai faced his first major test. According to the terms of a World Bank loan that had been negotiated before Mechai's arrival, PWA had to provide air-conditioned office space for the expatriate company that had won a bid to provide technical assistance. Mechai searched for an appropriate room that would require no renovations to save the installation of air conditioning. When he found acceptable space, he spoke with its 12 occupants and they agreed to move to another office nearby.

In any organization, space is a sensitive issue. This was particularly true in PWA, where the facilities were so poor. The image of Thais being evicted from desirable space, which was then air-conditioned to accommodate foreigners, created an opportunity for Mechai's enemies in PWA. Within days, a huge poster reminiscent of those frequently seen during the Cultural Revolution in China, appeared on the grounds of PWA, with an inscription in large letters denouncing Mechai: "The Governor disrespects Thais. He evicts Thais from a comfortable room and puts foreigners in because his mother is a farang (foreigner). He's not one of us."

When Mechai entered the PWA compound and saw the poster, which was impossible to miss, he said and did nothing. The poster remained until the demonstrators removed it of their own volition.

At the next quarterly meeting of the PWA's Bangkok headquarters staff, which Mechai had instituted to improve internal communications, he made his report to the staff outlining performance expectations and his proposals for change. Before the customary question and answer period, he peered very sternly at the 1,000 or so people in attendance and said, "I have a complaint to bring up with you. A poster was recently displayed which criticized me for having a farang mother. I strenuously object to that criticism. If you don't like my having a farang mother, you should talk with my father, not with me. I didn't select my mother, he did. I had no say in it."

The audience broke up as laughter filled the auditorium. Thereafter, the PWA staff knew that their pranks would never upset Mechai. The best they could hope for was a humorous response.

Improving staff morale was Mechai's first order of business. He believed that the great majority of PWA staff were basically decent, honest people with the potential to do good work. They just needed the right physical and organizational environment which could maximize their potential.

It was difficult to raise morale in PWA's deplorable facilities. So he invested all of his energy into getting a new office building for PWA. He brought in a camera crew (from PDA) to make a video of PWA's decrepit offices, accentuating the negative for dramatic effect. The tubes of chlorine, lined up row after row with no safety precautions, created a particularly poignant scene. With assistance from Songkran Krachangnetr, the video was presented to the Budget Bureau to accompany Mechai's request for funds to build a new office. Mechai told the Director that "the first Prime Minister in the world to die from a poison gas attack would be General Kriangsak Chamanand,[8] because his house is next door to the chlorine storage area." Funds to construct a new building were quickly appropriated. The new office was a "concrete" symbol of his commitment to the staff, and improved his credibility with them immeasurably.

Next, he sought to improve internal communications to replace the "black market" communications network he found so corrosive. Previously, the Governor was totally inaccessible to PWA's staff. Mechai instituted quarterly meetings with staff from the central and regional offices where he explained PWA's latest initiatives and gave employees an opportunity to question and criticize, which they took ample opportunity to do. He took his lunches in the employees' cafeteria so they could meet him informally and talk about their problems. He would "manage by walking around" to see for himself what the staff were doing.

During these peregrinations, he saw many women with children at their desks because they had no one to care for them at home during school holidays. So he created a PWA Foundation to run a daycare center on the premises. When companies gave gifts during holiday seasons, Mechai would raffle off the gifts and give the proceeds to the PWA Foundation, telling the companies that, in the future, rather than giving gifts, they could make donations to the Foundation. In addition to providing child care, the daycare center also took the children on trips to parks and zoos. Not only did the daycare center improve productivity, it endeared him to the mothers. They appreciated help for their children even more than help for themselves.

To make himself more accessible to the staff, Mechai traveled frequently to the PWA regional offices and water treatment plants to inspect facilities and meet staff. On one visit, to the waterworks plant in Chainat Province, he was inspecting water purification facilities when he noticed that so much sediment had accumulated in one of the flocculation tanks that it had created a small island in the middle. Obviously, it hadn't been cleaned for a while. Mechai always had sharp radar for a public relations opportunity. Here was one that could also be an abject lesson for PWA staff. Rather than admonish his managers publicly, he called for a "pakaoma", the traditional and ubiquitous sarong worn by all Thai men, which he donned in front of the entourage, climbed into the flocculation tank, and started shoveling the sediment out by hand. Soon he was joined by a Deputy Governor, senior regional managers, and of course, the press. The pictures in the newspaper of Mechai shoveling sediment from PWA's flocculation tank not only accentuated the absence of proper maintenance, but also portrayed him as a hands-on manager who was literally not afraid to get his feet wet.

These trips to the water treatment facilities had their down side. Traditionally, when the PWA Governor visited the regions, the Regional Director was expected to host a sumptuous feast to which all the local bigwigs were invited to fete the Governor. Where the funds were obtained for this banquet could only be surmised. Whose purpose it would serve was easy to deduce — certainly not the rank and file staff nor PWA's clients. One thing was certain. It was an elitist practice that had no place in a state-owned company; and it applied budgetary pressures on the Regional Directors that could only be met by irregular means. During Mechai's tenure as Governor, this practice was terminated. When Mechai visited the regions, the Regional Director still hosted a dinner. But now, Mechai purchased simple food in the local market with his own money, the dinner was held on the premises of the waterworks where all the staff lived, and all PWA staff and their spouses were invited to attend. Mechai met engineers and water quality inspectors, janitors and accountants, laborers and bookkeepers. And their wives. It demonstrated to the staff that the Governor was one of them, and held their interests paramount over "local bigwigs".

As the impact of these measures was internalized by PWA's staff, they began to view this new Governor in a different light. Unlike previous Governors, he seemed to have their best interests in mind. The new office building and daycare center for their children were tangible evidence of his priorities. Unlike previous Governors, he was accessible to them — either through regular meetings, visits to regional offices, or his frequent meanderings around the central office. He seemed honest and decisive. This new style was clearly reflected in better staff morale. But PWA staff were withholding judgment until they could see whether this new Governor was willing to tackle the other malignancy that was demoralizing staff and paralyzing the organization — corruption.

Attacking corruption in a large public organization is both legally and politically sensitive. Powerful vested interests with influential support may have instituted it and continue to benefit from it. It may be done within a procedural context that makes it morally reprehensible but legally defensible. Broad frontal assaults on corruption seldom work and may leave the organization weakened and demoralized. Instead, if it is excised cleanly with a sharp scalpel, the organization is more likely to survive and flourish.

Mechai chose the latter method for his campaign against corruption. On one hand, he made it emphatically clear that he would not tolerate corruption. On the other hand, he decided not to dig back and uncover past corrupt practices. It would be time consuming and disruptive with limited benefit. He decided on a different approach, which he announced to PWA staff: "Whatever happened before regarding corruption is history. I cannot change history. I can only change the future. I'll use my energy on something I can change. Everyone starts off with a clean slate with me. However, I will forcefully investigate and prosecute any dishonesty and corrupt practices that are uncovered, and where necessary, criminal charges will be filed, and jail sentences will be sought." He was serving PWA with a warning — if the corruption ceases, it will be forgotten. If it continues, it will be prosecuted to the full extent of the law.

There was a PWA waterworks manager in southern Thailand who chose to ignore Mechai's admonition. He had created his own empire for water delivery and payment as an extension of PWA, and was profiting enormously from this convenient arrangement. He had been warned before and had ignored those warnings with impunity. Why should this one be different?

Mechai seized upon this blatant challenge. A team of investigators was dispatched to scrutinize the waterworks manager's operations. When irregularities were uncovered, criminal charges were made and the manager was prosecuted, found guilty of corruption, and sent to jail — an appropriate punishment for his tawdry venture. For added effect, the imprisoned manager died ignominiously in jail of natural causes. This entire episode, occurring early in Mechai's tenure as Governor, served as a graphic symbol of the consequences of corruption in PWA under the new order.

The procurement of goods and services is the most easily subverted activity in any public organization. Accordingly, it was the area where Mechai targeted his anti-corruption campaign in PWA. Personnel holding positions with important procurement functions were rotated periodically to avoid conflicts of interest. He made all procurements transparent. Bid openings were public events and the press was invited. Bid-Evaluation Committees would make their deliberations public.

Mechai focused upon the purchase of water meters, PWA's largest recurring procurement with two million water meters purchased at each procurement. International bidding procedures required that a minimum of three bids were required for each procurement. One Thai company, which was the sole agent for a popular European-made water meter, was consistently winning all bids. The unsuccessful bidders were always small companies with no historical record of performance. Ostensibly, these procurements were meeting local bidding requirements.

Upon closer inspection, however, several irregularities were uncovered. The specifications for the water meters were written in such a way that only the meters supplied by the Thai company could fulfill the specifications. When Mechai sent PWA's labor union representatives to investigate the unsuccessful bidder, they found that these were only shell companies set up by the winning Thai bidder to provide the requisite three bid prices. Their offices were actually the homes of two employees from the Thai company. The procurements were fixed so that only the Thai company could win, and water meters were being procured at exorbitant prices.

Rather than protesting previous tenders, Mechai intervened in the next procurement of two million water meters. Specifications were rewritten so that several reputable brands could be competitive. The procurement was split in two and converted into an international tender. Other companies were notified of the revised specifications, and invited to submit bids. The winning bid price was 293 baht per meter (US$ 11.72), as compared to 630 baht per meter (US$ 25.20) being paid to the previous winning bidder for the same quality meter.[9] On a procurement of two million water meters, this represented a savings of US$ 27 million.

When this information was leaked to the press, it created something of scandal because it monetized the amount that was being diverted by corruption. Since Bangkok's Metropolitan Water Works Authority (MWA) was also purchasing even larger numbers of water meters from the same Thai company for 630 baht per meter, the scrutiny fell most heavily on it. The Governor of the Bangkok MWA was eventually sacked over this incident.

The third prong in Mechai's strategy was to eliminate inefficiencies. PWA had so many inefficient practices that it was difficult to know where to start. Mechai knew exactly where to start, with the most obvious and costly inefficiency — the price of water. People took water for granted and expected the government to subsidize it, which it was at two baht per cubic meter. But the subsidy was poorly targeted, and like most subsidies, benefited the rich, who used the most piped water, more than the poor.

If water prices were to be raised without a public outcry, people had to be convinced that it was a commodity worth paying for. This would require a public relations campaign to raise peoples' awareness of the value of water. Now Mechai was back in his element.

He used the same techniques to popularize the value of water as he had used to popularize contraceptives. Coin-operated condom vending machines were converted to dispense water. On H.M. the King's birthday, free water was given to anyone having a vasectomy at PDA vasectomy sites. Most people had no idea how large a cubic meter was. Mechai found that a commonly used jar, known to all Thais as a "peep", contained 20 liters. Soon the Governor of PWA could be seen on TV surrounded by 50 peep filled with one ton of water to graphically illustrate just how much water was in a cubic meter. He used images and symbols which common people could understand to demonstrate how cheap water actually was. "A liter of water cost one satang (100 satang = one baht)," he intoned . "A liter of Singha Beer (the local brew which could be found and consumed in any village in Thailand) cost 29 baht. A cubic meter of Singha Beer cost 29,000 baht. A cubic meter of water costs only two baht."

The subsidized cost of water, two baht per cubic meter, was a flat rate regardless of the quantity of water used. Consequently, government was subsidizing heavy commercial users like farms, factories, and restaurants that should be paying the real cost of water. One egregious offender was massage parlors. Every customer usually got a bath before receiving their massage or other ancillary services commonly provided at these establishments. To cut costs even further, many massage parlors had illegally installed pumps to steal water from PWA pipes while bypassing the water meters, a problem known as "leaks" in the water vernacular. A survey of provincial massage parlors found that the average establishment was paying only 2,000 baht per month, a pittance for an industry operating on such high profit margins.

The massage parlors would provide an appropriate symbol for inequities in the current pricing system while allowing Mechai to attack the problem of leakage. PWA staff visited massage parlors disguised as customers and estimated the water requirements for one bath. Based upon estimates of the number of customers per day, a monthly water utilization was calculated which translated into a monthly water bill several orders of magnitude higher than 2,000 baht per month.

With this data in hand, Mechai notified the police and the massage parlors were raided. Numerous leaks were detected and rectified, and punitive fines were levied on the owners. Forty percent of the fines were returned to PWA staff, who in turn donated 20% of their remittance back to PWA to purchase equipment. It was a public-relations coup that played well in the press and bolstered Mechai's argument for a revised pricing structure.

Mechai had done his public-relations homework by the time his proposal to revise the pricing structure was presented to the Cabinet. He proposed a sliding scale fee structure that charged two baht per cubic meter for low volume users and increased to 3.50 baht per cubic meter for high volume users. By targeting the subsidy more accurately and raising prices for commercial water users closer to real levels, he provided the politicians with the political cover they needed to embrace the new fee structure, which the Cabinet did by approving the pricing structure. This was the first price increase for rural piped water in 20 years. It would immediately provide an increased revenue stream for PWA.

There were other inefficiencies that could be wrung from the system to improve the bottom line. The contract of a European/Thai consortium was terminated for non-performance, serving notice that this Governor would not tolerate poor performance even by foreign companies. When the Provincial Electricity Authority (PEA) was delinquent with payment of its water bill, Mechai threatened that PWA would not pay its electricity bill in retaliation. PEA paid in full. He instituted a "leak" detection system that fined companies that had illegally tapped PWA pipes; and returned 40% of the fine to PWA employees who reported leaks. Since PWA was a government agency, he even found foreign donors who would provide grants to PWA for water trucks, equipment, training centers, and fellowships to supplement its meager investment budget. Seven years after Mechai left PWA, these grants were still rolling in. Slowly, PWA was becoming leaner and more effective. To improve efficiency further, however, he would need help from the unions.

Labor unions were firmly ensconced in Thailand's state-owned companies. Many management decisions required union approval. In some parastatals, they could even veto personnel appointments. Labor relations in PWA had always been rocky. The unions, skeptical of Mechai's appointment, were poised to oppose him. The incident where Mechai was denounced for favoring foreigners was the union's shot over the bow warning him that they were a force to be reckoned with.

Rather than confronting the unions, Mechai viewed them as a partner to be enlisted in his campaign to reform PWA. "Unions are like digestive juices," Mechai said. "If you don't give them something to digest, they'll digest the digestive system and cause ulcers." Previously, union negotiations had been delegated to one of PWA Deputy Governors. In the future Mechai negotiated with them directly. He provided the union with a room adjacent to his and invited four union officials on a rotating two-week basis to sit there, observe what he did, accompany him to meetings, dine with him, and discuss PWA problems. In the interests of transparency, he wanted the unions to know exactly what he did and why.

The union's first demand was veto authority over appointments of managers, a responsibility Mechai would not abdicate. "Let's make our roles clear from the beginning," he told the unions during their negotiation. "My job is to make appointments and supervise. Your job is to make sure that working conditions are good and the system is fair. I will do my job. You should do yours."

With their roles clarified, management and labor could seek common ground. Mechai explained his reform program to the unions and how it would benefit the workers. Once they understood what he was trying to do, they wanted to support him. Labor and management decided to work together.

Traditionally, the unions presented a list of demands to PWA management once per year, which were negotiated and resolved. Mechai found this arrangement cumbersome. "Why don't you make requests as they become necessary?" he advised the union. "Working conditions need to be improved here. Lighting is poor. Ventilation is poor. Why don't we agree in advance on conditions requiring improvement? Let the union make a request, I will approve, and you can advertise the concessions you've won in the union newsletter."

This was a win-win situation. Mechai gained the confidence of the unions. The union got improved working conditions and excellent press with its members. Everyone preferred cooperation to confrontation.

Working together, Mechai proposed and the union agreed to further measures to improve efficiency. They introduced strict working hours from 8:30 A.M. to 4:30 P.M. — a novelty in government offices. They agreed to a five-day, flexible time work schedule which included Saturdays and Sundays. In 1983 the PWA staff agreed to forego all overtime, generating the equivalent of 29 million baht in savings. They abolished a practice where relatives of PWA staff received a 25% margin on their evaluation scoring when they were hired. Mechai insisted that in a public organization, no one can have an advantage. The union agreed.

Once labor relations had been normalized and discipline enforced among managers and staff, employees took renewed pride in their organization. Morale was up, corruption was down, and efficiency was improving. Mechai was ready to proceed with the final prong in his strategy, management and organizational reform.

Like most public organizations, PWA had a cumbersome organizational structure that concentrated authority at the center, leaving managers with responsibility but no authority. There were three Deputy Governors and 15 Regional Directors. But Deputy Governors could only sign for expenditures below 50,000 baht; and Regional Directors below 10,000 baht. Everything else had to be signed by the Governor. Mechai knew this problem was acute when, shortly after his appointment, he had to sign a voucher for 42 baht to purchase a rubber stamp. Something clearly had to be done.

He started by rationalizing the organizational structure. The 15 regions, some of them overlapping, were reduced to ten. He eliminated the Deputy Governor for Administration. "I am the administrator," he said. "Those functions can report directly to the Governor." Instead he created an Assistant Governor for Corporate Planning and Finance and an Assistant Governor for Logistics which reported to him. He eliminated internal organizational contradictions. When he arrived at PWA, the Auditor's wife was Head of Finance, yet no one recognized the conflict of interest. It was quickly expunged.

Mechai's management philosophy was "delegation not abdication". He would delegate responsibility and authority to lower level managers, but he would not abdicate his responsibility for the bottom line. Deputy Governors were given authority to sign for expenditures up to ten million bath compared to 50,000 baht before. Regional Directors could sign for up to two million bath as opposed to 10,000 baht before. Simultaneously, he instituted a rigorous post-audit system that could routinely uncover irregularities. With the increased signatory authority, Regional Directors were required to submit the purchase price for goods and services so they could be compared by region and posted on a public notice board for everyone to see. Mysteriously, price disparities vanished within weeks, and purchase prices deviated toward the lowest prices. The power of transparency was amazing.

When Mechai arrived at PWA, it was an organization in turmoil. Morale was low, self-esteem was poor, productivity was down, and the organization was riven by corruption, distrust, and a hemorrhaging ooze of red ink. To counter these, Mechai used good example, communications, fairness, trust, transparency, consistent policies and practices, and his innate confidence in human nature. When these were accompanied by management and organizational reform, the result was a textbook case of organizational turnaround.

To substantiate this claim, it is best to use objectively verifiable indicators.[10] Mechai spent three years at PWA — 1983, 1984, and 1985. In 1983, it had an operating loss of 111.37 million baht. By 1984, the operating loss had been reduced to 58.72 million baht, and by 1985, his final year, PWA had an operating profit of 171.9 million baht, the first operating profit in its history. In 1986, the operating profit had increased to 357.68 million baht. Since then, PWA has not registered an operating loss in any single fiscal year. When PWA employees received an annual bonus in 1986, the union was rewarded for its cooperation and patience. Bonuses have been awarded annually ever since. The flow of red ink had been stanched.

When Mechai took the reins of PWA, it had 350,000 water connections serving 2.1 million people. In 1985, it had 500,000 connections serving three million people, an increase of 43%. From its high point of 17 staff per 1,000 connections in 1983, productivity improved to 14 staff per 1,000 connections. Today the number stands at 6 per 1,000 connections.

Profitability, productivity, and expansion of services — measured by these benchmarks, Mechai's tenure as Governor was singularly successful. His three-year term left PWA with other legacies that have endured to the present. The progressive rate fee structure he introduced is still employed, adjusted upwardly periodically to reflect the real cost of providing water to rural communities. The office building that he worked so hard to have constructed is still used today and stands as a symbol of PWA's renaissance. PWA is now recognized as one of the better run state-owned companies whose staff are respected for their high morale and esprit de corps. Most important, the momentum that he created for efficiency, honesty, and reform has been seized and accelerated by his successors.

When Mechai's proposed three-year appointment as Governor expired, the government was understandably pleased with the results. Labor was happy, staff were happy, morale was up, and PWA was making money. Mechai was invited to stay on longer, which he respectfully declined by reminding the Minister of Interior that "I said I would only stay for three years. My time is up." As quickly as he appeared as Governor of the Provincial Water Works Authority, Mechai vanished, to re-emerge in his real home, PDA.

Although Mechai had left PDA for three years, he had not forsaken it. He would still come back there some evenings to recharge his mental battery so he could fight another day at PWA. He would use PDA as a technical assistance arm to PWA. When he needed a video of its dilapidated office building, a PDA film crew was brought in to do the filming. When he needed condom machines adapted to dispense water, PDA technicians would make the changes. When he needed to create media events to convince people of the value of water, PDA public-relations staff would make the necessary arrangements. Since PDA assistance was provided pro bono, it actually became a donor agency to PWA, an odd twist of events since private voluntary organizations don't usually become donors to government.

After only a month back at PDA, another career opportunity presented itself to Mechai. He was asked to be the Deputy Minister of Industry. The April Fools Day Coup of 1986, à double entente which describes both the date of occurrence and the alleged perpetrators, resulted in several cabinet ministers being sacked, among them the Minister of Industry. After the coup, the previous Deputy Minister of Industry, Chirayu Issarangkura, was promoted to Minister, and he wanted Mechai as his Deputy. Only 45 years old, Mechai was being offered a Cabinet position at the highest echelon of government.

In addition to the policy responsibilities, the Deputy Minister of Industry was also in charge of Industrial Promotion Department of the Ministry of Industry. Its mandate was to promote rural industry. Most Deputy Ministers used this position to promote large industries in urban settings. Mechai saw this as an opportunity to promote small industry in rural settings, a natural extension of his CBIRD project. Mechai accepted Khun Chirayu's offer. His name was subsequently submitted to General Prem Tinsulanonda as Deputy Minister of Industry, and confirmed by the Cabinet.

As Deputy Minister, Mechai was placed in charge of the Industrial Promotion Department. As one of its responsibilities, the Industrial Promotion Department trained rural people in technical skills but had no mandate to place them. Trainees entered the program as unskilled people with no jobs and departed as skilled technicians with no jobs. Mechai suggested linkages with private companies to place trainees, but these never materialized. On occasion, government inertia was insurmountable even for Mechai. The idea planted a seed in his mind that would require several years to germinate.

During his tenure as Deputy Minister of Industry, Mechai participated in Cabinet deliberations, met visiting dignitaries, and served as the official representative of the government when requested by General Prem Tinsulanonda, the Prime Minister. In this capacity, he became acquainted with the King of Malaysia, a position occupied by the Sultan of Johore at the time.[11] The King was an avid golfer, and in Deputy Minister Mechai Viravaidya he found a kindred spirit. When golfing together, the King and Mechai liked to bet. Once the King was facing a long putt and Mechai said, "Your Royal Highness, if you make that putt I'll kiss that Rhino's backside," referring to a gift the King of Malaysia had given H.M. the King of Thailand. Fortunately, the King didn't make the putt.

On another occasion, the King and Mechai bet a year's supply of Thai durian, generally acknowledged as the world's best, on the outcome of their round of golf. When the King won that bet too, Mechai would dutifully take Thai durian to the Malaysian Ambassador in Bangkok for shipment to the King every month. On another round of golf they bet a lifetime's supply of Thai durian. When the King won that one too (the King handicapped himself generously), Mechai was in a bind. So he purchased six durian trees, sent them to Malaysia, and had them planted on the grounds of the King's palace. The King of Malaysia would now have Thai durian for the rest of his life.

In 1986 Crown Prince Vajiralongkorn of Thailand made state visits, each for 15 days, to Indonesia, Malaysia, and Canada. Mechai was assigned as the government's representative. His job was to speak for the government on policy matters and assure that all arrangements followed protocol. In the process he met Prime Minister Mahathir Mohammed of Malaysia, President Suharto of Indonesia, and Prime Minister Brian Mulrooney of Canada. He also met the King of Malaysia, who greeted Mechai like the old friends that they were and even took him to see how the durian trees were doing.

Within one year of Mechai's appointment as Deputy Minister of Industry, there were general elections in Thailand and General Prem had to reduce the number of ministers he appointed, while opposition parties increased their appointees.[12] Having the least Cabinet seniority, Mechai had to resign. During his short tenure, he was able to make some policy changes. He reformed the system for renewing business licenses, a notoriously lengthy and convoluted process in Thailand. Under his directive, if a license was not renewed within one week without good reason, it was considered automatically renewed. He also added a human touch to the office. Once, Mechai was sitting at the coffee table in his office when a woman entered on her knees to get his signature. This was a traditional form of obeisance usually reserved for royalty but used here as a gesture of respect sometimes reserved for Cabinet Ministers. In response, Mechai got down on his knees, waddled over to the woman, signed her document, and said, "If you have to kneel then I have to kneel too." Word of the incident quickly spread and the practice was abandoned.

After resigning his Cabinet position, another job opened in the Prem Government, as Government Spokesman. One of his aides suggested to General Prem, "Why don't you offer the position to Mechai? No one thinks on his feet like he does."

General Prem was hesitant. "Why should he accept? He has already been Governor of PWA and Deputy Minister of Industry."

The aide assured General Prem. "Mechai is not like that. If there is a job to be done and he respects you, he'll do it."

When General Prem offered Mechai the job of Government Spokesman, he accepted — because he respected General Prem, because he thought the job would be interesting, because Putri strongly supported the idea, and because he felt that if the government needed him, he should serve.

To function in his new role, Mechai needed to understand General Prem and how he governed to plan a communication strategy. General Prem was an honest and decisive leader who commanded the respect of the political classes and the people. His public persona was taciturn and stiff, not particularly suited to spontaneous communication with the press. Mechai tried the traditional press conference format, but General Prem was uncomfortable in this forum. It was quickly abandoned. Instead, Mechai became the government's predominate conduit to the press.

The position of Government Spokesman in Thailand was analogous to the Press Secretary for a President or Prime Minister in a western government. Mechai's principal responsibility was to report Cabinet decisions. He was not an apologist for the government, however. He confined his statements to factual accounts of Cabinet proceedings rather than defending particular decisions, which he viewed as the responsibility of the respective Cabinet Ministers. He created a transparent forum where Ministers could defend their decisions before the press. If the Ministers could successfully defend controversial policies, so much the better. If they could not, Mechai's philosophy was to let the chips fall where they may. In the interests of transparency and accountability, it was an efficient way to cull incompetent Ministers.

As Government Spokesman, Mechai maintained an excellent relationship with the press. They appreciated his candor and openness. They valued the access he created to Cabinet officials. They respected the equitable way all were treated. Under Mechai and his team, no exclusive interviews were granted, no special access provided, and no favors asked in return. He brought dignity and fairness to the office. And even fun, of course. Mechai had a red and blue traditional Thai jacket he would wear when briefing the press. When Cabinet proceedings were particularly dull and he had little newsworthy to report, he would wear his red jacket to tip off the press, who could then skip the briefing. When he wore his blue jacket, the briefing room was packed.

Mechai served as Government Spokesman for two years — 1987 and 1988. Although he was participating in government deliberations and reporting them to the press, the work was mostly routine, not particularly exciting, and he was making no real contribution to Thailand's development. Back at PDA, Mechai's visions were evolving toward fulfillment. The CBIRD project was being consolidated in new sites rather than expanding in new directions. Management was strong and, as his six-year absence had proved, Mechai's presence was not essential to maintain PDA's operations.

From 1982 until 1988, Mechai had spent six years in senior government positions — three in PWA, one as Deputy Minister of Industry, and two as Government Spokesman. In the process he collected six solid years of experience as a senior government executive and policy maker. He had learned the machinations of the political arena and how to make it work. He had made excellent contacts at the highest levels of government, contacts he would need to further his development ideals.

After six years, he also needed a rest. He needed new challenges. He needed to recharge his battery. He needed time to think about the future and to develop the new ideas blossoming in his mind.

It was quite opportune when he was approached by Harvard University to join its Visiting Scholars Program in 1988 at the Harvard Institute for International Development (HIID). This program was established to allow development practitioners to spend one year at Harvard among academics to mingle the theoretical with the practical. It was no surprise that Mechai accepted Harvard's offer. It allowed him to resign gracefully from government. He would use the time to teach and write. Most importantly, he would use the time to prepare intellectually for two of the greatest challenges of his life.

*The Tung Nam (water tank) Project*

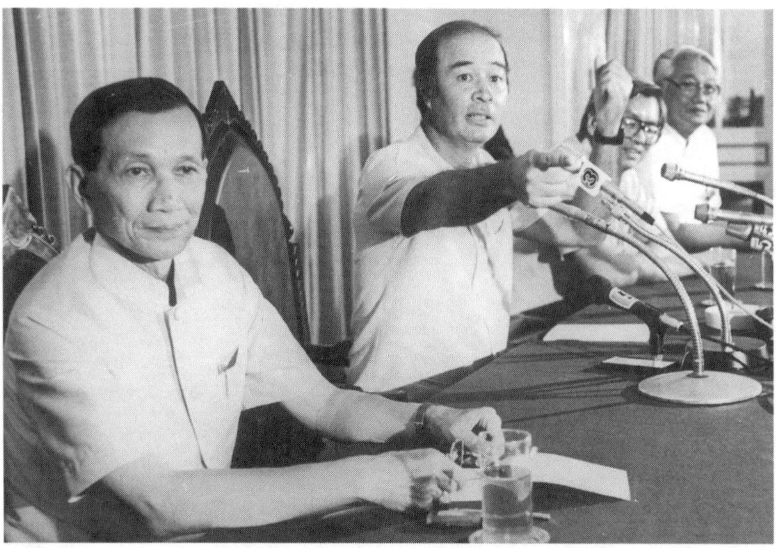

*As Government Spokesman Mechai (center), PM's Secretary General Prasong Soonsiri (left), and Minister of the PM's Office Chirayu Issarangkura (second from right) at a Government House Press Conference*

*Three newly appointed cabinet ministers at swearing in audience with H.M. the King. From left Deputy PM General Prachuab Soontarangoon, Chirayu Issarangkura, Anan Chaisaeng, and Mechai*

*Briefing the media while accompanying the PM General Prem Tinsulanonda in Moscow, 1987*

*Mechai as Government Spokesman with General Prem Tinsulanonda*

# NOTES:

1 The FPPC had two components: the Urban Program and the Rural Program. The Urban Program operated out of 231 schools and 300 factories in Bangkok. Using stool samples, it tested people for parasitic infestations and treated all positive cases. In 1979, it was expanded to include basic medical and dental exams at affordable prices. The Rural Program began with mass treatment of intestinal parasites in target villages. When follow-up surveys revealed high reinfestation rates 3-6 months following treatment, this strategy was abandoned because high running costs and unsatisfactory results made the prospects for self-sufficiency dubious. Instead, PDA began building latrines and installing village water supplies to attack the root cause of parasite infestation.

2 Agro-Action was by far the largest donor to PDA's rainwater catchment projects, providing the capital to build 90% of the nearly 9,000 systems built between 1980 and 1985. The other donors were Appropriate Technology International (ATI) which provided the seed money to pilot test the construction methods and revolving fund payment system, the German Relief Association, and USAID.

3 The animal- and crop-raising schemes introduced by CBIRD were ingenious arrangements to increase household incomes. The animal-raising schemes provide a vivid example. Village families entered into a contract with PDA to raise domestic farm animals — pigs, chickens, ducks, geese, fish, even rabbits. PDA advanced livestock, feed, vaccines, and technical advice for their care at no cost. When the animals reached maturity, PDA would arrange buyers for the livestock. From the selling price, the cost of livestock purchase, feed, and vaccines was remitted to PDA. The farmers retained the balance as their profit. The farmers provided their labor.

PDA provided capital, technical advice, and assistance with marketing. This was a very attractive arrangement for farmers.

4 The CBIRD projects are located in Ban Phai and Nong Nam Kriang (Khon Kaen Province); Maha Sarakham (Maha Sarakham Province); Phutthaisong, Nang Rong, and Lam Plai Mat (Buri Ram Province); Sapthai, Chakkarat, and Korat (Nakhon Ratchasima Province); Nong Pruk (Surin Province); Chiang Rai and Wiang Pa Pao (Chiang Rai Province); Phitsanulok (Phitsanulok Province); and Sai Yok (Kanchanaburi Province). As this book was being written, PDA was preparing to develop a fifteenth CBIRD center in Krabi Province. The CBIRD centers in Khon Kaen, Maha Sarakham, Buri Ram, Nakhon Ratchasima, and Surin Provinces are all in the economically depressed Northeast.

5 All CBIRD projects introduced prior to 1990 are self-sufficient. Only those introduced after 1990 have not had sufficient time to become self-sufficient.

6 Throughout this section, budget and cost figures will be quoted in Thai baht. To convert these amounts into US dollars, use the exchange rate US$ 1 = 25 baht.

7 Mechai's decision to be considered for appointment as Governor of the Provincial Water Works Authority (PWA) was in no way related to his involvement in the provision of rural water supply through the Tung Nam Project. When asked why he chose to work at PWA, he said, "Because that was the only organization that invited me."

8 General Kriangsak Chamanand was Prime Minister of Thailand from 1977 to 1980, at which time he was replaced by General Prem Tinsulanonda. In 1984, when Mechai was making his presentation to the Budget Bureau, General Kriangsak was actually a former Prime Minister.

9 Interestingly, the Thai bidder that had formed the shell companies decided to participate in the revised bid and actually was selected as the winning bidder for one of the tender packages, but at the much more reasonable price of US$ 11.72 per meter.

10 The data in this section was provided by Dr. Wanchai Ghooprasert, who is currently Deputy Governor of the Provincial Water Works Authority and who served as Director of the Planning Division from 1983 to 1985 when Mechai was Governor.

11 The monarchy in Malaysia resides in its various sultanates. The position of King is bestowed on a rotating five-year basis on the various Sultans. When Mechai was Deputy Minister of Industry in Thailand, the Sultan of Johore held the position of King.

12 During the Prem Government, political parties were allowed to exist and proliferate. In the original political cohabitation agreement between General Prem and the political parties, General Prem controlled three fourths of Assembly and Cabinet appointments. To promote democratic participation in government, periodic elections were held to provide legitimacy to the political parties. Based upon results of each election, new power-sharing arrangements were negotiated between General Prem and the parties. When Mechai entered the Cabinet in 1986, General Prem controlled 50% of Cabinet appointments. Following their strong showing in the 1987 election, the political parties were given a greater share of Assembly and Cabinet appointments while General Prem's percentage of appointees was decreased to 25%. It was at this point that Mechai had to resign from his position as Deputy Minister of Industry.

## 9

# AIDS IN THAILAND

*The first case of Acquired Immune Deficiency Syndrome (AIDS) in Thailand was reported in 1984. The patient was a Thai homosexual who had been living in the US. In the following four years, only a handful of new AIDS cases were reported, mostly confined to gay men who contracted the disease abroad or from tourists.*

The early days of the AIDS epidemic before 1984 were like the dark ages. Little was known about the etiology, mode of transmission, or the causative agent of this virulent disease. The epicenter of the epidemic seemed to be in New York and San Francisco among gay men, where the overwhelming majority of cases had been identified. Other cases of AIDS appeared among Haitians, hemophiliacs, and heroine addicts. Clinicians had few tools in their arsenals to deal with the ravages of this disease. A diagnosis of AIDS was equivalent to being condemned to a slow, painful death.

Researchers worked tirelessly to unravel the puzzle this new disease presented. The first breakthrough came in 1985, when a team of researchers led by Luc Montaignier in France and Robert Gallo in the US, isolated the causative agent of AIDS, the Human Immunodeficiency Virus (HIV). The second breakthrough came shortly thereafter when a diagnostic test was developed that identified antibodies to HIV in the blood. With these tools in hand, scientists were able to explain the epidemiology of AIDS.

When the first cases of AIDS appeared in Thailand, there was little concern either by the government or the public health community. AIDS was viewed as a disease of gay men in developed countries. There was even misguided speculation that Asians possessed a natural resistance to HIV. The Thai government reasoned that this was simply not a Thai problem. Complacency and denial were the order of the day.

While serving as official spokesman for the Prem Government from 1986 to 1988, Mechai was an interested observer as the AIDS drama unfolded internationally. When blood testing for HIV was expanded, certain "high-risk" groups were identified — gay men, injecting drug users, and persons having blood transfusions. Next, modes of viral transmission were identified — through sexual intercourse (heterosexual and homosexual), shared needles, blood transfusions, and vertical transmission from pregnant women to the fetus. These findings were potentially ominous for Thailand, where high-risk behaviors provided the vehicle for much broader transmission of HIV. Still the government did little.

In some quarters it was felt that the government's indifference was due to economic reasons. The year 1987 was designated as "Visit Thailand Year", and the country's nascent economy expected a significant boost from the many tourists who would visit the country. The government had organized a massive worldwide advertising campaign in 1986 to lure tourists to Thailand's many attractions. In 1987, there were few diagnosed AIDS cases, and no immediate indication that this disease presented a public health threat to the country. Government data acknowledged that there were only 11 full-blown cases of AIDS, and an additional

100 persons who had tested positive for HIV. The government feared that even the slightest hint of such a threat would jeopardize the potential tourist bonanza that "Visit Thailand Year" promised. The government preferred to deny the problem entirely.

For his part, Mechai was alarmed by the government's silence. With the modes of HIV transmission clearly defined, Thailand seemed at risk despite the few reported cases of HIV and AIDS. If the virus was spreading so rapidly in developed countries like the US, where heterosexual transmission had been confirmed, was it possible that Thailand would be spared? He was concerned by the government's inertia and felt that more had to be done immediately if Thailand was to avert or modulate an impending AIDS epidemic. Mechai, however, was not an expert on AIDS, and could not assess the establishment's assertions that AIDS was not a threat to Thailand. More importantly, he was the official Government Spokesman. While he was no apologist for the government, it was his job to articulate its policies, not to criticize them publicly.

Nonetheless, since he was still associated with PDA while Government Spokesman, Mechai could use his platform at PDA to address his concerns about an explosive increase in HIV and AIDS in Thailand. In 1987 with limited funding of its own, PDA mounted a campaign to educate the public about AIDS. Audio tapes, video cassettes, books, and pamphlets explaining the modes of HIV transmission and how it could be prevented, were distributed to media representatives, government organizations, and some private companies. PDA staff gave lectures and held discussions at public and private institutions. As the Secretary General of PDA, not as Government Spokesman, Mechai established himself as an activist and vocal advocate for HIV/AIDS prevention. "If Thais remain unaware of the dangers of AIDS, it will soon be too late to prevent the deadly disease from spreading," he warned in 1987. "We have to try to keep the disease under control. If we don't do it now, it may be too late." PDA mobilized itself to combat the AIDS epidemic. Still, the government moved slowly.

When Theo Ponayootoo and Chip Meyers, both Harvard faculty members working at the Thailand Development Research Institute (TDRI), approached Mechai with the offer to be a Visiting Scholar for one year at Harvard in 1988, Mechai accepted. It provided the graceful exit from government that he sought. It also provided the opportunity for him to learn all he could about AIDS. He would need this knowledge for yet another challenge.

Cambridge Common serves as the social, intellectual, and commercial center of Cambridge, Boston's neighboring city located on the Charles River in Massachusetts. Directly to the East, bordered by Massachusetts Avenue, lies Harvard University. Founded in 1636, Harvard is the oldest institution of higher learning in the US. Its graduates include six US presidents, famous artists, renowned authors, and heads of governments throughout the world. Its Faculty has produced 30 Nobel laureates, all adding to its cachet as one of the most prestigious educational institutions in the US.

When Mechai arrived at Harvard in July 1988, his original plan was to use his one year sabbatical as a Visiting Scholar to select and edit the twenty best GNP articles into a book. In addition, he would offer several seminars. Mostly, he would reflect and strategize on the next phase of PDA development strategy.

As events transpired, two issues would dominate his agenda at Harvard. He wanted to learn as much as possible about HIV/AIDS. The Thai government's lethargy on this matter disturbed Mechai. Unless the government took concerted action quickly, he feared an impending national disaster. He also wanted to crystallize his thinking about the role of private business in development.

He turned his attention to AIDS first. To advocate for swift government action on AIDS, he had to become knowledgeable on the topic. He had to learn the epidemiology and pathophysiology of the disease, its etiology, modes of transmission, high-risk behaviors, and means of prevention. For this he turned to the massive resources available at Harvard. In addition, he discussed HIV and AIDS with old friends like Sheldon Siegal of the Rockefeller Foundation, Nicholas Wright of Rutgers Medical School, and Allan Rosenfield at Columbia University. He identified sources of donor financing for the preventive interventions he wanted to introduce on his return to Thailand.

He also monitored the situation in Thailand closely. The year 1988 was a turning point in the spread of HIV in Thailand. The National AIDS Prevention and Control Program was housed in the Department for Communicable Disease Control of the Ministry of Public Health. Staffed by epidemiologists, the Department used a classic communicable disease control approach toward AIDS — reporting cases of HIV and AIDS to a central registry, and monitoring high-risk groups for HIV. Until 1988, both AIDS cases and HIV were found primarily among the homosexual male population. In 1987, the Medical Services Department of the Bangkok Metropolitan Authority (BMA) began testing injecting drug users (IDUs) for HIV. When testing began in December 1987, 4% of the sample of IDUs tested positive for HIV. In March 1988, the figure rose to 16%. By September 1988, the number of HIV positive cases had risen precipitously to 43%. This data indicated that Thailand had passed the first wave of the epidemic, among homosexuals, and had already entered the second wave, with the virus spreading rapidly among IDUs.

In response to these findings, the Thai MOPH established a National Sentinel Surveillance Survey to track the prevalence of HIV among five high-risk groups — IDUs, brothel prostitutes, males attending STD clinics, women attending antenatal care clinics, and blood donors. A sentinel surveillance system is an excellent epidemiologic tool to track the progression of a communicable disease. The data it generates, however, is retrospective i.e. it tracks previous transmission patterns by identifying the number of present cases. It does nothing to alter the course of future transmission. For HIV/AIDS, that could only be done with a massive education campaign to change behaviors among high-risk groups. In this critical area, the government's response was still inadequate.

Toward the end of his sabbatical year at Harvard, Mechai was invited to make a keynote address to the International Conference on AIDS being held in Montreal in June 1989. He used his keynote speech to sound an alarm about AIDS in Thailand. Using data on HIV transmission coming from Thailand, Mechai predicted that the HIV/AIDS epidemic in Thailand would pass through the standard progression of six waves — the first wave of infected male homosexuals, followed over time by IDUs, female prostitutes, male clients of female prostitutes, partners of males infected by female prostitutes, and finally the children of infected women. Because of the ubiquitous sex industry and the predilection that Thai men have for using prostitutes, he predicted that HIV transmission into the general population would be explosive, with dire consequences for Thailand. He called for a massive education program that mobilized all segments of Thai society to prevent HIV from erupting into the general public.

When Mechai returned to Thailand in July 1989, he was horrified to see that the government was still in a state of apathy and denial about AIDS.[1] The government of Prime Minister Chatichai Choonhavan, which came to power in July 1988, continued the same official silence about the impending epidemic as its predecessor.[2] The government still lacked a coherent anti-AIDS strategy. Instead, the AIDS Prevention and Control Program remained in the sheltered confines of the Ministry of Public Health, still treating AIDS as a medical problem instead of the behavioral problem it presented.

This does not imply that there was total silence on the issue. Individual voices were raising public concerns about the threat of AIDS. Pichit Rattakul, a former Deputy Science Minister and Democratic Party MP, warned that "the AIDS situation has reached the point where the MOPH alone cannot control the spread of this killer disease. Fighting AIDS is everybody's business." Minister of Public Health Chuan Leekpai stunned the country and its prodigious sex industry in October 1988 when he proclaimed that AIDS was indeed a serious problem for Thailand, and the sex industry should be repressed to prevent further transmission. After the Malaysian government issued health warnings for its citizens traveling to Hat Yai, a southern Thai city with a thriving sex industry, Thai businessmen vehemently attacked Malaysia for trying to kill its tourism industry. Rather than siding with the Thai businessmen, Chuan confirmed the HIV figures for southern Thailand, claiming that Thailand should not be defending its sex industry. At the same time, Princess Chulabhorn, the third daughter of H.M. King Bhumibol Adulyadej, condemned the sex industry and said that Thailand must do something about its AIDS problem.

However, no one in the government or the military came out in defense of these pleas for action. Chuan came under exceptionally heavy attack from the Hat Yai businessmen. The Governor of the Tourism Authority of Thailand (TAT), Dhamnoon Prachuabmoh, suggested that Chuan and the Hat Yai business community should keep their argument private so as not to damage tourism. Chuan was criticized so harshly for his statements that he was hanged in effigy. Newspapers predicted the end of his political career.[3] While on a European tour, Prime Minister Chatichai announced again that AIDS was not a problem in Thailand.

Mechai could not tolerate such duplicity any longer. Despite the official denials, he knew that AIDS was a problem for Thailand, and an extremely serious one if nothing was done about it. Thailand was fertile ground for the risk factors for HIV transmission. There were an estimated 200,000 to 400,000 IDUs in Thailand at this time. Data from the MOPH National Sentinel Surveillance System for June 1989 indicated that 33% of IDUs had already been infected with HIV. Thailand had a prodigious sex industry that was internationally renowned and a magnet for western tourists. Estimates of the numbers of prostitutes in Thailand ranged from the government figure of 80,000 to a more credible estimate of 200,000 supported by survey data. The sex industry was ubiquitous in Thailand. Beginning as a domestic phenomenon, its growth was stoked by the Vietnam War and the tens of thousands of American GIs either stationed in Thailand or visiting the country on R&R. Brightly lit and colorfully decorated massage parlors could be found in every provincial capital. Bars laden with prostitutes lined the streets of cities like Pattaya, Phuket, and Hat Yai. Brothels could even be found in some villages.

To complicate matters, "The Thai male's propensity to consume commercial sex is immense," Mechai asserted. Indeed, Thai men frequented prostitutes with numbing regularity. Surveys revealed that 95% of Thai males had visited a prostitute by the time they were 19 years old. It was literally a rite of passage for them. Marriage did not seem to dampen their appetites. After work while drinking with their friends or when traveling in the provinces, Thai men used prostitutes as nonchalantly as visiting a friend. Prostitution was woven into the country's social fabric —

"institutionalized by big business, an economic necessity for poor 'up-country' girls, accepted as normal for married Thai men, and a titillating attraction for foreign tourists."[4]

If promiscuous sexual behavior was normative among Thai men, then once HIV infection reached a critical mass among prostitutes, it would spread rapidly into the general population in the fourth, fifth, and sixth waves of the epidemic. The news on this front was not encouraging. The National Sentinel Surveillance data from June 1989 indicated that 6% of the prostitutes tested nationwide were already infected. If Thailand was to get serious about combating AIDS, the clock was ticking and time was running out.

When Mechai returned to Thailand in June 1989, he decided that the time to do something about AIDS could no longer be postponed. The government must be directly challenged to take stronger action. Those individual voices clamoring for action needed a vocal advocate around whom their movement could coalesce. The battle had to be taken public into the media. With his public persona, his association with condoms from his family planning crusade, and his media savvy, Mechai Viravaidya was ideally suited to lead this battle. And the time for action was now.

There were powerful vested interests aligned to oppose him. His anti-AIDS campaign must inevitably take on Thailand's sex industry, which had influential proponents. The triumvirate of brothel owners, police, and politicians had financial interests in propagating and expanding the sex industry. By stressing its positive impact on tourism and employment, they equated it to a vital economic activity for the country. Official government policy was complicitous in perpetuating this fallacy. Thailand had long been a popular tourist destination because it offered a relatively cheap and accessible sex industry with little official interference. Tourism authorities burnished Thailand's image as a Southeast Asia's tourist Mecca by stressing its excellent service industry. The pictures of Bangkok's Go-Go Bars and Patpong's raucous street scene featured in foreign magazines implied the range of services that tourists could obtain in Thailand.

To outflank the opposition, Mechai took his campaign public immediately and took his message right to the top. "Condom Night with Mechai" in the Patpong entertainment area attracted huge crowds and media attention. "We must unite in this war against AIDS," Mechai proclaimed over loudspeakers. "We lost the old capital (Ayutthaya) to Burma twice in our history and were able to take it back, so we can win the fight against AIDS."

Nearby, helium-filled condom balloons floated in the air to attract attention to a display of photographs and information on AIDS. Using tried and true techniques from past family planning campaigns, his staff invited passersby to blow up condoms to win T-shirts. Captain Condom, a Harvard MBA student dressed in a Superman-like costume festooned with condoms, cruised the Go-Go Bars imploring the inhabitants to practise safe sex. There was a Safe Sex Knowledge and Compassion Test, where passersby threw darts at boards with names of venereal diseases on them. A Queen was crowned in the Miss Condom Beauty Contest. "I want to promote the Miss Condom Beauty Contest to rival Miss Universe," said Mechai. "It will save more lives." Mechai stopped at bars and nightclubs and distributed condoms to the girls, telling them "This (condom) will save your life. If you're not careful, you'll die."

The humor that was a trademark of his family planning campaign was absent in his AIDS media and PR blitz. When asked by the press about its absence, Mechai said, "In family planning we were constantly using humor. But you can't use humor with AIDS because there's nothing funny about people dying."

The local and international media turned out in droves to hear Mechai's straight talk about AIDS. "An open AIDS campaign in Thailand will not scare off tourists because in large cities like New York, London, and Paris there is a higher rate of AIDS but people still go there. The issue is to fight it seriously and this will reassure tourists that the deadly disease isn't being neglected. If AIDS really scares off tourists, then it's good because only sex tours will be scared off. Thailand has three years to fight the disease because by that time prostitutes would have spread the disease too extensively to stop it." He chose Patpong because it epitomized Thailand's sex industry and was sure to attract media attention. The press obliged, and his message was beamed throughout the local and international media.

Next he took his message to the two most powerful men in the country, Prime Minister Chatichai Choonhavan and Army Chief General Chavalit Yongchaiyudh. Mechai was asked to brief the Cabinet of Prime Minister Chatichai, where he asked the Prime Minister to chair a National Committee on AIDS. Chatichai's response was not unexpected. "Mechai, if I became Chairman of the National Committee on AIDS, people would get a hell of a shock and it might cause panic," General Chatichai explained. To which Mechai replied, "I would get a hell of a shock if you don't." Chatichai didn't, his refusal exemplifying the government's inaction.

Mechai had gone to General Chavalit in a last ditch effort to obtain media time to broadcast AIDS prevention messages. All 488 radio stations and six TV stations in Thailand were controlled by the government. Two thirds of these were controlled by the military. The Minister in charge of Government Media had issued a clear policy directive prohibiting the broadcast of any AIDS related news on government-owned stations. The military stations were his last chance.

General Chavalit's response was more sympathetic. He listened attentively as Mechai explained the impending threat and his proposals to combat it. The General was concerned by the discrepancy between the MOPH official statistics for HIV positives, reported as 10,000 in 1989, versus more realistic estimates based on survey data that ranged from 150,000-200,000. He was alarmed by Mechai's warning that, if Thailand did not bring the AIDS epidemic under control in the next three years, the entire country would be affected. General Chavalit was also concerned by the military's burgeoning list of HIV positive recruits — estimated at over 200 by August 1989.

General Chavalit and his advisors took one day to consider Mechai's proposals. On August 14, 1989 he announced one of the seminal decisions in Thailand's battle against AIDS. Acting in collaboration with the MOPH, PDA, and private companies, the Army would spearhead the mobilization of a national effort to combat the growing AIDS menace. Some 326 radio stations controlled by the Army plus the Army-run TV Channel 5 and Channel 7 would launch a three-year nationwide educational campaign to prevent further spread of HIV. Ogilvie and Mather, an international advertising firm, created public service ads for HIV prevention pro bono. A grant from the Rockefeller Foundation was used to produce them. Soon, AIDS prevention messages had broken the government imposed radio silence. To underscore the importance it attached to the AIDS threat, the military agreed to change its HIV testing policy. Previously, new recruits testing HIV positive would be dressed in red shirts and ostracized with a dishonorable discharge. At Mechai's suggestion, the military discontinued this practice. Rather than stigmatize recruits with HIV, the military educated them to prevent further transmission and allowed them to remain in the Army. By throwing its full support behind this national mobilization effort, the military leadership was serving notice that the HIV/AIDS threat could no longer be ignored.

Since the other radio and television stations were controlled by various other government agencies, they now had the chance to follow the military's example. Inertia and complacency continued to plague the government's official response. Channels 3 and 9, controlled by the government's Mass Communications Organization of Thailand (MCOT), refused to grant permission to air the AIDS prevention messages because the government feared the adverse consequences a public education effort might have on tourism. The Director General for Communicable Disease Control asserted that the number of new HIV infections had begun to level off and would soon decrease. Cabinet Ministers criticized Mechai and others for being so vocal about AIDS because of the damage it could do to the tourist industry.

Support from the military was an important victory in Thailand's campaign against AIDS. However, it was only the first battle in what was shaping up as a full-scale war. Mechai realized that constant pressure and activism was required to counter the government's inherent indifference.[5] Over the next 16 months — from November 1989 until February 1991 — Mechai would be the focal point for Thailand's anti-AIDS activism. Where he had once been identified as Thailand's family planning crusader, now the press and the public would label him as Thailand's anti-AIDS campaigner.

He would not have to fight the battles alone. Other prominent personalities like Prawase Wasi, a physician and university professor who had received the prestigious Magsaysay Award for his work with NGOs in primary healthcare, joined Mechai in calling for a total mobilization of all sectors, public and private, to combat the deadly disease. Dr. Praphan Phanupak, Director of AIDS Prevention and Control for the Thai Red Cross, was a vocal advocate for concerted action against AIDS. Minister of Public Health Chuan Leekpai supported Mechai's proposal that Members of Parliament use part of their annual local development funds for the fight against AIDS in their respective provinces. Chuan continued to raise concerns over the growing number of HIV cases among prostitutes, and reiterated his pleas for concerted government action to avoid a national disaster.[6]

If the government wanted more proof of the serious threat that HIV and AIDS presented, it came in February 1990. A study by Dr. Vicharn Vithayasai at Chiang Mai University based upon random surveys in the northern provinces of Chiang Mai, Lampang, and Lamphun, revealed that 59-91% of HIV positive cases had contracted the virus through sexual contact, in sharp contrast to MOPH figures for the whole country showing only 10% of persons with HIV contracted the virus sexually and 84% by intravenous drug use. Alarmingly, 44-72% of prostitutes surveyed in Chiang Mai were HIV positive.[7] When the prostitutes were stratified by price, 72% of prostitutes charging 30-50 baht (US$ 1.25-2.00) were HIV positive, 30% of prostitutes charging 51-100 baht tested positive, and for prostitutes charging more than 100 baht, the figure was 16%. It was the lowest priced prostitutes, the ones frequented by farmers, fishermen, students, and working men, that posed the greatest risk. Some 44% of all prostitutes who tested HIV positive were less than 20 years of age. By the time prostitutes had worked 6-12 months, 70% were infected with HIV. One percent of pregnant women in Chiang Mai tested positive for HIV.

These findings were confirmed by the MOPH National Sentinel Surveillance data. By June 1990, 14% of brothel prostitutes in the national survey tested positive for HIV, up from 6% only one year before. In August 1990, a survey of 26,000 men aged 19-21 eligible for military service found that 2% were HIV positive. The threat of HIV/AIDS was no longer an empty one. Mechai and his supporters could no longer be accused of sensationalizing the threat. The sex industry could no longer be protected on the grounds of national economic interest. HIV had spread into the general population. There were no longer discrete high-risk groups. Now everyone was at risk — from teenage boys to newborn infants to middle-aged housewives. When asked to identify the groups at risk for AIDS, Mechai responded, "We have no high-risk groups. We only have a high-risk nationality."

With these findings, any further negligence by the government was criminal. Mechai immediately challenged the Prime Minister. "General Chatichai will go down in history as either the savior or the real unwitting devil of the AIDS plague." The *Nation* newspaper, one of Thailand's English language dailies, proclaimed, "Wake up, Prime Minister Chatichai! The lives of millions of people depend on you."

Denial was no longer an option for the government. Action was the only option, specifically a total national mobilization against AIDS. Hiding the truth was no longer tenable. Given the social, cultural, political, and economic dimensions of the disease, confining the National AIDS Prevention and Control Program in the MOPH was now absurd. It did not make sense to blame the most vulnerable — IDUs, homosexuals, or prostitutes. AIDS was a national problem. The only logical way to combat it was to educate the people about how the disease is spread and how they could protect themselves.

However, the Chatichai Government was paralyzed by bureaucratic inertia and responded with only lukewarm measures. It asked the MOPH to draw up an AIDS prevention strategy as part of the Sixth and Seventh National Economic and Social Development Plans. An anti-AIDS bill, drafted by a committee headed by former Prime Minister Tanin Kraivichien, was being prepared for submission to the cabinet. In 1991, a budget of US$ 4.7 million was allocated for anti-AIDS activities, 75% provided by foreign donors. No action was proposed to curb Thailand's flourishing sex industry, the root cause of the problem.

Speaking for the government, Dr. Thira Ramasut, Director General for the Communicable Disease Control Department in the Ministry of Public Health, defended these half-hearted measures in August 1990. "The government is approaching the AIDS problem step by step in accordance with the degree of the problem, suitability, and timing, while in the implementation of each action attempting to cause as little impact on the country as a whole. Data about AIDS was gradually released to avoid causing unnecessary panic and also to prevent some countries from using the information against Thailand. Secondly, we try to blend our policy with that of WHO and integrate the global AIDS program with that of our country. Thirdly, the problem of preparedness of our service(s). We have limited resources, therefore it is not possible to mobilize all the available resources at once. Budget was allocated according to the projects proposed, beginning with a three-year period and, meanwhile, resources came from international organizations," he explained.

Mechai was angered by this bureaucratic obfuscation and appalled by the government's tepid response to the real threat of HIV/AIDS. He characterized it as "using a small water pistol for a very large fire. At this rate we'll go down gallantly, but we'll go down." He publicly criticized Prime Minister Chatichai for being "more interested in golf than in AIDS." Rather than modulating criticism, the government's new anti-AIDS measures only intensified it.

A chorus of voices criticized the AIDS bill. Tanin's draft bill, which had already been approved by the Juridical Council and the Cabinet and was supported by the MOPH, contained measures requiring households to report people with AIDS to health authorities, allowed health officials to forcibly test anyone suspected of having HIV, and proposed to confine people with AIDS to "therapeutic centers". Calling the draft law worthless, and draconian, Thai and foreign scientists said "coercive measures against people with AIDS have no scientific basis and have been shown to be counterproductive in many countries." The *Nation* newspaper editorialized that "In the guise of protecting public health, the draft (law) proposes measures that would engender an atmosphere of fear and mistrust, pushing AIDS victims underground and guaranteeing that the disease spreads farther and faster than it already has." For his part, Mechai called the draft law "naive and written by well-meaning people who did not consult people with AIDS. We have to treat AIDS sufferers with sympathy and compassion, not confine them to jail or detention centers."

Mechai's strongest criticism was reserved for the absence of any government action to curb the sex industry. He called it an "industry of death" that, unless reformed or regulated, would cause a national catastrophe. Special venom was directed at sex tourism from Germany, Japan, and Australia. "If you want to die, go on sex junkets to Thailand," he warned the potential victims.

Again, Mechai went on the offensive, this time against Thailand's sex industry. He recommended compulsory temporary closure of all brothels so that the proprietors and prostitutes could be educated about safe sex and condom use. Surveys had shown that although most prostitutes had heard about HIV/AIDS, they had serious misconceptions about how its transmission could be prevented. He would then allow the brothels to be reopened in a regulated, legalized industry.

His next target was the attitude of Thai men towards sex. "Within the next few years, Thailand will have more than one million persons with HIV. It is worse than any war. It will destroy every fiber of our social and economic life. We need a movement so intense that it will uproot men's sexual habits to curb AIDS. When male teenagers in western countries are going on their first date, in Thailand they are visiting their first prostitute." He wanted to change ingrained male attitudes against condom use. There is a saying in Thailand that "real men box without gloves." Mechai proposed an intensive education program in the last three years of primary school and the first three years of secondary school as a major subject aimed at changing male attitudes toward prostitution and safe sex. He wanted to present prostitution as a health issue and as a form of degradation of women.

In the 12 months since he returned to Thailand, Mechai had campaigned assiduously for concerted action against HIV/AIDS. Despite his warnings about the impending national disaster that would kill millions of people, the government continued to drag its feet. Now he tried a new strategy. The mortality associated with AIDS, especially among younger people, would have economic implications that could no longer be ignored. HIV and AIDS would first disable and then kill economically productive younger people, strain the labor supply, and burden the country's healthcare system. The associated costs could change the face of Thailand's economy.

This strategy struck an immediate chord in the business community. Mechai urged businesses to take care of their own workers rather than waiting for the government; and suggested that each company protect its customers because, in Mechai's frank assessment, "Dead staff don't produce and dead customers don't buy (your products)." The result was PDA Corporate Education Program. More than 100 private companies enrolled in the program. PDA trained their human resources staff about AIDS. Support groups were formed in each company to deal with the AIDS cases that would eventually appear. Companies were urged to use their distribution networks to spread information about HIV/AIDS to their customers. In this way, Thailand's Avon ladies became the country's most visible and effective peer educators.

When Mechai saw how private companies reacted to the potential economic implications of AIDS, he decided that this strategy might finally wake the government from its lethargy. However, he would need reliable figures to quantify its economic implications if he wanted to convince the government. He assembled a team of economists and social scientists at PDA to estimate the direct and indirect costs of AIDS to Thailand's economy. Their findings were startling.

Mechai chose the International Congress on AIDS held in Bangkok in December 1990 to announce the findings publicly. Assuming that there were 150,000 persons with HIV in 1990, a very conservative estimate, that rapid transmission of HIV began in 1987, and that transmission would peak in 1994, his team projected that there would be 2.1 million Thais with HIV by 2000, 460,000 deaths from AIDS, and the direct and indirect costs of the disease[8] would reach US$ 8 billion by 2000. If transmission did not peak until 1996, a much more likely scenario given the government's inertia, there would be 3.4 million Thais with HIV, 588,000 deaths, and the disease would cost the economy US$ 10 billion in direct and indirect costs by 2000.[9]

The study concluded that, unless significant behavior change occurred, the AIDS epidemic was likely to alter the performance of the Thai economy. It predicted high rates of worker absenteeism by persons infected with HIV; shortages of labor that would increase both wage rates and production costs while simultaneously making Thailand less attractive to foreign direct investment; a reduction in foreign exchange remittances from Thailand's overseas contract workers; a decline in the personal savings rate and Thailand's aggregate investment as individuals spent more on medical care relative to income and the government invested more on social and health services rather than investing in infrastructure and other productive enterprises; and a decrease in tourism.

These findings were explosive. When the costs of the AIDS epidemic were stated in stark economic terms, it was impossible for the government to ignore them any further. The negative impact on tourism from directly confronting the epidemic would be inconsequential compared to the impact on the entire economy if it was not. In December 1990, Mechai was invited to brief Prime Minister Chatichai's Cabinet on the AIDS epidemic. As Mechai knew from his stint as Government Spokesman, it was extremely rare for an outsider to be invited to brief the Cabinet. This was his chance to influence government policy. He enlisted support from friends inside the government, especially in NESDB, for his proposals. He reiterated his call for total mobilization to combat AIDS. "If AIDS prevention and control is to work, it must be multisectoral," he implored the Cabinet. "It is not a medical problem. It is a behavioral problem and any institution that can affect behavioral change must be involved." Again, he asked Prime Minister Chatichai to become Chairman of a National AIDS Committee. Again, Chatichai refused.

This time, however, General Chatichai created a National AIDS Advisory Committee, the first one in Thailand's history, and appointed Mechai as Chairman. The Committee was charged with responsibility for developing a National Plan for the Prevention and Control of HIV/AIDS. The Prime Minister asked the Committee for concrete anti-AIDS measures that could be implemented immediately. NESDB was assigned as its Secretariat. The Committee was provided office space in Government House and a budget to develop the National Plan. Mechai was given total freedom to appoint the Committee's 14 members, which he used to make it multisectoral. Mechai's crusade for a concerted national effort against AIDS had almost reached fruition. He was now in a position to guarantee that the government took the requisite action.

The National AIDS Advisory Committee, chaired by Mechai Viravaidya, assembled at PDA offices in December 1991 while awaiting permanent office space to commence its deliberations. All sectors were represented. There were also persons with AIDS and HIV on the Committee. NESDB provided staff support. In addition to developing the National Plan for HIV/AIDS, the Committee was asked to scrutinize the draconian anti-AIDS measures contained in the government's anti-AIDS bill. It was also requested to provide the government with more accurate estimates of the number of persons infected with HIV, persons with AIDS, and deaths from AIDS. The Committee's deliberations were going extremely well, with great excitement for its potential — until January 1991. As happened so frequently in Thailand, politics interfered with the best intentions when the military staged a coup d'état, removed Chatichai from office, and the work of the National AIDS Advisory Committee, started only one month before, was terminated.

While the Chatichai Government dragged its feet on fighting AIDS, it was quite adroit at reaping the benefits of the economic boom sweeping Thailand in the late 1980s. By 1990, the Thai economy was enjoying its third year of double-digit growth. It needed massive infrastructure improvements to accommodate further economic growth. More roads had to be built, modern communications systems installed, power stations and dams constructed to expand power generation, and mass transit systems developed. With rapid economic growth, the public exchequer swelled and the country's improved credit rating gave the government ample access to capital to finance its large infrastructure projects.

Under regulations adopted by the Chatichai Government, individual Ministers were given total control of these projects with little independent supervision. In an atmosphere of huge capital transfers to finance massive infrastructure projects, bidders were willing to pay — and Ministers were willing to accept — substantial kickbacks to obtain lucrative contracts. Allegations that political merchandise was up for sale — such as garment export quotas, transport concessions, and votes in Parliament — became commonplace. Stories of corruption among government ministers became so widespread in the press that the Chatichai Government became known as the "Buffet Cabinet". They would take all they could eat from the state, then come back and take more.

Powerful forces within the military, however, were suspicious of the Chatichai Government, not only for the increasingly blatant corruption, but also for its perceived hostility to the perquisites, preserves, and preferences of the military. General Suchinda Kraprayoon, who replaced General Chavalit as Chief of the Army in 1990, was openly antagonistic to Chatichai, and attempted to undermine his government. The mounting tension between the government and the military came to a head over proposed government appointments that would tilt the balance of power away from Suchinda and toward Chatichai. On February 23, 1991, Chatichai was arrested by the military on his way to meet H.M. the King. General Suchinda seized control of the government in the name of "restoring good administration and stopping corruption."

The coup leaders anointed themselves as the National Peace-Keeping Council (NPKC). They sensibly decided to appoint a provisional government that would restore the government's administrative credibility, rewrite the constitution, and prepare for a democratic transition to an elected government. Anand Panyarachun, a highly respected retired career diplomat and successful businessman, was appointed as Prime Minister of the interim government.

The public's reaction to the coup was equivocal. The business community was concerned that a government installed by the military would damage the booming Thai economy that relied on export earnings and foreign investment. The people, on the other hand, were weary of the corruption and nepotism of the Chatichai Government and sought stable, clean government above all else. All were ecstatic over the appointment of Anand Panyarachun as Prime Minister, a stroke of genius in retrospect. Anand had an unimpeachable reputation for honesty, integrity, and competence among the general public, businessmen, and the international community. Anand promised a government of technocrats and businessmen that would pursue an agenda of economic reforms while preparing the country for democratic elections. Everyone welcomed the Anand Government enthusiastically.

The coup d'état could not have been more ill timed for Mechai. Nearly two years of constant struggle to put AIDS prevention at the vanguard of the government's policy agenda was jeopardized when the work of the National AIDS Committee he chaired was terminated by the coup. Given the vagaries of Thai politics, it was impossible to predict what the future held.

It only took several days for him to find out. Immediately after the official announcement that Anand would lead an interim government, an Army General called Mechai and asked him to come to the Central Security Command in Bangkok. Prime Minister Anand wanted to speak with him.

Mechai had known Anand both professionally and personally. His impeccable reputation for competence and integrity in the Foreign Ministry was common knowledge. He had previously been the Permanent Secretary of the Ministry of Foreign Affairs and Thai Ambassador to the United States. Anand was well acquainted with Putri's father, also a former Thai Foreign Service Officer in the United States, and had known Putri since she was a child. Plus Mechai's mother, Dr. Ella, had been the personal physician for Anand's wife, hence the Panyarachun and Viravaidya families were well known to each other.

The meeting with Anand was brief. He offered Mechai the position of Minister in the Prime Minister's Office in the Anand Government, responsible for Tourism, Public Information, and Mass Communications. Anand had three criteria for selecting Ministers for his government. First, they had to have previous government experience at senior policy levels, so they knew how to work within the bureaucracy. Second, they had to have achieved success in their careers. Finally, and most important, they had to have a record for honesty that was beyond reproach. Anand knew that Mechai fulfilled all three criteria. He also knew Mechai as a man with ideas. He wanted him in his government.

In the Thai government, many government agencies normally assigned to line ministries report directly to the Prime Minister through Ministers in the Office of the Prime Minister. NESDB, the National Security Council, the Department for Technical and Economic Cooperation (DTEC) are a few examples. The Minister for Tourism, Public Information, and Mass Communications was one of four Ministers in the Prime Minister's Office in the Anand Government. It was this position that Mechai was offered, and accepted, in the Anand Government. He proposed one addition to his portfolio — that he be given responsibility to coordinate the National AIDS Prevention and Control Program. Prime Minister Anand agreed that a total national effort was necessary to stem the spread of AIDS, and gave Mechai the authority to mobilize it. Politics creates peculiar ironies. Thailand's indefatigable anti-AIDS crusader, who had campaigned tirelessly to make an indifferent government take concerted action against the disease, was now the senior government official responsible for the national program.

The period from February 1991 until October 1992 was the Prague Spring for HIV/AIDS control in Thailand. Taboos, restrictions, and prohibitions fell by the way side under Minister Mechai Viravaidya. The impossible was now possible. Government reticence, indifference, and duplicity were replaced by openness, honesty, political commitment, and the financial resources needed to combat AIDS. Most observers acknowledge that the actions taken by the Anand Government constituted the critical turning point in Thailand's struggle against AIDS.

The anti-AIDS program that Mechai introduced was quite predictable. It contained the same measures that he had been demanding from the government over the previous two years. On the policy level, a new National AIDS Committee was established, with the Prime Minister as Chairman and the Minister of Public Health as Deputy Chairman. Having the Head of State chair the Committee ensured that all government ministries would participate. Thailand joined Uganda as the only countries in the world where the Head of Government chaired the National AIDS Committee at this time, testimony to the priority these governments gave to HIV/AIDS control. Co-Secretaries of the Committee were the Permanent Secretary in the Office of the Prime Minister and the Permanent Secretary of the Ministry of Public Health. Membership was multisectoral, representing government, business, and the private non-profit sector. Agencies like the Thai Bankers Association, the Federation of Thai Industry, the Chamber of Commerce, and the Tourism Authority of Thailand joined colleagues from government, NGOs and even people with AIDS on the National AIDS Committee to mobilize a national effort against AIDS.

An AIDS Policy and Planning Coordination Bureau was established in the Office of the Prime Minister, assisted by NESDB, to coordinate preparation of a National AIDS Prevention and Control Plan. This made the Office of the Prime Minister, not the Ministry of Public Health, the focal point for all AIDS programming and budgeting. Plans were developed with every government ministry, businesses, and the private sector to determine their role in the national AIDS campaign. The plan was backed up with money. The previous government had allocated 62 million baht (US$ 2.5 million) of Thai government funds in the 1991 budget for AIDS. The Anand Government, guided by the new National AIDS Control Plan, increased that figure to 1.2 billion baht (US$ 48 million). The money flowed from the Prime Minister's Office directly to every ministry department and to NGOs, assuring that no bureaucratic bottlenecks would impede the flow of funds.

Reporting on this achievement, the *Bangkok Post* noted, "This latest development is little short of revolutionary, if he (Mechai) can see it through. Probably for the first time, all sectors of society — government, private sector, non-governmental organizations, educational and religious institutions — will join forces in an effort to tackle a menace which experts predict could bring about a national calamity if left unchecked."[10]

Education was the backbone of the National AIDS Prevention and Control Plan. There were two major themes. The first was prevention — what is AIDS, how is it transmitted, and what to do if you get it. The second theme was understanding and compassion for people with AIDS. Mechai's position was that "the public must come to understand that HIV-infected people are just like everyone else; that they pose no danger through casual contact; and that they deserve love, care, attention, and respect."

A massive public education program employing all 488 government radio stations and 15 television stations provided free air time to broadcast 30 second spots for AIDS education messages every hour. In return, Minister Mechai, who was the Deputy Chairman of the Broadcasting Commission that regulated advertising time, allowed the stations 30 seconds of additional advertising time per hour as an incentive, an arrangement the stations found most agreeable. Since the content of the public information campaign came from the Office of the Prime Minister, the anti-AIDS messages were uniform and accurate. Every day radio stations throughout Thailand broadcast 73 hours of AIDS information. More than two hours of daily television broadcasting was devoted to AIDS. The airwaves were literally saturated with information about AIDS. The public was deluged with it.

Government officials in all ministries were educated about HIV/AIDS. In departments having direct contact with the public — e.g. Agricultural Extension, Police, Social Welfare, Labor — government officials disseminated information about AIDS to their clients. AIDS education was introduced as part of the course work in all educational institutions in the final two years of primary school through high school. All teachers were educated about AIDS and trained to teach their students on the subject.

The private sector joined the effort enthusiastically, responding to Mechai's oft repeated warning that "Sick staff can't work and dead customers don't buy." In an extension of PDA Corporate Education Program, private companies of all stripes provided AIDS education to their employees and distributed educational messages to their customers. Some companies inserted messages in product packages. Bank tellers distributed brochures to their clients. Plans were even being made to program Automatic Teller Machines to display AIDS messages to users.

Since Minister Mechai was also in charge of the entertainment industry through the National Motion Picture Committee, he solicited the help of movie producers, television actors, singers, musicians, and movie stars in the anti-AIDS campaign. Soon there were benefit concerts for AIDS and songs with AIDS education messages. The Thai Motion Picture Federation pledged their full support. Mechai subsidized movies that incorporated AIDS themes in their plots. Movie theaters broadcast AIDS messages free of charge during the advertisements prior to their feature films.

If education was the backbone of the National AIDS Prevention and Control Plan, then classical public health measures were its central nervous system. Seroprevalence surveillance of HIV was continued and expanded throughout the country to monitor the course of HIV transmission. Strict protocols were proposed to ensure the integrity of the county's blood supply. Because sexually transmitted diseases (STD) facilitated HIV transmission, rigorous measures were adopted to detect and treat them. If a locality had more than ten brothels, funds were allocated for an STD clinic. The plan contained provisions for a nationwide100% condom policy, which mandated that any customer who visited a brothel must use a condom. If men subsequently presented at an STD clinic for treatment, and transmission was traced to a brothel, the Ministry of Public Health and the police could use the blandishments at their disposal to enforce adherence to the policy.[11] Sex workers at brothels were randomly tested for STDs. The first and second offenses elicited a warning. Subsequent offenses resulted in temporary closure.

Ironically, Mechai also became Chairman of the Tourism Authority of Thailand (TAT) when he joined the Anand Government, as it was in his portfolio of state-owned agencies. This was the same Tourism Authority of Thailand that opposed him so vehemently when he urged openness about AIDS and action against sex tourism. His tenure as Chairman was exemplified by the slogan "Tourism with Dignity". While other TAT chairmen focused upon building hotels and promoting tourism at all costs, Mechai devoted his tenure as Chairman to waging a vociferous and relentless campaign against AIDS, eradicating sex tourism, raising the dignity of Thai women through Women's Visit Thailand Year, conserving the environment, and protecting wildlife.[12]

When it came to sex tourism, he didn't mince words. During a television interview, he referred to sex tours as "...Sperm Tours. I suggest they (sex tourists) don't buy a ticket to Thailand. They should buy rat poison and stay at home and take it instead." Such candor, coming from the outspoken Chairman of TAT, was quoted in the media around the world, bringing international opprobrium upon Thailand's sex tourism industry.

The Anand Government was in a race against the clock. Its tenure was finite — 14 months in total — long enough to introduce needed reforms and prepare for a general election. Simultaneously, a new constitution was prepared and approved to govern the upcoming elections. Still, 270 laws were passed during that 14-month period, equivalent to 12 years worth of legislation by previous governments. The Anand Government concentrated upon economic reforms to facilitate Thailand's export-oriented businesses. It introduced a value-added tax, reduced corporate and individual income taxes, and cut tariffs on capital goods from 31 to five percent. It made the Thai baht openly convertible, removed exchange controls, and established a Securities and Exchange Commission to oversee the rapidly expanding Bangkok Stock Exchange. It accelerated infrastructure projects, and advocated for an Asian free trade area to stimulate the region's economies.

In addition to his AIDS work, Mechai had other responsibilities that occupied his attention. Among his most important policy contributions were statutes to remove censorship from the media, laws to protect wildlife, increased budget for the Bangkok Zoo, and much to the chagrin of the TAT, he abolished a golf course in the Khao Yai National Park. Working closely with the National Energy Policy Office and the Petroleum Authority of Thailand (PTT), he organized the public education program that gained public acceptance for the law requiring exclusive use of unleaded gasoline in Thailand.

One of his biggest responsibilities was to organize and distribute broadcast time in the government-run media. Under normal circumstances, this was a lucrative perquisite handed out to political cronies. Under Mechai's purview, a transparent system of public bidding for broadcast time was introduced. For political parties campaigning in the general election to be held in 1992, he made sure that broadcast time was distributed evenly and fairly to all legitimate candidates regardless of party affiliation or size of their campaign war chest, an example of campaign finance reform before it became fashionable. It was his contribution to fair and democratic elections.

When the elections were held in March 1992, the Anand Government prepared to hand the reins of power to the newly elected government. It had navigated the economy through a stormy passage, passed economic reforms that would guarantee the economy's growth for years to come, and finally engaged Thailand in the war against AIDS. It would be left to the next government to continue its work and maintain the momentum of reform.

Events, however, conspired to thwart this scenario. Like military leaders before him, General Suchinda had created a political party, called Samakkitham (Unity), to represent the military's interests in the general election. The election returned Samakkitham as the largest party with a mandate to form a government. Its leader, Narong Wongwan, was preparing to form a government when it was revealed that he had been denied a visa to the United States because of suspected involvement with drug traffickers. Narong immediately withdrew. In the ensuing leadership vacuum, General Suchinda's name was proposed as Prime Minister. Unwisely, he accepted.

This was a strategic blunder. When he engineered the coup that removed the Chatichai Government in February 1991, General Suchinda had eschewed any personal ambition for power by claiming publicly that he would not install a military government, especially one led by him. His appointment of the respected Anand Government assuaged the public's apprehension about the military's encroaching influence in Thai politics. When he reneged on that promise in March 1992, it signaled the military's intention not only to interfere in politics, but also to institutionalize its role once again.

Demonstrations demanding Suchinda's withdrawal began in April 1992, led by ex-Bangkok Governor General Chamlong Srimuang's Palang Dharma Party. The demonstrations continued unabated, increasing in intensity until 17 May 1992, when 200,000 demonstrators assembled in Sanam Luang Park and demanded Suchinda's resignation. For the next three nights there was chaos in the streets of Bangkok. CNN and BBC carried live coverage of soldiers shooting directly into the crowds and protesters burning and looting buildings. This was poisonous to Thailand's economic aspirations. Many countries issued travel advisory warnings for Thailand. The stock market plummeted. The government's credit rating on the international bond market tumbled. Chaos in the streets quickly translated into disaster for the economy.

On May 20 H.M. King Bhumipol Adulyadej summoned Suchinda and Chamlong to his residence, and ordered them to stop the violence and restore order. Suchinda resigned ignominiously. Thc protests and the violence ceased.

This outcome still left Thailand with no government. Rather than allowing the elected Parliament to resolve the problem and risk further unrest and instability during the stalemate, H.M. the King appointed Anand Panyarachun to return and head a second interim government — henceforth known as the Anand II Government — until new elections could be held.

When he left his position as Minister in the Prime Minister's Office in March 1992, Mechai was exhausted. He had been working 18-hour days for 14 months to fulfill his obligations as Minister. When the political unrest of May 1992 occurred, Mechai was attending a Population Council meeting in New York City. One evening he was having dinner with Allan and Clare Rosenfield when Clare told Mechai that she had heard that Anand had been reappointed as Prime Minister. When he returned to his hotel later that evening, he received an urgent phone call from Thailand telling him to return to Bangkok immediately. With the appointment of the Anand II Government, Mechai had been reappointed as Minister in the Prime Ministers Office with his former portfolio. Actually, Anand had called Putrie to see if Mechai would accept reappointment, and she had accepted in his absence.

News of the Anand II Government was warmly received. The Thai people were ecstatic to have the Anand Government, and the integrity it represented, back in office. The capital markets were euphoric after the announcement. The international community pledged their complete support. Given the alternative almost foisted upon them, the people viewed the Anand II Government as if it were a savior.

Given the popular support his government received from the local, business, and international community, Anand Panyarachun could have easily parlayed his popularity into political power and built a dynasty. Others had done it before him with much less popular support. Anand would have none of that. He was an honest man committed to democratic principles. He used the three-month life span of the Anand II Government to replace military leaders involved in the May violence, rescind the perquisites military figures enjoyed from state-owned enterprises, and rewrite the election rules to modulate vote buying.

When Mechai returned as Minister, he immediately revitalized the anti-AIDS campaign. However, his principal responsibility in the Anand II Government was to prepare for the election of September 1992. Again, he distributed broadcast time to the candidates equitably, and made sure that the contesting political parties had equal access to public facilities for election rallies. The Democratic Party emerged as the largest party in the election, and subsequently formed a government with Chuan Leekpai, the man who as Minister of Public Health in 1988 spoke out against the sex industry and government indifference about AIDS, as Prime Minister.

Although Mechai was not involved in the anti-AIDS program of the Chuan Government,[13] and some of the innovations and reforms instituted during his tenure as Minister were reversed by subsequent governments, it is widely accepted that the AIDS Prevention and Control Program initiated by the Anand Government under Mechai's leadership was a milestone in Thailand's struggle against HIV/AIDS. To this day, Thailand still has a multisectoral National AIDS Committee chaired by the Prime Minister. NESDB continues to prepare a National AIDS Prevention and Control Plan that emphasizes compassion, understanding, and education. Although the focal point for AIDS prevention and control has shifted back to the Ministry of Public Health, the Thai government continues to allocate significant resources for a multisectoral AIDS campaign. By 1997, the Thai government was allocating 2.5 million baht (US$ 100 million) annually to fight AIDS. Thailand and Brazil have been recognized as the only two emerging economies that have allocated the substantial government resources required to effectively combat AIDS. The 100% Condom Policy has been implemented and enforced with resounding success. Every subsequent government has addressed the AIDS problem openly and honestly.

A convincing body of statistical evidence indicates that Thailand has turned the corner in its struggle against AIDS since 1992. The incidence of STDs has fallen, condom use has increased, the use of prostitutes by Thai men has been curtailed, and the numbers of new HIV cases has decreased.

The first indication of change came from falling STD rates. In 1989, the MOPH reported 410,406 STD cases, a rate of 7.69 cases per 1,000 population. By 1997, there were only 22,765 reported STD cases, a rate of 0.38 per 1,000 population.[14] The number of STDs has fallen so dramatically that pharmaceutical companies complained that the market for their antibiotics to treat STDs had dried up in Thailand.

Next came reports on condom usage between men and their female sex worker partners. A study among Thai military conscripts revealed that 61% of conscripts in 1991 used a condom for their most recent encounter with a prostitute. By 1995, 92% of conscripts reported using condoms.[15] Other studies confirmed high rates of condom use among sex workers. Commercial sex acts protected by condoms increased from 25% in 1989 to 94% in 1993.[16] By the late 1990s, condom use had become the norm during commercial sex.

The 1990s saw a tidal change in male sexual behavior. National and regional surveys buttressed by data from Thailand's behavioral surveillance survey reported declines in the use of female sex workers among all groups of Thai men. Nationally, the number of men reporting sex with a female sex worker in the past year fell from 22% in 1990 to 10% in 1993. In the nationally representative survey of Thai military conscripts, 57% of conscripts surveyed in 1991 reported using a female sex worker in the previous year. That number had fallen to only 24% of conscripts in 1995. Similar changes in sexual behavior were found among factory workers and vocational students.[17]

By the late 1990s, that old Thai adage was being disproved. Real Thai men were boxing less, and when they boxed, by and large they boxed with gloves. But was behavioral change translating into reduced HIV transmission? The national survey of HIV among military conscripts provided incontrovertible evidence that the tide had turned. HIV prevalence among Thai military conscripts peaked at 4% in 1993, then fell to 2% in 1996. In a subsample of military conscripts from northern Thailand, where the epidemic was more severe hence the scope for change was greater, HIV prevalence peaked at almost 8% in 1992 and had fallen to 3% by 1996.[18]

Following Thailand's efforts at HIV/AIDS control in the 1990s, nearly one million Thais have been infected with the HIV virus. This number is 395,000 lower than it would have been without the intensive efforts of the past decade. AIDS is still a scourge in Thailand. Had nothing been done, it could have been much worse. A recent article in *Time* magazine about AIDS in Thailand leads off with their assessment that "nearly 400,000 Thais owe their lives to Senator Mechai Viravaidya."[19]

Ominously, as Thailand enters the 21st century, many of its past successes are being reversed. There is recent evidence of a resurgence in HIV infections in some regions and among army conscripts. HIV prevalence among pregnant women continues to rise, from 1.7% in 1997 to 2% in 1999. Critically, the Thai government has reduced its expenditures for AIDS since the Asian Economic Crisis. Its AIDS budget has fallen by 28% since 1997. Public expenditure on HIV/AIDS prevention has declined by half in that time.[20] When asked to comment on the government's shortsightedness in allocating funds to AIDS prevention, Mechai said, "This is one case where stupidity is proving to be worse than corruption."

It is not possible to attribute Thailand's impressive success in combating AIDS to any individual or event. It has been the result of a national effort combining resources from the public, private, and NGO sector. Also, the battle against AIDS has not been won. It has reached an impasse where transmission is falling because high-risk behaviors have been curtailed. Constant vigilance is required to maintain the standoff. There is no room for complacency, as the recent resurgence in HIV infection emphatically demonstrates. What is clear is that activism, concerted national action, and significant Thai government resources that have fought this epidemic to a standoff in the 1990s have replaced the indifference and denial that characterized Thailand's approach towards HIV/AIDS in the 1980s. For that, Mechai Viravaidya bears much of the responsibility.

*The Anand Cabinet being sworn in by H.M. the King*

*Prime Minister Anand joining the anti-AIDS campaign*

*Miss Condom and Captain Condom on the street in Patpong*

*The launch of "Thailand Fights AIDS" at Patpong*

*"Condom Night with Mechai" in the Patpong area*

*Army Commander-in-Chief General Chavalit Yongchaiyudh (left) offering Mechai total cooperation of military-operated radio and TV stations for AIDS education*

## NOTES:

1 There was a vibrant public debate about the HIV/AIDS epidemic in Thailand that was being played out in the local newspapers and international media. All data, quotes, and details in the subsequent section covering the period 1989 to 1992 have been gleaned from articles found in Thai newspapers and the international press from June 1989 to February 1992. A list of the articles and the publications in which they appeared is contained in Appendix 2.

2 After eight years in office, General Prem Tinsulanonda stepped aside as Prime Minister after a general election in July 1988. As more MPs were elected to Parliament, they campaigned for a Prime Minister representing the majority in Parliament. As the largest party in Parliament, the Chart Thai Party headed by Chatichai Choonhavan, successfully formed a government in 1988. The government of General Prem had brought Thailand eight years of political stability during a time of political and economic turbulence in the region. In the early 1980s, the government exercised strong fiscal control during the recessionary period following the end of the Vietnam War and the withdrawal of the US military presence. External borrowing was limited, debt was managed conservatively, and the currency was stabilized. An environment conducive to business development was established that laid the groundwork for Thailand's impressive economic growth of the 1990s. Most important, the Prem Government laid a foundation for democracy which eventually led to its replacement by a civilian government through peaceful democratic means, a rarity for Thailand during this period of its history.

3 History would show that the pundits could not have been more wrong. Chuan Leekpai would lead his Democratic Party to victory in parlia-

mentary elections and become Prime Minister in September 1992. In October 1997, Thailand would again turn to Chuan as Prime Minister in the aftermath of the Asian Economic Crisis that decimated Thailand's economy that year.

4 For an excellent article that objectively summarizes the public debate about HIV/AIDS during this period, see "AIDS in Thailand," *British Medical Journal* 300 (17 February 1990): p. 415.

5 During this period, the Chatichai Government gave lip service to the increasingly vocal demands for action against HIV/AIDS, but its proposals were always hollow measures lacking substance and budget. For example, in October 1989, the Council of Social Affairs Ministers "declared war on AIDS with a resolution making control and prevention of the incurable virus a top national priority." Neither specific proposals nor a budget accompanied this resolution. The MOPH requested 149 million baht (US$ 6 million) in the 1990 budget for a rehabilitation and welfare center for HIV/AIDS sufferers. The proposal was dropped by the Budget Scrutiny Committee. Although the government ostensibly appeared to be taking some action on HIV/AIDS during this time, and organizations like WHO were praising it for its exceptional efforts, its reaction was still characterized as "indifferent" by activists like Mechai who demanded real, concerted action backed up with the money needed to get things done.

6 It may seem paradoxical that, on the one hand the Director General for Communicable Disease Control in the MOPH reflected the official government indifference to HIV, while on the other hand the Minister of Public Health was sounding alarms to combat the official indifference. In Thailand there is a dichotomy between the Minister of Public Health and the bureaucracy. The Minister of Public Health is an appointed political position, traditionally held by non-physicians representing one of the political parties in the governing coalition. In his case, Chuan Leekpai was a

lawyer representing the Democratic Party in the governing coalition. The MOPH bureaucracy, from the Undersecretary and Director Generals on down, were physicians and health personnel serving as full-time, career civil servants. The bureaucracy held the real power. The Minister of Public Health could try to cajole it, to influence it, but he could not control it.

7 Where data from this survey is presented in ranges, these represent the ranges for 95% confidence intervals.

8 In this analysis, the direct costs are defined as the systems costs (the cost of blood testing, education and prevention programs, HIV testing by the Thai military and other groups, and training of healthcare workers) and personal healthcare expenditures (the costs of healthcare for people with AIDS). The indirect costs are a measure of the burden on society of an increase and redistribution of mortality due to AIDS, defined as the foregone contribution these individuals would have made to the economy and society.

9 For a detailed explanation of these projections and how they were derived, see Mechai Viravaidya, S. Obremsky, and C. Myers, "The Economic Impact of AIDS on Thailand," *Economic Implications of AIDS in Asia*, ed. David Bloom and Joyce Lyons (United Nations Development Programme, Regional Programme Division, Regional Bureau for Asia and the Pacific, 1993).

10 For a comprehensive article describing the National AIDS Control Program initiated by Mechai, see Wasant Techawongtham, "A Plan for All-Out War Against AIDS," *Bangkok Post*, November 29, 1991.

11 The 100% Condom Policy was introduced on a pilot basis in Ratchaburi Province and several nearby provinces in 1989. Owners of sex establishments were encouraged to instruct or order their sex workers to use condoms for all sexual encounters. If the owners were uncooperative and STDs were traced to sex establishments,

police were authorized to order temporary or indefinite closure of those establishments. The National AIDS Committee under the Anand Government approved the nationwide expansion of the 100% condom program in August 1991. Although the 100% Condom Policy was introduced in the National AIDS Control Plan prepared by the Anand Government, it was not fully implemented until after the Anand Government left office. When it was implemented and enforced by subsequent administrations, it had a resounding impact upon HIV transmission in Thailand.

12 Mechai's tenure as Chairman of the Tourism Authority of Thailand is nicely described in the *Bangkok Post*. See Imtiaz Muqbil, "Mechai — the Man Who Changed Thai Tourism," *Bangkok Post*, March 30, 1992.

13 Although the Democratic Party under Chuan Leekpai formed the government, the Health portfolio was given to the Social Action Party (SAP), one of the partners in Chuan's governing coalition. The Minister of Public Health and the Director General for Communicable Disease Control disliked Mechai for subverting the MOPH role in HIV/AIDS. They campaigned vigorously to have the program returned to the Ministry of Public Health. When they succeeded, Mechai was not invited to be a member of the National Aids Committee.

14 Wiwat Rojanapithayakorn, "Thailand: Promising Results," *Integration* (Fall 1998): 21-23.

15 K. Nelson et al, "Changes in Sexual Behavior and a Decline in HIV Infection Among Young Men in Thailand," *New England Journal of Medicine* 335(1996): 297-303.

16 R. Hanenberg et al, "Impact of Thailand's HIV-Control Program as Indicated by the Decline of Sexually Transmitted Diseases," *Lancet* 344 (1994): 243-245.

17 S. Mills et al, "Assessing Trends in HIV Risk Behaviors in Asia," *AIDS* 12 suppl. B(1998): S79-86.

18 Nelson et al, 1996.

19 Robert Horn, "Back to No Future," *Time* magazine, October 16, 2000.

20 For an excellent review of the current status of AIDS in Thailand, see "Thailand's Response to AIDS: Building on Success, Confronting the Future" prepared for the World Bank Thailand Office, October 2000.

# 10

## LOOKING TO THE FUTURE

*While serving as Deputy Minister of Industry in charge of the Industrial Promotion Department in 1986, Mechai suggested linkages with private companies to place its trainees. These never materialized. While serving as Government Spokesman, he took the idea one step further, proposing a plan to use the resources and expertise of private companies to promote economic development in rural Thai villages. Thailand was experiencing rapid economic growth in the late 1980s, and his plan would allow private companies to share some of their benefits with the underprivileged. He took the idea to General Prem Tinsulanonda, who liked it. However, rather than giving Mechai responsibility for implementing this idea, General Prem placed NESDB in charge. "You are the Government Spokesman," he explained to Mechai. "Let NESDB do it."*

So NESDB did it. However, NESDB was a planning agency, not an implementing agency, and not particularly adept in its public relations with private companies. NESDB arranged a large conference to discuss the concept, invited more than 100 private companies, and even had General Prem give the keynote speech. He encouraged the private companies to identify areas where they could help rural villagers, and asked them to approach NESDB with their ideas. NESDB would make linkages with the villages.

Unlike Mechai's original proposal, the NESDB plan left the initiative with the private companies. Private companies are in business for profit first and foremost. Altruism and philanthropy are secondary, and very minor objectives. Leaving the initiative with the companies was a strategic blunder with predictable results. Not a single cooperative project emerged from the 100 companies that attended the conference. The idea fell flat on its face.

This result did not surprise Mechai. He was convinced that the concept was sound — private companies have the resources and skills to aid rural villagers, and an undeniable social responsibility — but the implementation was all wrong. There had to be a catalyst to foster linkages between private companies and rural villagers, and the catalyst had to be proactive. Experience had shown that NESDB could not be the catalyst. Mechai doubted that any government agency could effectively play that role. But he was too busy with his duties as Government Spokesman to develop the concept any further at this time.

During his sabbatical year at Harvard, however, he had both the time and inclination. First, he wanted to crystallize and adapt his long-term development strategy in view of the rapid economic growth and changes in the Thai economy brought about by globalization. In Mechai's view, there were three waves of development. In the first wave, when physical infrastructure and human resources were being developed, government was the catalyst. In the second wave, when software was needed to bring benefits for the rural population, private voluntary organizations using resources from international organizations were the catalyst. Thailand had already passed through the first two waves. Government infrastructure was vastly improved and foreign aid was declining in inverse proportion to Thailand's economic growth. Now he was pondering a third wave of development where the private sector would play the pivotal role, with government creating a climate conducive for development and NGOs bridging the gap between the private sector and the rural poor.

In Mechai's view, private businesses had a social responsibility to help those people who had been denied an opportunity to benefit from Thailand's economic growth. Although Thailand's GNP had grown by 14% in 1988, and would experience sustained average growth of almost 10% until 1997, the benefits were not distributed evenly. In 1989, the per capita income in Bangkok exceeded US$ 4,000, while in the Northeast it was only US$ 500. Almost 40% of the population in the Northeast lived below the poverty line of US$ 173/year. In relative terms, the gap between the rich and the poor was widening dramatically. The income share of the top 20% of the population had increased from 49% in 1976 to 55% in 1989. During the same period, the income share of the bottom 20% of the population had declined from 6% to 4.5%.

Rapid economic growth was creating two Thailands, with disparities not dissimilar to those Dr. Samak observed on his visits to the countryside with his father 70 years before, only now the disparities were systemic and highly visible. In "Thailand One", prosperous urban couples have tea on expansive front lawns; they have several luxury cars in their garage; they live, work, and travel in air-conditioned comfort. They can afford to send their children to private schools and universities, and give them pocket money to buy fast-food snacks, which cost more than the wage millions of Thais earn for a day of hard labor. In "Thailand Two", people live in houses without plumbing, they ride in the backs of open trucks and crowded buses, and their children, who must leave school at age 12 when free education ends, start working to supplement family income. In "Thailand One", people drink bottled drinking water that costs more per liter than gasoline. In "Thailand Two", people have to fetch their drinking water from remote sites, and the water is not as clean as the liters of water urban dwellers run down the drain while taking a shower.[1] These two Thailands are worlds apart. Affluent city dwellers reap the benefits of economic growth while rural villagers struggle to meet basic needs.

Where drastic income disparities exist, social tensions are inevitable. Rural Thai farmers were leaving their villages and migrating to urban areas to participate in the economic miracle, straining urban services and infrastructure while simultaneously jeopardizing Thailand's agricultural self-sufficiency. With few income opportunities in the Northeast, young women migrated to cities looking for jobs. Some were forced to resort to prostitution, exacerbating the growing HIV/AIDS problem. This migration was splitting families, proliferating urban slums, and destroying the social fabric of village life because only the aged remained in the villages. Economic growth was not worth social disaster.

To Mechai, asking private businesses to help leaven these disparities did not seem unreasonable. Economic growth had left them with surplus resources and skills that they could transfer to villages that needed their help. The challenge was to do this in a way acceptable to the private companies and useful to the villages without resorting to outright charitable donations.

When Mechai returned to Thailand in 1989, he prepared the blueprint for his grand design with assistance from the Harvard Business School. He called it Thai Business Initiatives for Rural Development — TBIRD for short (pronounced "tee-bird"). From 25 years of experience in rural development and countless discussions with rural people, Mechai concluded that villagers needed exposure to four skills that are abundant in private business — organization, production, financing, and marketing. For example,

Thai farmers can organize themselves to produce rice and other crops, but must borrow money at usurious interest rates for seed and fertilizer, and depend upon middlemen to market their produce. Private business could assist at each stage of the process, not with money only but with their time and business skills.

TBIRD had five objectives: (1) imparting economically relevant skills to rural people; (2) raising villagers incomes; (3) reducing migration; (4) decreasing the gap between rich and poor; and (5) providing opportunities for the private sector to become partners in rural development. It was business with a social conscience. Mechai would eventually coin it "the privatization of poverty alleviation". Typically, a private company could assist with traditional development activities focusing upon basic needs (water, sanitation, nutrition), then move on to some income generating activity, e.g. in agriculture, manufacturing, or services.

The TBIRD concept was proposed to the Ford Foundation and funded for a three-year pilot period from 1990 to 1993. Mechai had learned a lesson from the experiment with NESDB. There had to be a proactive catalyst to foster linkages between private companies and rural villagers. In his grand design, PDA would be the promoter and facilitator, and Mechai would be its most vocal salesman. The TBIRD concept was novel and pioneering, but Mechai was a well-known personality from his successful career in family planning and government. He was serving on the Board of Directors of several private companies and had many contacts in the business community. He used these connections to market TBIRD.

Convincing private companies to participate was difficult, even with Mechai's persuasive skills. Their standard response was "Our job is to make a profit. The government's job is development." Or "we know how to run a business, but we don't know how to do rural development." Mechai appealed to their social conscience as good corporate citizens, sometimes in his characteristically blunt and candid fashion. "I cannot imagine that you would rather see dogs in your house eat better than the villagers," was his familiar refrain.

The breakthrough came when he convinced the Swedish Motor Company (Volvo Thailand) and Bangkok Glass Company to sponsor villages. Both companies were managed by Mechai's personal acquaintances, facilitating the cooperation. The Bangkok Glass Project is instructive of the possibilities TBIRD held both for the villagers and the company. Bangkok Glass is a manufacturer of bottles used for pharmaceuticals, cosmetics, and beverages. It chose to work in a poor northeastern village called Ban Na near the Cambodian border, a linkage arranged by PDA. The first challenge was to build trust between the two, overcoming fears about mutual intentions. By joint agreement, it was decided that the first priority was to improve village infrastructure — financed by Bangkok Glass with either grants or loans and with villagers contributing their labor. From this point, their collaboration progressed to income generating activities. Bangkok Glass provided capital for villagers to raise chickens and cultivate mushrooms. Profits were used for school lunch programs.

Once a mutual relationship of trust and respect had been established, Bangkok Glass brought its business experience into play by fostering employment opportunities related to its core business. It installed a simple machine to produce brushes used to clean glass molds at its factory. It trained Ban Na villagers to use the machine, supplied them with materials to produce glass brushes according to factory specifications, and purchased the brushes from the villagers. By 1994, the operation had grown into a mini-factory, supplying all glass-mold brushes used in the Thai glass industry, and has exported brushes to Germany.

The benefits of this arrangement worked both ways. Rolf Von Buren, the Managing Director of Bangkok Glass, described the benefits that this cooperation afforded his company. "Our participation in the TBIRD project had profound intangible benefits for our company. Management is always viewed critically by its employees, especially in a foreign-owned company with Thai employees. When we allocated funds for our TBIRD program, and let our staff run it themselves, it improved management's image with the staff. When our employees saw that we wanted to help poor villagers and then saw what could be done with the money, it created an interplay between management and staff that improved morale and trust in the company."

Bata, an international manufacturer and retailer of footwear, took the TBIRD concept one step further. Bata based its TBIRD project in Buri Ram Province near PDA's CBIRD center in Nang Rong District.[2] Its ultimate aim was to produce footwear at a manufacturing facility in Buri Ram to be sold under the Bata label.

This idea was nothing short of revolutionary. Manufacturing had always been centered in urban areas having the requisite infrastructure and human resources. Buri Ram Province was an agrarian province in Thailand's depressed Northeast that had only rudimentary manufacturing capacity even in its urban centers. Bata was proposing to bring its shoe-manufacturing operation to rural Nang Rong District.

With PDA assistance, Bata established a training facility in the village of Nong Bod, which evolved into a small factory employing 32 workers, most of whom were young women aged 18-25, earning about US$ 120/month, the same wage Bata paid its factory employees in Bangkok. For young women in the rural Northeast, whose prospects rarely exceeded a life of backbreaking work in agriculture or migrating to cities to work in the sex industry, a fixed monthly income in a manufacturing job in their own villages was a godsend. It liberated them from seasonal agricultural income, which often left families at the mercy of money-lenders, and provided an alternative to the sex industry.

When villagers in neighboring sub-districts saw the success of the Nong Bod factory, they approached TBIRD about setting up factories in their villages. Bata and TBIRD established factories in three more villages. In these cases, the shoe factories are operated by village cooperatives that administer all aspects of production and pay their own overhead costs. Bata purchases each pair of shoes from the cooperatives at a market-based price, an arrangement which assures long-term sustainability. By 1998, Bata had six facilities in Buri Ram Province owned by cooperatives employing 400 people who earn up to three times more than the average wage in northeastern Thailand.

Impressed by Bata's success with rural manufacturing, Pan Asia Footwear Company joined the TBIRD project in 1994 and brought its shoe manufacturing to Buri Ram Province. Pan Asia was a large shoe manufacturer in Thailand employing 33,000 people around the country. However, high turnover rates and the cost of retraining workers had increased its production costs so significantly that it was considering moving its entire manufacturing operation to Vietnam. When Pan Asia executives saw the workmanship of Bata shoes in Buri Ram, and especially the loyal and productive workforce with low turnover, they decided to shift some of their production to Buri Ram. Pan Asia's experience in Buri Ram was so positive that it decided to keep its shoe-manufacturing operation in Thailand.

The experience of Bata and Pan Asia illustrates the potential that linkages between private companies and rural villagers could bring to both parties. The villagers got stable employment paying good wages. Bata and Pan Asia got a high-quality product with stable labor costs. This wasn't corporate charity. It was good business.

It also started a trend within TBIRD. Seven of the CBIRD centers in the Northeast now have modern manufacturing facilities located on their premises employing 6,600 workers. The factories are clean, well-illuminated, and briskly ventilated. Companies installing factories at CBIRD centers must agree to provide a fair minimum wage, good working conditions for the work force, and standard benefits. In return, they receive a dedicated and productive work force and harmonious labor relations. The factories bring ancillary benefits to the communities. The manufacturing facilities at the Chakkarat CBIRD center in Nakhon Ratchasima Province in northeastern Thailand provide a vivid example.

Within the past two years, five companies have located their manufacturing facilities at the Chakkarat center, employing more than 2,000 workers. More than half are women. Their monthly wages bring more than US$ 240,000 per month of purchasing power to this rural, predominantly agrarian district of approximately 70,000 people. The Honda, Suzuki, and Kawasaki motorcycles lined up in the parking area demonstrate where some of that purchasing power is going. Vendors can be found on the premises selling fruits and other consumables to the workers. The vendors take home US$ 12 in profits per day, a tidy income in this part of the country. When the workers depart for home at the end of the day, the vendors lining the streets are so numerous that traffic policemen have been deployed to the previously isolated road in front of the center to sort out the congestion. Other businesses have sprung up in Chakkarat's district center to provide services to this economically empowered work force. The factories have had a ripple effect through the economy, improving the well-being of the entire district, not to mention the increased tax revenues going to the government.

While PDA's role as catalyst in TBIRD was crucial, it was important not to overplay it. Once a contact was arranged between a company and a village, PDA let them decide how their collaboration would proceed. PDA was careful to avoid scripting the collaboration, letting the companies and the villagers identify needs and how they could help.

Mechai was primarily responsible for marketing TBIRD at the beginning, although this responsibility has now been delegated to his competent staff. He went to companies where he had friends and enlisted them first. He got advertising companies to suggest their best clients and presented TBIRD to them. When American Express asked him to do an advertising campaign, he agreed only if they would sponsor a village. When companies asked him to serve on their Boards, his quid pro quo was that 2-5% of their profits must go to rural development through TBIRD. During the three-year pilot period, PDA contacted 200 companies and 32 agreed to sponsor projects. In 1992, with several successes under his belt, Mechai proposed the TBIRD concept to the government's National Rural Development Committee. After an evaluation by NESDB, the government endorsed the TBIRD concept as one of its sanctioned rural development approaches. Now the Ministry of Industry is using TBIRD to match private investment with its rural labor force.

In 1994, the German NGO Agro-Action provided an additional three years of funding to allow for further expansion of TBIRD. Its investment of US$ 500,000 has leveraged 16 times that amount in local contributions, and an additional US$ 17.5 million through income generating activities.[3] TBIRD now has 135 sponsors supporting 139 integrated development projects. Multinational companies like 3M, American Express, Ericsson, Bristol Myers-Squibb, IBM, Singer Sewing Machines, and Mobil Oil sponsor TBIRD villages. Thai companies like Dusit Thani Hotel, Nakornthon Bank, Thai Farmers Bank, Siam Unisys Co., and the Thai Oil Co. do likewise. TBIRD received an endowment of US$ one million from the Petroleum Authority of Thailand (PTT) to ensure its long-term sustainability. When the contribution of these private companies to Thailand's rural development is monetized on an annual basis, it exceeds the level of all United Nations development assistance to Thailand.

TBIRD has promoted local initiatives in manufacturing, small agribusiness enterprise, local reforestation, gender issues, education, and revolving micro-credit loan funds. It has mobilized resources from private companies to address local challenges. It has generated employment opportunities in rural areas that have reversed urban migration, strengthened local communities, and drastically reduced poverty. It is a graphic example of the privatization of poverty alleviation. With its potential, there is much more that can be done.

The consultations between villagers and private companies that were at the core of TBIRD spawned a plethora of community development projects — village cooperatives, vegetable banks,[4] school-lunch programs, animal raising, village manufacturing, silk production and weaving, furniture repair, village water supply, and school improvement to name just a few. However, two recurring themes kept surfacing — environmental degradation and education. Thailand's rapid economic growth over the past four decades has been accompanied by serious depletion of its natural resources and degradation of its environment. Deforestation, either for commercial logging or agricultural expansion, has disfigured the landscape. The ecological consequences have been soil erosion, flooding, and the loss of wildlife habitats. In 1975, forests covered 40% of Thailand's total land area. Today, only 25% has tree cover. The poor, rural northeastern region has been disproportionately affected, retaining a forest canopy over only 12% of its land area.[5] Although a government ban on concessionary logging in 1989 ameliorated the problem, illegal logging continues to deplete forests.

Environmental degradation is not confined to deforestation, however. Industrial waste effluent and excessive use of fertilizers and pesticides have polluted rivers and contaminated water tables. Motor vehicle emissions and industrial pollution have dramatically compromised air quality, as any recent visitor to Bangkok can attest. Poor sanitation and waste management pollute the environment and threaten public health.

As these problems escalated, Mechai decided to turn his attention toward environmental protection and conservation. He obtained funding for six environmental projects, all located in the Northeast. Soon PDA was involved in reforestation, irrigation, water resources development, and environmental sanitation. These projects had one common denominator. They were centered around the community and its institutions, based on the assumption that natural resources and natural habitats are better protected and managed in a sustainable way when the local people have a stake in their conservation.

PDA's most ambitious environmental management project was the Student Environmental Education and Demonstration (SEED) Project, funded in 1997. Located in four northeastern provinces, SEED aims to create a new generation of environmentally conscious citizens. Under this project, teachers were trained in environmental education, primary and secondary schools had environmental issues integrated in their curricula, and "Environment Days" were held in nearly 1,000 schools. Village-level environmental protection societies were created to implement local conservation activities. Nearly 1,000 hectares of land were reforested, with the support of private businesses, of course.

Following the enactment of Thailand's new constitution in 1998 and the opportunity it creates for political reform, PDA will use its CBIRD centers to train villagers about civil society. The objective is to contribute to a new generation of politically aware people demanding responsiveness from their politicians. Plans are also being formulated to use the CBIRD centers to raise the peoples' awareness about corruption so that they will demand good governance from politicians and the government bureaucracy. There is a new age of political maturity dawning in Thailand, and PDA will likely be at its vanguard.

If these methods sound familiar, it is because they are essentially the same methods Mechai used for family planning, refugee relief, AIDS control, and community development. Raising awareness through education and public relations, stressing individual responsibility, seeking participation and ownership by the local people as the ultimate stakeholders — these principles, which Mechai began developing when he traveled throughout Thailand working for NESDB in 1966, remain the foundation of his work in development until today.

After three decades of community development work, Mechai was publicly recognized by several international institutions for his indefatigable efforts to help Thailand's rural poor. In 1994, he received the Ramon Magsaysay Award for Public Service for "mounting creative public campaigns in Thailand to promote family planning, rural development, and a rigorous, honest, and compassionate response to the plague of AIDS."[6] In 1995, *Asiaweek* magazine profiled Mechai as one of "the shapers of the new Asia" when it named him as one of the 20 Great Asians 1975-1995.[7] In 1997, he received the United Nations Population Award for his "outstanding contribution to the awareness of population questions and to their solution."

By the time he received these awards, Mechai had received seven honorary doctorate degrees from universities in Thailand and Australia, and was serving on the Board of Directors of eight companies.[8] Added to his work with TBIRD and the environment, he was one busy man. He was not too busy, however, to return to public life as the Chairman of the Board of the Telephone Organization of Thailand and Krung Thai Bank.

The Telephone Organization of Thailand (TOT), located in the Ministry of Transport and Communications (MOTC), is the largest state-owned enterprise in Thailand in terms of revenue. Its contribution to government revenue is as large as the second, third, and fourth largest state-owned enterprises combined. It has 26,000 employees stationed throughout the country. When the Chairman of its Board of Directors, Dr. Sumet Tantivejkul, resigned in February 1998 after serving only one year of his three-year term, the Minister of Transport and Communications asked Mechai to become Chairman for the remaining two-year tenure. Although Mechai was not an engineer, he had a proven record of service and success in other state enterprises, like the Provincial Water Authority (PWA) where he served as Governor (CEO), and the Petroleum Authority of Thailand — Exploration Production (PTT-EP), where he had been Chairman of the Board of Directors. Consequently, when Mechai was appointed Board Chairman in 1998, the press, TOT staff, and the unions welcomed the appointment.

Mechai used his tenure, which terminated in February 2000, to promote transparency and good governance in TOT. The previous Chairman had installed a union member as an official observer on the Board of Directors. Mechai increased the number of union members as observers. He opened all contracts to public scrutiny, inviting university legal experts to study them at TOT expense to uncover contracts considered unfair to the public (no universities accepted this offer). He eschewed the perquisites offered Board Chairman in state enterprises, declining the Mercedes car that came with the position, refusing to accept lifetime free telephone calls given as a benefit to all Directors, and donating his Director's fee to a fund that could be used by TOT for developmental purposes.

Soon after his appointment as Chairman, press stories began appearing about collusion and corruption in a large TOT project to install a telephone backbone network for the entire country. The project had already been tendered and approved by the TOT Board, NESDB, and the Cabinet, hence it was a fait accompli in the true sense of the word. Because of the press murmurings, he decided to review the project and bidding process nonetheless.

Several irregularities were immediately uncovered. The project had divided the country into six separate regions. In each region there was a separate contractor to install fiber optic cable and telephone equipment. This was neither the most rational nor economic way to do things. Allegations of collusion were inevitable.

When the procurement was examined, the cost of fiber optic cable in the winning bid was found to be 40% above the market price. Without even reviewing equipment procurements, these findings were taken to the Board, which decided that TOT would purchase cable and equipment itself and have winning contractors do the installation only. This would result in huge savings for TOT. Not unexpectedly, the winning companies objected to this arrangement because it required modifications to the bid's Terms of Reference. Rather than entertain these objections, the Board decided to cancel the procurement, revise the Terms of Reference, and revamp the selection process to make it more transparent.

There were two reasons for this decision. First, the price was too high. Second, demand for telephone networks had subsided subsequent to the Asian Economic Crisis of 1997, hence the prices would be even lower now. Mechai asked World Bank telecommunications specialists to advise him on the next steps. They supported the Board's decision to cancel the project because there were better technical approaches that could be used, and a more transparent bidding and procurement process was in the public's best interest. In reality, there was no legal basis for cancellation. The Cabinet had already approved the project. Yet when Mechai proposed cancellation, there was no opposition in the press or government, leading some observers to comment that the project was so transparently bad that its proponents didn't even bother to object.

With additional assistance from the World Bank, which wasn't financing the project but saw their assistance as a contribution to good governance, the specifications for the project were rewritten with only two types of contractors — one for fiber optic cable and one for telephone equipment. The concept of regions was discarded. To avoid possible collusion, the bidding process was separated into two stages, a technical proposal and financial proposal. The eventual winner must have passed the technical requirements and tendered the least expensive financial bid. The World Bank specialists estimated the total project cost at substantially less than the 15 billion baht price tag on the first tender. When the winning bid for the new tender was announced in October 2000, the winning bid price was 7.58 billion baht, half the original bid price.

In August 1998, the Governor of the Bank of Thailand, the country's central bank, rang up Mechai to ask him to take the position of Chairman of the Board of Krung Thai Bank, Thailand's largest state-owned commercial bank. Krung Thai Bank had formerly been under the aegis of the Ministry of Finance. The Asian Economic Crisis of 1997, which started in Thailand and reverberated throughout the region, revealed the precarious state of the bank's loan portfolio and finances, a situation shared by most other Thai banks at the time. The International Monetary Fund (IMF) had stipulated reform of the Krung Thai Bank as one of the conditions of its bailout package for Thailand.

Mechai's mandate as Chairman was to implement the reform measures required of Krung Thai Bank.

Under the Ministry of Finance, Krung Thai Bank's performance had been dismal. The level of reported Non-Performing Loans (NPL) as a percentage of the total loan portfolio was dangerously high, but the exact figure was unknown. Good lending practices were violated with impunity. Charges of corruption, nepotism, and cronyism resounded in the press. The IMF singled out Krung Thai Bank in its bailout package, specifying that the entire Board of Directors previously stacked with government officials must be replaced, ownership immediately transferred to the Bank of Thailand, and Krung Thai must be privatized within two years.[9]

Both the Bank of Thailand and the IMF strongly endorsed Krung Thai Bank's reform.[10] The Governor of the Bank of Thailand recognized that, if Thailand was to recover quickly from the economic crisis, its financial services sector must be repaired. Repair would entail financial services sector reform. Banking reform comprised three principal elements: good corporate governance, operational independence, and adherence to world's best banking practices — the end of nepotistic cronyism and directed lending.[11] As the largest bank in Thailand, Krung Thai Bank played an integral role in its financial services sector. Its 600 branches and 18,000 employees were distributed geographically throughout the kingdom. It comprised 20% of the banking sector and had approximately US$ 25 billion in assets. Reforming the financial services sector had to start with Krung Thai Bank. As an ancillary benefit, if banking reform was successful in the country's flagship bank, it would be a vivid example of what could be done, and lead the way for reform in other state-owned and commercial banks.

The Governor of the Bank of Thailand also reckoned that reforming Krung Thai would force Thailand's family-owned banks to admit the actual value of NPLs on their books, thus increasing the costs of recapitalization. Raising the necessary capital would bring in outside investors as shareholders and dilute family ownership, creating a climate conducive to transparency and better corporate governance. If implemented properly, banking reform would precipitate a virtuous circle of efficient lending to the most productive sectors that would promote economic growth, which in turn would attract more capital for efficient lending.

When Mechai was approached to become Chairman of the Board of Directors, ownership of Krung Thai had already been transferred to the Financial Institution Development Fund (FIDF), a legal entity attached to the Bank of Thailand. The previous Board of Directors had already been removed and Mechai would have to propose new candidates, only one of whom could be a government official. The Chairman and the four Executive Directors would be full-time positions — i.e. at least three days per week — to unravel the non-performing loans problem, revise lending practices, restructure the bank, and privatize it. It constituted a significant challenge. Mechai decided to accept.

His appointment created a stir in the press. At the press conference announcing his appointment, the most obvious question was asked first. "Why were you selected as Chairman of the Board? You are not a banker and have no banking experience."

In answering the question, Mechai chose to ignore his most obvious qualifications — previous positions as Chairman of state-owned companies and private businesses, his executive experience in government, private firms, and PDA — and cut to the central issue. "After the financial crisis, anyone with banking and finance skills is either in jail or close to going to jail. I was the only one left," he responded in his usual light-hearted fashion. "If you can't have a banker, at least you can have someone who is honest," he responded to the laughter rippling through the audience.

Ironically, it was exactly these attributes that made someone like Mechai ideally suited to become Chairman of this troubled bank. Thailand's financial services sector was not enamored with the reforms agreed with the IMF, which would threaten the cozy relationships between the banks, the politicians, and favored borrowers that had precipitated the economic crisis. As an outsider, he was not hampered by political constraints. His record during 30 years in public life demonstrated that he was daring enough to take on the establishment despite the forces arrayed against him. Perhaps he was also naive enough to believe that he could succeed.

Indeed, there were powerful vested interests aligned to impede the reform measures Mechai was mandated to implement. The first was Thailand's powerful Minister of Finance, Tarrin Nimmanahaeminda. His brother, Sirin Nimmanahaeminda, had been President and CEO of Krung Thai Bank for the previous six years and presided over the bank's decline. Any irregularities or improprieties uncovered during investigations required by the reform process might implicate Sirin. At best his competence would be questioned and his reputation attacked. At worst he could be held criminally negligent. Tarrin opposed the reforms in order to protect his brother.

Senior officials in the Ministry of Finance and the Bank of Thailand also opposed Krung Thai Bank's reform. These were the senior executives and board members running Krung Thai with Sirin during its decline. They would be implicated by association if the magnitude of the bank's ill health was fully disclosed. The Ministry of Finance, as an institution, was opposed because they feared that full disclosure of Krung Thai's NPLs would cause a knock-on effect across the sector that would precipitate systematic collapse in the banking sector, a fear that experience from other countries has proven unjustified.

Finally, senior staff at Krung Thai Bank would obstruct reform actively and passively. Many were ex-BOT officials or personal friends of Sirin seconded to Krung Thai as plum positions in their retirement. They enjoyed significant remuneration and benefit packages at Krung Thai, privileges they were loath to forfeit to the accountability measures and meritocracy proposals reform would introduce. With their cozy old boys network of insider relationships and executive perquisites threatened by reform, they would close ranks to oppose it.

All of these vested interests viewed the new Chairman of the Board as a threat, especially if a witch-hunt led to culpability of senior MOF officials and even the Minister's brother. For his part, Mechai had no intention to conduct a witch-hunt. Rather, he would have his hands full reforming and restructuring Krung Thai Bank. His first order of business was to propose new Directors. For this he turned to people with track records of success and reputations for honesty. Several good candidates were rejected by the MOF, a portent of the combative relationship the MOF would have with Krung Thai's new Board Chairman.[12] Once a Board of Directors had been appointed, however, Mechai could proceed with his reform and privatization agenda.

As Board Chairman, Mechai enlisted CLSA Emerging Markets,[13] the largest global emerging markets investment bank, to assist Krung Thai Bank to fulfill the MOF's commitments to the IMF. Even the selection of CLSA was a break from past practices. Previously, Sirin selected advisors himself. Neither their competence nor any subsidiary arrangements were disclosed for public scrutiny. In the interest of transparency, Mechai chose CLSA based upon a public tender process open to the public. CLSA proposed a restructuring package for Krung Thai Bank that included revenue enhancement, good governance, meritocracy, and branch rationalization. Restructuring was an essential prerequisite for privatization. Although the restructuring plan and privatization contained bromides that were difficult for the financial services sector to swallow, it was approved by the Ministry of Finance and Bank of Thailand in early 1999.

The next problem was non-performing loans and lending practices. Krung Thai had just absorbed two commercial banks, First Bangkok City Bank (FBCB) and Bangkok Bank of Commerce (BBC), both in danger of failing. The government had made a political decision not to let any banks fail, not only to protect the banks' clients but also for fear of contagion to other banks, so Krung Thai was forced to bail out sick banks. This was a misguided policy. To the contrary, the government should allow banks to fail, both to weed out inefficient institutions and to allow capital flight to quality banks so that credit could be distributed more efficiently. FBCB had massive liabilities that Krung Thai was forced to absorb.

The FIDF, now Krung Thai Bank's majority shareholder, wanted to know the size of its combined non-performing loans after the merger before providing funds to recapitalize it; and mandated Krung Thai Bank to hire an independent firm to audit the NPLs. Accordingly, a Terms of Reference was prepared and the Board of Directors selected PricewaterhouseCoopers (PWC) in January 1999 from a list of six reputable accounting firms to determine the level of NPLs in Krung Thai's portfolio and to examine its lending practices. Both the BOT and the MOF agreed to the PricewaterhouseCoopers audit, the first time an agency outside the BOT and Auditor Generals Office audited Krung Thai Bank.

The audit findings were devastating. Krung Thai Bank's loan portfolio can be classified into five categories according to BOT's regulations: (1) Pass loans requiring 1% provisions; (2) Special mention loans requiring 2% provisions; (3) Substandard loans requiring 20% provisions; (4) Doubtful loans requiring 50% provisions; and (5) Loss loans requiring 100% provisions. It was found that over half of the total loan portfolio in the combined bank were non-performing loans. Krung Thai's level of NPLs was much higher than the standard and acceptable commercial bank levels. In fact, Krung Thai Bank's NPLs were the highest among Thai commercial banks. Indeed, the bank was in a very serious and risky situation. The situation at First Bangkok City Bank, one of the banks being absorbed by Krung Thai, was even worse. Almost all of its loans were non-recoverable. With such a heavy burden of NPLs, Krung Thai Bank would require a very high recapitalization amount to keep it afloat, all of which must come from the taxpayers.[14] With regard to its credit practices, of the 13 basic principles that were considered good lending practices, Krung Thai failed to meet minimum levels of performance on ten. This was a very sick bank requiring emergency resuscitation.

With a sound restructuring and privatization plan and an accurate reckoning of the bank's NPLs, Mechai had all the elements in place to proceed with the reform measures. From his experience at the Provincial Water Works Authority, he also knew that reform measures required the full support of Krung Thai Bank's staff, especially the rank and file, if they were to succeed. Using his considerable skills of salesmanship and persuasion, Mechai went on the road to enlist their support. He traveled to Krung Thai Bank branches around the country, explaining the precarious position of the bank's finances and the restructuring plan that had been devised to rectify it. He established a telephone hotline for staff to communicate their concerns. He used radio as a medium to communicate regularly with staff. He involved unions in selecting advisors and consulted with them on key management decisions. He even rented the national basketball stadium to address 9,000 Krung Thai staff at one time. In his view, transparency was the best policy. The unions and the bank's staff agreed to support the reform measures.

The prospect's for financial services sector reform in Thailand now seemed quite positive. The nation's largest bank now had an activist Chairman committed to reform. A sensible restructuring plan had been approved by the MOF and BOT. Krung Thai Bank's unions and staff supported the plan. The omens for Thailand's economy were auspicious.

The forces opposing reform had not been subdued, however, and their opposition could not be taken lightly. The PWC audit of Krung Thai's NPLs was politically sensitive and this information had to be handled carefully. After the Board of Directors was informed of the audit results, Mechai immediately brought the findings to the Governor of the Bank of Thailand. Although the Governor supported reform, he also had political constraints. There was pending legislation to make the Bank of Thailand an independent central bank, a world's best practice essential for financial sector reform. This legislation required MOF approval. The Governor feared that disclosure of the PWC audit report would incur the wrath of Minister Tarrin and endanger the central bank legislation. Also, several of his staff had been threatened with legal action by the MOF, another reason for caution.When the Governor saw the PWC audit report, he said he wanted nothing to do with it.

Suspecting political stonewalling, Mechai immediately sent official copies of the draft PWC Audit Executive Summary to the Governor of the Bank of Thailand, the FIDF, and the Permanent Secretary of the Ministry of Finance. For good measure, he made sure to collect signed receipts that proved that the documents had been officially submitted and received. He might need them in the future.

Soon thereafter, Mechai was at the golf course waiting for a friend to play golf. At the next table were three Senators and the

Secretary General of the Senate, all of whom were well known to Mechai because of his position as an appointed member of the Senate. One of the Senators queried Mechai,

"I heard that a recent PricewaterhouseCoopers audit of Krung Thai Bank indicates that the bank is in serious trouble."

"All banks are in serious trouble right now. There is nothing unique about Krung Thai," said Mechai.

The Senator pressed further,

"Could you testify before the Senate and release a copy of the audit report?"

"Surely. Just send me a letter of request to testify and I would be glad to comply."

The whole exchange only lasted several minutes before the Senators were called for their tee time. Mechai did not think their request was unusual. While Chairman of the Board of TOT, he had frequently been requested to testify before the Senate and submit documents. It was a parliamentary body responsible for the supervision of government agencies. It was his duty to testify.

Mechai received the Senate's request to testify and submit the draft PricewaterhouseCoopers Audit Executive Summary on the Friday before the hearing to be held on Tuesday August 10, 1999. Although he felt certain that he was authorized to submit the Executive Summary report, he asked the Assistant Secretary to the Board of Directors to consult with a board member who was a legal expert to assure its propriety. Mechai went to his office that Friday to meet with Krung Thai's top management and to prepare for the testimony. While awaiting the decision of the legal expert, the Assistant Secretary to the Board of Directors asked PricewaterhouseCoopers to make 80 copies of the draft Audit Executive Summary just in case Krung Thai had to distribute the report at the senate hearing. To protect Krung Thai Bank customers named in the report, he had all client names replaced with generic reference to their business (e.g. real estate, manufacturing, etc.) in the 80 copies.

Later that same afternoon, Minister of Finance Tarrin called Mechai asking to see him. When Mechai arrived at the Minister's office, he was met by a grim-faced Minister Tarrin, the Permanent Secretary of the MOF, and a coterie of senior MOF officials.

"It is now known that certain elements opposed to the government want to use the Krung Thai Bank issue to discredit the government. Also at issue is the PricewaterhouseCoopers Audit Executive Summary of Krung Thai Bank's non-performing loans," the Minister explained.

Mechai informed Minister Tarrin that he had been requested to testify at a Senate hearing on Tuesday and to submit a copy of the Audit Executive Summary. "Copies are being made right now with client names replaced with generic reference to their business for confidentiality while I check the legality of releasing the report. I think we should be transparent about this. All banks are in trouble and we know the lending procedures are faulty."

Although their views on transparency diverged, Mechai decided that he would appear at the Senate hearing and release the report if it was legally authorized. Prior to the hearing, however, the legal expert on the Board of Directors informed Mechai that existing commercial banking law precluded his releasing the draft Audit Executive Summary to the Senate. He could testify at the Senate hearing, but he could not release the report.

The following Tuesday Mechai, accompanied by the new President of Krung Thai Bank, who replaced Tarrin's brother, and several senior executives of the bank appeared, before the Senate.

"Have you brought the Audit Executive Summary report?" the Senator asked Mechai.

"Under existing banking law, I am not authorized to release it."

The Senator then passed Mechai a document. "Is this the copy of the Audit Executive Summary report done by PricewaterhouseCoopers that was submitted to the Board of Directors?"

Mechai looked at the document handed to him by the Senator. "Yes, I believe that this document is the same as the draft version submitted to the Board." Mechai responded. "Can you tell me how you obtained this copy?"

The Senator replied, "I can't reveal that, but I have my sources."

That question would reverberate in the press over the next months, with accusations and countercharges going back and forth. "Who leaked the report to the Senate?" The content of the report and reform of Krung Thai Bank became a secondary issue as the government and its opponents parried for political advantage over the leaked PricewaterhouseCoopers audit report. Mechai became one of the suspects. One of the Senators at the golf course, who coincidentally was a member of the Board of Directors of Krung Thai Bank that had been replaced in accordance with the IMF agreement, claimed that Mechai had handed the report to another Senator at the golf course that day, who was chairman of the Senate Investigation Committee. Although the other Senators present denied the claim, it gained cachet in the press, and was used by the Ministry of Finance to discredit Mechai. The Governor of the Bank of Thailand, the Minister of Finance, and the Permanent Secretary disclaimed any prior knowledge of the report, despite the receipts Mechai produced to prove that the reports had been officially hand-delivered and received. The controversy dragged on.

What got lost in the press furor was the irony. Here was the Chairman of the Board of a publicly-owned bank being accused of giving a report on the bank's ill health to the people's parliament mandated to monitor public institutions. The sentiment that emerged in the local press was that, rather than being viewed as an infraction, it might be viewed as a civic duty.

During this confusion, the Ministry of Finance managed to regain control of voting rights for Krung Thai Bank's Board of Directors, despite IMF stipulations to the contrary. The Governor of the Bank of Thailand viewed it as a headache that he gladly relinquished to the MOF. Now that the MOF controlled voting rights, it also held all the cards. The forces against reform were positioned to sabotage it. According to Krung Thai Bank's bylaws, the Chairman of the Board must be elected annually. Although Mechai's tenure as Director was four years, his position as Chairman must be renewed every year. Mechai's tenure as Chairman was due to expire at the end of August 1999, at which time Mechai was sure the MOF would try to oust him as Chairman. He met with sympathetic colleagues in the Board. "They will definitely try to oust us. Why don't we resign first?"

Which is exactly what they did, on the very day the FIDF decided to remove the entire board. The new Board of Directors appointed by the MOF investigated the leaked audit report, and even made an official complaint to the police to find the culprit. But no charges were ever brought against Mechai. Rather than dealing with the NPLs and lending practices problems identified by the PricewaterhouseCoopers audit, the new leadership of Krung Thai Bank tried to refute its findings. There were even allegations that they falsified documents in the process, though this was never proven. They subsequently canceled the PricewaterhouseCoopers contract to continue the audit, and prevented the draft audit of Krung Thai's NPLs from ever being released publicly. Until now, the IMF-mandated reforms have been sidetracked and it is business as usual at Krung Thai Bank. A momentous opportunity for financial sector reform in Thailand was squandered.

Two significant events unfolded in the following months. First, the House of Representatives investigated the Krung Thai Bank NPLs and credit practices issues for one and a half days during the Censure Debate in December 1999. Second, the Bank of Thailand filed charges against Sirin Nimmanahaeminda, the former President of KTB and brother of the Finance Minister, alleging corruption and violation of prudent credit approval procedures. The Counter Corruption Commission rendered a guilty verdict on the case in early December 2000.[15]

The real losers in this entire affair were the Thai people. Equitable and efficient access to credit is essential for any economy. Because of its size and geographic distribution, Krung Thai Bank is the dominant source of credit in Thailand. If the reform measures had been implemented, Krung Thai Bank would have become an efficient lender with adequate capital to assure that credit reached the most productive sectors of the economy. It would likely have pulled the rest of the banking sector along with it. Efficient lending leads to efficient production, which spurs economic growth and alleviates poverty.

Instead Thailand remains saddled with a moribund banking sector that has reverted to the vicious cycle of nepotism, cronyism, and corrupt lending practices. As a result, its recovery from the economic crisis is slower than it could have been, its economic growth is not being driven by the most efficient sectors of the economy, and Thailand's comparative advantage in some sectors has not been optimized for lack of credit. The people of Thailand must pay for this inefficiency, especially the poor, either to recapitalize failing banks or by their lack of credit. The virtuous circle that could have been has been replaced by the vicious cycle of sick banks and lack of credit that still exists. The status quo prevailed.

Although financial services sector reform was stymied, Mechai could still claim some achievements at Krung Thai. He was a populist leader willing to confront an entrenched opposition. As a result, some restructuring measures were pushed through and some NPLs were recapitalized. He forced a debate on disclosure, transparency, good corporate governance and recapitalization into the public arena, a dialogue that is essential for the eventual health of Thailand's economy. He used his skills as a communicator to connect with the staff at Krung Thai to enlist their support for reform, an asset that future leaders can build upon. Was his tenure at Krung Thai a success? If success is measured by a popular leader who worked indefatigably for the best interests of the bank and ultimately the country, then on balance he surely was.

In the Thai government, the upper house of Parliament or Senate was an appointed body with little more than the supervisory power it exercised in the Krung Thai Bank case. Mechai had been appointed to the Senate twice, most recently in 1995. That changed with the new constitution of 1998, which created an elected Senate with real influence and power. The elected Senate can impeach government officials, sanction government, appoint and dismiss members of independent organizations such as the Counter Corruption Commission and the Electoral Commission, monitor government operations, and reject legislation proposed by the lower house. The new constitution put some teeth into a toothless tiger.

Elections to the newly constituted Senate were scheduled for March 2000. To guarantee the Senate's independence, the new constitution stipulated that candidates could not be government employees and must have no affiliation with a political party. There would be 200 elected Senators, 18 from Bangkok.

Following his campaign for a seat in Parliament in 1972, Mechai had eschewed electoral politics. He had been courted by several political parties over the years but always spurned their advances. He valued his independence and preferred to avoid the compromises that association with a political party would ultimately entail. The elected Senate, however, with its built in independence, provided the perfect electoral platform for Mechai. Running for the Senate would end speculation about his political aspirations. He decided to run for one of Bangkok's 18 Senate seats.

The Senate election was scheduled for March 4, 2000. On the day before submitting his application for candidacy in late January, Mechai checked with the Election Commission to assure that he fulfilled the criteria for candidates. His term as Chairman of the Board of TOT ended on February 20, 2000 and he wanted to make sure that the position did not jeopardize his eligibility. The constitution stated that candidates could not be employees of the government or state-owned enterprises. The bylaws of TOT specifically stated that the Chairman of the Board was neither a government employee nor an employee of a state-owned enterprise. Plus his term as Governor ended on 20 February, two weeks before election day. He was prepared to resign if necessary, but was assured by a member of the Election Commission that it would not be necessary.

On the appointed day, more than 250 persons applied to run for the 18 Senate seats from Bangkok. Once the dust settled and the candidates learned who their opponents were, one of them appealed to the Election Commission that Mechai's candidacy contravened the law by virtue of his position as Board Chairman of TOT. The Election Commission upheld the appeal and removed his name from the election rolls. Mechai's quest for a Senate seat had stalled before it even got started.

There was an uproar in the press over this decision, so Mechai held a press conference to answer questions. Rather than attacking the ruling, he vowed to abide by the decision. The Election Commission was new, he explained, they meant well, and he pleaded with the press not to criticize them. "They are like a new bride who hasn't become very adept at cooking yet." For its part, the Election Commission was grateful for the absence of vindictiveness, and even suggested Mechai appeal their decision to the Constitutional Commission, a suggestion he politely declined. He has plenty of other things to do. He would abide by the ruling.

Subsequently, the Election Commission disqualified an additional 32 candidates, all serving as University Trustees. Their reasoning was that Trustees have collective authority to appoint a university president, hence they are government employees. These candidates appealed the decision to the Constitutional Court. In a blanket decision, the Court ruled that University Trustees and Board members are not government employees, and reinstated their candidacies. Although Mechai never appealed, the Constitutional Court included his case in their decision, and reinstated his candidacy. He was cleared to run again.

He still faced one major problem. After being disqualified in late January, Mechai's name had been struck from the electoral rolls sent out to all the election districts and each home. He was reinstated only one week before election day. This gave him seven days to spread the word that he was back in the race.

In the interests of equity, election law forbade any campaigning or political advertising. Candidates could not use any media, advocate platforms, or make campaign promises. All they could do was distribute cards of predetermined size and shape with their photograph on one side and a summary of their professional accomplishments on the other. Placards of predetermined size could be posted at voting booths. These restrictions severely impeded Mechai's efforts to get the word out about his reinstated candidacy. He would have to rely primarily on name recognition.

On election day, many voting booths had still not listed Mechai as a candidate and many people still thought he was ineligible. However, enough voting booths had reinstated his name and enough voters recognized it to place him ninth out of 18

Senators elected from Bangkok. Senator-elect Mechai is now preparing for his six-year term in office.

Mechai has already formulated his policy agenda for the Senate. He will advocate for poverty alleviation, good governance, and civil society. He lobbied for and won Senate approval to elect the Senate President for two-year terms only, even though the law allows the Speaker to be elected to a six-year term, to preclude dominance by any individual. He will hold town hall meetings to keep political issues of concern to the people at the vanguard of the Senate's agenda. He will use his Senate seat to monitor government performance, curb the perquisites of senior government officials, and curtail profligate spending. The Ministry of Finance will probably wish that Senator Mechai was still Chairman of the Board of Krung Thai Bank.

Although these pursuits occupied much of Mechai's time, poverty alleviation and providing opportunities for the poor through PDA remained his passion. Guaranteeing its continuity became his highest priority. Toward the end of the 1990s, Mechai and his two closest associates, Tavatchai Traitongyoo and Sudha Chatchavalvong, developed a strategy for sustaining PDA in the future. Their planning was based upon one overlying assumption: that donor's support for NGOs like PDA will decline, hence PDA's future must be built upon a foundation independent of external donors.

The basis for their strategy was the relationship between the PDA group of companies, such as the Population and Development Company (PDC) and PDA. By law, NGOs like PDA cannot engage in business activities. All registered for-profit activities, from clinics to family planning paraphernalia to the Cabbages and Condoms Restaurant, were run by PDA-associated companies, whose charter stipulated that profits must be donated to PDA and used for charitable purposes. In effect, these companies became reliable donors to PDA.

Their strategy was to create more private companies whose charter also stipulated that their profits could only be donated for charitable purposes. Once the profits from these companies reached a critical mass, their contributions would compensate for the anticipated decline in donor funding.

PDA has established 15 for-profit companies that generate funds for its work as a non-profit association.[16] There is a chain of Cabbages and Condoms Restaurants run by these companies, plus other income-generating activities like marketing, trade, and manufacturing that make use of PDA nationwide network. Some of the companies endeavor to maximize profits. Others, working with economically-challenged communities, only seek to optimize profits.

Making this transition has not been easy. In most instances, PDA staff were seconded to run the private companies. In the process, Mechai had to replace their NGO orientation with a profit-oriented business mentality that seeks to optimize profits. PDA now provides 1,000 scholarships for students to study business at high schools and universities, and hires them to work in the companies when they graduate. In the future, it will undoubtedly hire many people with business skills.

PDA now receives a significant amount of its operating revenues as grants from its associated businesses, serious progress toward becoming sustainable independent of donor funds. Mechai has devised a strategy to replicate PDA's experience with other NGOs in a project called NGO Sustainability. Rather than giving grants to NGOs that keep them strapped to the funding treadmill, Mechai has proposed a strategy for donors to contribute toward their sustainability.

He envisions two stages. During the first stage, donors would provide grants for NGOs to obtain technical assistance to identify viable business opportunities and register businesses. In the second phase, the donor would provide the equity and working capital for the business in the form of long-term, low interest loans and grants. In this way, donor funds can revolve to other NGOs for business, rather than being consumed in one-off projects. PDA would provide technical assistance and supervision, sharing its experience with other NGOs as they developed their business skills.

Mechai has devoted the past 35 years to improving the quality of life for Thailand's underprivileged. Some may question his results, others may question his methods, but no one can question his motives. With his talents and the opportunities available to someone born to his station, he could have easily become a celebrity or wealthy businessman. Instead, he has dedicated his life to helping the poor. As he enters the 21st century and completes his sixth decade, there is every indication that he will continue doing so until he is no longer able. He never forgot his mother's admonishment when he was only seven, as the old Chinese women crossed the road, "If these people, who have been blessed with education and wealth, won't help this poor old lady, who will?" Mechai has spent his life answering that question.

Many people have dedicated their lives to the poor with equally impressive results. What is unique about Mechai is the way he did it. His methods were unorthodox. Sometimes he shocked the establishment. But he always made them laugh. He was not averse to taking chances, even when they put him at personal risk, if he thought the ends justified the means. In the process, he became the social conscience of a nation. Political leaders consult with him. Business leaders cooperate with him. The Thai people listen to him. He can be assertive and insistent when necessary, or charming and endearing when the occasion requires. Everything he does has one objective — to help the poor.

Mechai enjoyed several advantages as he pursued this objective. Foremost is the love and support that he continues to receive from his family. Although she has a demanding career of her own (Putrie is now the Secretary General of the Privy Council) and never becomes directly involved in Mechai's work, Putrie has always been his loyal confidant and advisor of first resort. Before making any major decision or launching any new initiative, he would always consult Putrie first, confident that her advice would be thoughtful and insightful; that it would consider the social and political milieu in which they lived; and above all, that it would be brutally frank.

Looknoo is the joy of their lives. She has matured into a level-headed adult with a mind of her own. Following her graduation from Melbourne University, she is pursuing a Master's degree in Museum Studies at University College in London. Regardless of the path she chooses, her contribution will be significant.

He has also been fortunate in the colleagues who joined him to pursue his dreams. Tavatchai Traitongyoo has worked with Mechai for 34 years. Their skills are mutually complementary. Where Mechai is creative, energetic, and sometimes impulsive, Tavatchai is steady and deliberate. Sudha Chatchavalvong joined in 1974, became Managing Director of PDC in 1977, and along with Tavatchai, has spearheaded business development in the private companies. Together, Tavatchai and Sudha are Mechai's most senior and trusted advisors. When he was absent, they ran the organization. They are a sounding board for the endless ideas he generates, helping him to identify the most promising and prioritize. When projects must be implemented, they take direct responsibility.

When Mechai launched CBFPS in 1974, he was extremely fortunate to recruit a cohort of loyal staff. Sophon Siriwong, Vilas Lohitkul, Praween Payathvipapong, Vilas Techo, Sunida Chattanont, Songnam Ritwana, and Tanothai Sukhdis were idealistic young graduates when they joined the fledgling community-based contraceptive distribution program. Over the years, they have evolved and adapted with the organization, willing to tackle the variety of challenges that Mechai posed — whether it was refugee relief, better marketing, animal raising, AIDS education, or business development. They are now the senior staff running PDA and the private companies. They will be the leaders of the future.

Finally, all of his actions have been guided by a consistent philosophy. Mechai believes that you must identify and address the root cause of a problem in order to solve it. Dealing with problems indirectly just wastes time. When the population problem confronted Thailand, many suggested that increasing incomes and better education would ameliorate the problem over time. Mechai said that the root cause of the population problem was too many births, hence all of his efforts were aimed at getting contraceptives to the people to reduce the number of births. Unprotected sex with prostitutes caused the rapid spread of AIDS in Thailand, so Mechai focused on that problem first. Traditional development theory postulates that poverty is caused by slow economic growth. For Mechai, economic growth alone was insufficient to reduce poverty, because its benefits were not distributed evenly. It led to urban industrialization, which forced rural people to migrate to cities for jobs, creating urban slums and depleting rural societies. His approach to rural development, embodied in TBIRD, brings economic growth directly to rural villages, allowing villagers to prosper in their indigenous environment.

As this biography was being researched, every person interviewed was asked the same question: What does the future hold for Mechai? The range of answers was disparate. Some predicted a high position in government. Others predicted a prominent role in an international organization. Others saw his future in business. With his new role in the Senate, it could even be in politics.

There was one common thread to all the answers. Whatever Mechai does in the future, his paramount objective will be the same — to improve the quality of life for Thailand's poor. The vehicle he chooses to achieve it may vary, but the objective will always be the same.

It is not easy to summarize Mechai's life, but his friend Henry David stated it most simply when he said, "Mechai's life is a wonderful example of what can be accomplished by one man with imagination, good humor, and strong motivation."

*The TBIRD shoe factory in Nang Rong District, Buri Ram Province*

*PDA vegetable bank*

*Mechai with his former headmaster of GGS Sir James Darling*

*Mechai greeting staff at Krung Thai Bank after an address*

*Mechai with Dr. Malcolm Potts*

*Mechai with Dr. Allan Rosenfield*

*Mechai's campaign poster for Senate election, 2000*

*Mechai, Looknoo, and Putri at Harvard University, 1988*

## NOTES:

1 These descriptions of "Thailand One" and "Thailand Two" were taken from a monograph prepared by the United Nations Economic and Social Commission for Asia and the Pacific (ESCAP) titled "Business for Development: The HRD Approach of the Thai Business Initiative for Rural Development," Bangkok, 1995.

2 Most of the TBIRD projects were established in the proximity of one of PDA's CBIRD centers, as Bata did in Nang Rong. This was a convenient arrangement because PDA had already introduced community development programs in these areas and had the trust and respect of the villagers. The CBIRD centers also had infrastructure for training and administrative support services that would be essential for the kinds of collaboration Bata was envisioning, to bring manufacturing capacity to rural areas.

3 Lohitkul V, and Nichols J, "TBIRD: Promoting Thai Rural Based Industry," *Business Day*, 9 June 1998.

4 The vegetable bank was one of TBIRD's most unique innovations, particularly suited to the arid conditions in northeastern Thailand. Rice and cassava are the traditional crops grown in the Northeast — rice for consumption and cassava for animal feed. Without irrigation, farmers can only grow one crop per year. The vegetable bank concept was developed by PDA to provide farmers with additional income during the dry season, when most migration occurs, by surmounting the problems of scarce rainfall and limited irrigation. Bristol-Myers Squibb, a pharmaceutical company, sponsored a TBIRD project in Ban Nong Kok, Buri Ram Province in 1991 that scaled up the vegetable bank concept to a replicable level.

The vegetable banks are irrigated, cooperatively run, and intensely cropped vegetable gardens. Water for year round irrigation is obtained from a deep well which is dedicated for use in gardens where vegetables, herbs, or even flowers can be grown. If water is conserved conscientiously, a single well can irrigate up to fifty 800-square-meter plots during the dry season. Because the produce is grown during the dry season, it commands a respectable market price. A single 800-square-meter plot can provide a family with 200 baht of supplemental income per day, significantly higher than the average daily wage in the Northeast.

In the vegetable bank sponsored by Bristol-Myers Squibb at Ban Nong Kok, the government provided four hectares of unused public land for the gardens. Bristol-Myers provided a low-interest loan to pay for initial site construction — construction of the well, installation of the pump and irrigation system, and training for the villagers. Forty-three families joined the project and each received an 800-square-meter plot of land. The villagers repaid the loan for initial site construction through a charge for the water they used. The project was so successful that it has been implemented in over ten sites.

The vegetable bank concept has certain limitations that constrain its replication. A village may not have enough arable land or sufficient water to sustain a site throughout the dry season. It may be too far from a market to make the vegetable bank viable. Where conditions are conducive, vegetable banks have been shown to be a powerful method to raise incomes and improve living standards.

5 *Forestry Statistics of Thailand 1994*, Data Center, Information Office, Royal Forest Department.

6 1994 Ramon Magsaysay Awards Presentation Ceremonies, Manila, Philippines, 31 August 1994.

7 "20 Great Asians 1975-95 and 20 for the Future," *Asiaweek* 21 no. 22, 2 June 1995.

8 Mechai was Chairman of the Board of four companies — Petroleum Authority of Thailand Exploration and Production Co., Eastern Water Resources Development and Management Co., Lam Soon (Thailand) Co., and Business Day Newspaper. He was a Director on the Board of Mobil Oil (Thailand), Capital Nomura Securities, Motivation Asia (Thailand) Ltd., and Jasmine International Public Co.

9 In a joint statement issued by the Ministry of Finance and the Bank of Thailand on August 14, 1998 titled "Financial Restructuring for Economic Recovery", Krung Thai Bank was ordered to absorb two severely undercapitalized government-owned banks with a large proportion of non-performing loans — First Bangkok City Bank (FBCB) and the Bangkok Bank of Commerce (BBC). Under the heading "Operational Restructuring of Krung Thai Bank", the report goes on to recommend that "the government recognizes that KTB (Krung Thai Bank) also needs to be restructured and recapitalized, with the ultimate intention of preparing KTB for privatization within two years. With this objective, KTB will implement a comprehensive restructuring plan. A new KTB Board will be appointed on end-August 1998, with all but one member of the Board from outside the public sector. KTB will also establish a new full-time Executive Board. A comprehensive plan for the restructuring of KTB will be developed by outside experts by end-November 1998."

10 The IMF had other motives for advocating privatization of Krung Thai. It also saw the sale of Krung Thai as a fantastic revenue opportunity for the government. Experience in other countries had demonstrated that the sale of state-owned banks could pay for the entire cost of financial services sector restructuring. Although this was not entirely the case with Krung Thai, its sale

would generate significant revenues that the government could use for restructuring.

11 Nepotistic cronyism was the practice, common in Thailand among state-owned and commercial banks, of lending to business ventures of political allies and their associates. Directed lending was the practice, especially among family-owned banks, of lending to associated family enterprises. Both lending practices were usually done without proper due diligence and frequently resulted in non-performing loans.

12 Although the FIDF was the majority-shareholder of Krung Thai Bank at the time, in practice the appointment of Directors still needed approval by the Ministry of Finance. This was one of many contentious issues that caused a power struggle between Krung Thai Bank and the MOF.

13 CLSA stands for Credit Lyonnais Securities Asia.

14 The information and data in this section were taken from the unofficial translations of public documents. Sources of information include newspaper articles on the Krung Thai Bank's NPLs audit findings, and the Report of the Senate Sub-Committee on Finance and Banking which was issued to the public following the hearing in August 1999. Both the press and the report discussed the summary of the NPLs audit in the following manner: "It was found that 65% of the total loan portfolio in the combined bank were non-performing loans. Krung Thai's loan portfolio contained 70% NPLs. Under prudent credit lending criteria, PWC found that 65% of Krung Thai Bank's portfolio were Loss Loans and 5% were Doubtful Loans. An additional 14% of its loans were classified as Substandard. The situation at First Bangkok City Bank, one of the banks absorbed by Krung Thai Bank, was even worse — 94% of its assets were Loss Loans. With such a heavy burden of NPLs and their extraordinarily high level of pro-

vision requirement, Krung Thai Bank would require 417 billion baht (US$ 10.7 billion) to properly recapitalize the bank, versus 185 billion baht in new equity earmarked by the Bank of Thailand and FIDF for recapitalization.

15 The Counter Corruption Commission rendered its verdict against Sirin in December 2000. After the electoral defeat of the Chuan Leekpai Government in January 2001 and Tarin's replacement as Minister of Finance, the staff of Krung Thai Bank made a petition to have the entire Board of Krung Thai Bank replaced. No action has been taken to this time.

16 The companies associated with PDA are the Population and Community Development Co., the Rural Small Scale Industries Development Co., Nang Rong Pattana Co., Sarakham-Ban Phai Development Co., Rural Environmental Sanitation Development Co., Vieng Pa Pao Pattana Co., Health North Co., Health Northeast Co., All North Co., Phutthaisong Development Co., Punoi Pattana Co., Lamplaimat Development Co., Hu-Kwang Bay Development Co., Sapthai Development Co., and the Jakkarat Development Co.

# APPENDIX 1

## GNP articles (1968-1976)

| | Date | Title | Publication |
|---|---|---|---|
| 1 | 9/3/68 | U.S. Presence: Imagined Hostility | *Bangkok World* |
| 2 | 1/4/68 | Development Expenditures, Foreign Loans and Grants | *Bangkok World* |
| 3 | 28/4/68 | Severe Drought Forces Reduced Growth Targets | *Bangkok World* |
| 4 | 2/5/68 | Foreign Trade and Balance of Payment | *Bangkok World* |
| 5 | 4/5/68 | Development of Agriculture | *Bangkok World* |
| 6 | 6/5/68 | Development of Transportation and Communications | *Bangkok World* |
| 7 | 7/5/68 | Development of Power | *Bangkok World* |
| 8 | 8/5/68 | Development of Public Health, Community Facilities and Social Welfare | *Bangkok World* |
| 9 | 10/5/68 | Development Administration | *Bangkok World* |
| 10 | 26/5/68 | Thai Press Move for Immediate Population Policy | *Bangkok World* |
| 11 | 14/7/68 | Adjustment to U.S. Withdrawal | *Bangkok World* |
| 12 | 28/7/68 | A Labor of Love — on Government Service | *Bangkok World* |

| | Date | Title | Publication |
|---|---|---|---|
| 13 | 18/8/68 | Implications of Nixon-Agnew Victory | *Bangkok World* |
| 14 | 15/9/68 | How Thais Spend Their Income | *Bangkok World* |
| 15 | 7/10/68 | Thai Economy — 1967: Part I | *Bangkok World* |
| 16 | 1/12/68 | Lonely Advocates of Birth Control | *Bangkok World* |
| 17 | 15/12/68 | Revolutionary Concept in Local Housing | *Bangkok World* |
| 18 | 23/12/68 | Provincial Participation in State-Owned Enterprises | *Bangkok World* |
| 19 | 30/12/68 | 1968 Thai Economy Falters | *Business World* |
| 20 | 6/1/69 | Drought — Agriculture Dampens Overall Growth | *Business World* |
| 21 | 3/2/69 | Beyond the Elections | *Business World* |
| 22 | 11/2/69 | Thai Development Future Not Bleak | *Business World* |
| 23 | 17/2/69 | Will Bangkok Be Choked to Death?: Traffic Part I | *Business World* |
| 24 | 24/2/69 | Traffic Improvement Proposal | *Business World* |
| 25 | 4/3/69 | Diseconomies of Traffic: Part III | *Business World* |
| 26 | 17/3/69 | Traffic Survey Must Begin Now: Part IV | *Business World* |
| 27 | 24/3/69 | Corruption Understood: Prebendalism Part I | *Business World* |
| 28 | 31/3/69 | City Environment Planning and Guidance | *Business World* |
| 29 | 21/4/69 | Shortsighted Approach to Civil Service Reform: Prebendalism | *Business World* |
| 30 | 28/4/69 | Does Civil Service Commission Want to Increase Salary? | *Business World* |
| 31 | 7/5/69 | Catalyst in Thailand's Development Effort | *Business World* |
| 32 | 10/7/69 | Guide to Future Thai Development: Part IV | *Business World* |
| 33 | 15/7/69 | Infrastructure: by Virtue of Its Being There | *Business World* |
| 34 | 19/8/69 | The Economic Consequences of the Peace (in Vietnam) | *Business World* |
| 35 | 28/8/69 | The Controversial 1970 Budget | *Business World* |
| 36 | 3/9/69 | Should the Rice Premium Be Abolished? | *Business World* |
| 37 | 10/9/69 | Commercialization of Thai Wats | *Business World* |

| | Date | Title | Pubplication |
|---|---|---|---|
| 38 | 18/9/69 | Salt Water Intrusion: A Threat to City Water Supply | *Business World* |
| 39 | 15/10/69 | Teamwork: Japan's Secret Economic Weapon Part II | *Business World* |
| 40 | 22/10/69 | Zaibatsu: Engine of Japanese Industrial Expansion Part III | *Business World* |
| 41 | 27/10/69 | Past and Future Development of the Thai Economy: Part I | *Business World* |
| 42 | 28/10/69 | Urban and Rural Sectors: Part II | *Business World* |
| 43 | 29/10/69 | Past and Future Development of the Thai Economy: Part III | *Bangkok World* |
| 44 | 27/11/69 | No Shortcuts to Development | *Business World* |
| 45 | 18/12/69 | Blueprint for Global Development Part I: Pearson Commission | *Business World* |
| 46 | 19/12/69 | Commission's Recommendations Part II: Pearson Commission Report | *Business World* |
| 47 | 25/12/69 | Recommendations on Aid Administration, Population and Education | *Business World* |
| 48 | 2/4/70 | The Third Plan: Deciding Factor in Thai Economic History | *Bangkok Post* |
| 49 | 16/4/70 | Red Light for Baby Boom (On National Family Planning Policy) | *Business World* |
| 50 | 2/8/70 | Perils of Prebendalism — Is There a Solution? Part I | *Bangkok Magazine* |
| 51 | 9/8/70 | Behind Corruption: Problems of Prebendalism Part II | *Business World* |
| 52 | 16/8/70 | The Miracle Workers Part II: Excerpts from Diary of an Expert | *Bangkok Magazine* |
| 53 | 23/8/70 | The Vendor Economy | *Bangkok Magazine* |
| 54 | 30/8/70 | Behind the Insurgency Problem | *Bangkok Magazine* |
| 55 | 6/9/70 | Thailand: Consequences of Counter-Insurgency | *Bangkok Magazine* |
| 56 | 13/9/70 | Technology Backfires: On Polluted Environment Part IV | *Bangkok Magazine* |

| | Date | Title | Publication |
|---|---|---|---|
| 57 | 20/9/70 | Fouling Our Own Nests (On Polluted Environment): Part II | *Bangkok Magazine* |
| 58 | 27/9/70 | Bangkok: The Troubled City | *Bangkok Magazine* |
| 59 | 11/10/70 | War on Middlemen | *Bangkok Magazine* |
| 60 | 8/11/70 | Irrigation: The New Approach | *Bangkok Magazine* |
| 61 | 6/12/70 | Difficult Times Ahead (On Recession of 1970) | *Bangkok Magazine* |
| 62 | 3/1/71 | Where Has Development Taken Us? | *Bangkok Magazine* |
| 63 | 10/1/71 | A VIP on R+R by O. Wattana Siam | *Bangkok Magazine* |
| 64 | 22/5/71 | Tourism: TOT's 148 Million Baht Misconception | *Bangkok Magazine* |
| 65 | 11/4/76 | Abortion in Thailand | *The Nation* |
| 66 | 18/4/76 | Abortion: Part II | *The Nation* |

# APPENDIX 2

## Newspaper and magazine articles about HIV/AIDS epidemic in Thailand (1989-2000)

| | Date | Title | Author | Publication |
|---|---|---|---|---|
| 1 | 27/8/87 | Mechai Launches AIDS Campaign | | *Bangkok Post* |
| 2 | 8/6/89 | Thai Perspectives Aired at World's Biggest AIDS Conference | Promporn Pramualratana | *Bangkok Post* |
| 3 | 14/8/89 | Army to Join War against AIDS Menace | | *Bangkok Post* |
| 4 | 14/8/89 | Test on Drug Addicts Reveals Slight Increase in AIDS Cases | | *The Nation* |
| 5 | 15/8/89 | Warning on AIDS Spread | | *The Nation* |
| 6 | 30/8/89 | All Army Personnel to Have AIDS Tests | | *Bangkok Post* |
| 7 | 2/9/89 | Army Set to Launch Blitz against AIDS | Paisal Sricharatchanya | *Bangkok Post* |
| 8 | 4/9/89 | Pragmatism and AIDS | Post Opinion | *Bangkok Post* |
| 9 | 7/9/89 | Condom Night with Mechai a Big Hit in Patpong | | *Bangkok Post* |
| 10 | 18/9/89 | Thailand's War on AIDS | Ron Moreau | *Newsweek* |

| | Date | Title | Author | Publication |
|---|---|---|---|---|
| 11 | 21/9/89 | Mechai Calls for Tax Fund to Fight AIDS | | *Bangkok Post* |
| 12 | 21/9/89 | "AIDS Spreading Rapidly" Says Health Official | | *The Nation* |
| 13 | 21/9/89 | 261 Soldiers Test Positive for AIDS | | *The Nation* |
| 14 | 22/9/89 | Mechai Warns of "Dead City" | | *Bangkok Post* |
| 15 | 24/9/89 | Campaign against AIDS Puts Curb on Sex Trade | Denise Young | *Seattle Times* |
| 16 | 26/9/89 | Thailand Steps Up Fight against AIDS | John Berthelsen | *Asian Wall Street Journal* |
| 17 | 13/10/89 | Combatting AIDS a Top National Priority | | *Bangkok Post* |
| 18 | 2/11/89 | The Lust Frontier | Paul Handley | *Far Eastern Economic Review* |
| 19 | 2/11/89 | Survey: People Still Lax about AIDS | | *The Nation* |
| 20 | 3/12/89 | Mechai's Anti-AIDS Campaign | Denis Gray | *The Nation* |
| 21 | 3/12/89 | Thailand Wages War against AIDS | Denis Gray | *The Daily Yomiuri* |
| 22 | 22/1/90 | Miracle Man of Thailand | Charles P. Wallace | *Los Angeles Times* |
| 23 | 26/1/90 | Thailand Launches Anti-AIDS Campaign | Denis Gray | *Asahi Evening News* |
| 24 | 2/2/90 | 72% of Poor Chiang Mai Prostitutes Have AIDS | Ann Danaiya Usher | *The Nation* |
| 25 | 2/2/90 | Mechai: Govt's AIDS Figures "Misleading" | | *Bangkok Post* |
| 26 | 6/2/90 | Premier Chatichai, Wake Up Now! | AIDS Watch | *The Nation* |
| 27 | 15/2/90 | Mechai Urges Private Sector to Join Fight against AIDS | Paisal Chuenprasaeng | *The Nation* |
| 28 | 13/3/90 | Mechai, Touching the Untouchable | Suda Kanjanawanawan | *The Nation* |

| | Date | Title | Author | Publication |
|---|---|---|---|---|
| 29 | 6/6/90 | AIDS Education for Officials | | *Bangkok Post* |
| 30 | 7/8/90 | Mechai Calls for Closure of "Industry of Death" | | *Bangkok Post* |
| 31 | 9/8/90 | Mechai Calls for Sex Industry Shutdown | | *Bangkok Post* |
| 32 | 10/8/90 | Curb AIDS Horror, Close Vice Dens | Post Opinion | *Bangkok Post* |
| 33 | 11/8/90 | AIDS: the Menace We Can No Longer Ignore | Ampa Santimatanedol | *Bangkok Post* |
| 34 | 16/8/90 | Thailand's War on AIDS | Lois Jensen | *The Nation* |
| 35 | 26/8/90 | "Dead Customers Don't Buy" | | *Manager* |
| 36 | 1/10/90 | Hilltribe Girls Pose AIDS Risk — Survey | | *Bangkok Post* |
| 37 | 10/11/90 | Cops and Rubbers | | *The Economist* |
| 38 | 21/12/90 | Govt Urged to Scrap AIDS Bill | Ann Danaiya Usher | *The Nation* |
| 39 | 22/12/90 | AIDS to Cost Thailand Billions | James Fahn | *The Nation* |
| 40 | 22/12/90 | Mechai Warns of Repaid Raise in AIDS Patients | | *Bangkok Post* |
| 41 | 24/12/90 | Echoes of an Ugly Past | | *The Nation* |
| 42 | 2/2/91 | PDA Estimates 2 Million AIDS Cases by Year 2000 | Tulsathit Taptim | *Bangkok Post* |
| 43 | 19/2/91 | PM's Team to Lead AIDS Fight | Sorrayuth Suthassanachinda | *The Nation* |
| 44 | 29/9/91 | A Plan for All-Out War againt AIDS | Wasant Techawongtham | *Bangkok Post* |
| 45 | 30/3/92 | Mechai — the Man Who Changed Thai Tourism | Imtiaz Muqbil | *Bangkok Post* |
| 46 | 16/10/00 | Back to No Future | Robert Horn | *Time* |

# BIBLIOGRAPHY

"AIDS in Thailand." *British Medical Journal* 300 (17 February 1990): 415.

Barmé, Scot. *Luang Wichit Wathakan and the Creation of a Thai Identity.* Institute of Southeast Asian Studies, 1993.

Bate, Weston. *Light Blue Down Under — The History of Geelong Grammar School.* Oxford University Press, 1990.

Chanda, Nayan. *Brother Enemy — The War after the War.* Collier Books, 1986.

Chandler, David P., *A History of Cambodia.* 2nd ed. Silkworm Books, 1994.

Chandler, David P. et al. *In Search of Southeast Asia: A Modern History.* University of Hawaii Press, 1987.

Darling, James. *Richly Rewarding — An Autobiography.* Hill of Content Publishing PLC., 1978.

ESCAP. *Business for Development: The HRD Approach of the Thai Business Initiative for Rural Development.* United Nations Economic and Social Commission for Asia and the Pacific (ESCAP), 1994.

Hanenberg, R., et al. "Impact of Thailand's HIV-Control Program as Indicated by the Decline of Sexually Transmitted Diseases." *Lancet* 344 (1994): 243-245.

Haseman, John B. *The Thai Resistance Movement during the Second World War.* Chalermnit Press.

Hulse, David L. "The Integration of Community Based Family Planning and Development in Thailand: the Role of the Population and Community Development Association." JOICFP Documentary Series 17, 1985.

Karnow, Stanley. *Vietnam: A History*. Viking Penguin Press, 1983.

Leonowens, A.H. *Anna and the King of Siam.* Trubner and Co., 1870.

McNamara, Robert S. and Brian Van De Mark. *In Retrospect: The Tragedy and Lesson of Vietnam.* Random House, 1995.

Mills S., et al. "Assessing Trends in HIV Risk Behaviors in Asia." *AIDS* 12 suppl. B(1998): S79-86.

Narkavonnakit, Tongplaew. "Rural Abortion in Thailand: A National Survey of Practitioners." *Studies in Family Planning* 10 no. 8/9 (August-September 1979).

National Statistics Office. *Statistical Handbook of Thailand.* National Statistics of Thailand, Office of the Prime Minister, 1984.

Nelson, K., et al. "Changes in Sexual Behavior and a Decline in HIV Infection among Young Men in Thailand." *New England Journal of Medicine* 335 (1996): 297-303.

Panyarachun, Anand. "AIDS and Social and Economic Progress in the Asian and Pacific Countries." Third International Conference on AIDS in the Asia and Pacific, Chiang Mai, September 1995.

Phongpaichit Pasuk and Chris Baker. *Thailand: Economy and Politics.* Oxford University Press, 1995.

Rojanapithayakorn, Wiwat. "Thailand: Promising Results." *Integration*, Fall (1998): 21-23.

Rosenfield, A.G. "Thailand: History of the National Family Planning Program." 25th Anniversary of Thailand's National Family Planning Program, Bangkok, July 1996.

Rosenfield, A.G. and C. Limcharoen. "Auxiliary Midwife Prescription of Oral Contraceptives." *American Journal of Obstetrics and Gynecology* (December 1972).

Smithies, Michael. *Descriptions of Old Siam.* Oxford University Press, 1995.

Syamananda, Rong. *A History of Thailand.* Thai Watana Panich, 1993.

The Population Council, "Abortion in Thailand: A Review of the Literature." May 1981.

UNDP. "Economic Implications of AIDS in Asia." HIV/AIDS Regional Project, 1993.

Warner, Roger. *Backfire: The CIA's Secret War in Laos and Its Link to the War in Vietnam.* Simon & Shuster, 1995.

World Bank. "Thailand's Response to AIDS: Building on Success, Confronting the Future." World Bank Thailand Office, October 2000.

Wyatt, David K. *Thailand: A Short History.* Yale University Press, 1984.

1994 Ramon Magsaysay Awards Presentation Ceremonies, Manila, 31 August 1994.

*Asia Weeks.* 2 June 1995.

*Business Day.* 9 June 1998.

*The Economist.* 3-9 May 1997.

## READ MORE IN POST BOOKS

For complete information about books available from Post Books and
how to order them, write to us or visit our website at the following address:
Post Books, The Post Publishing Plc. 136 Na Ranong Road,
off Sunthorn Kosa Road, Klong Toey, Bangkok 10110, Thailand.
Tel: (662) 240-3700 ext. 1691-2 Fax: (662) 671-9698
e-mail: postbooks@bangkokpost.co.th
http: //www.bangkokpost.net/postbooks

### Softcovers:

**Good Morning, Buddha** *Phra Peter Pannapadipo*

*5" 1/2 x 8". 212 pp. 2000.*

Buddha — a fully-awakened one — is not confined to the altar, immortalised in bronze or gold, remote and untouchable. The qualities that make a Buddha do not come from "out there" but are already "within" each of us. This book propounds that, to uncover them, it is necessary to make the practice of Buddhism part of our everyday life, the basis of our every thought, word and action.

**Phra Farang:** An English Monk in Thailand

*Phra Peter Pannapadipo*

*5" 1/2 x 8". 380 pp. 2000. 4th printing (extended edition).*

An English Buddhist monk describes his experiences in an unfamiliar culture in a lively and gripping style. Readers will find the author's treatment of Dhamma easy to understand, his soul-searching moments touching and thought-provoking. But it is the author's remarkable sense of humour that sets this book apart from most others on a similar subject.

**One Step at a Time:** Buddhist Meditation for Absolute Beginners

*Phra Peter Pannapadipo*

*5" 1/2 x 8". 168 pp. 2000. 2nd printing.*

Written with the objective of making meditation more accessible to those who do not have easy accesss to a guide or an instructor, this book presents Buddhist meditation in a very straightforward and practical way while offering basic guidance frequently overlooked by even very knowledgeable instructors or authors. A good start for those looking for nothing more than peace within.

**The White Umbrella** *Patricia Elliott*

*5" 1/2 x 7". 404 pp. 1999.*

A dazzling true tale of modern Burma told through the life story of a woman who has been called Princess, Mahadevi, First Lady, MP, rebel leader and refugee... Her journey — from quiet Shan hills to the presidential palace in Rangoon to the halls of power in Asia and Europe; and finally to the violent, drug-laden netherworld of the Golden Triangle — is a revelation about Burma, Southeast Asia, and about what happens when the games of superpowers are played out in real life. With a prologue by Bertil Lintner, maps and B/W photographs.

**The Black Swan** *Anthony Aikman*

*4" 1/2 x 7" 1/8. 152 pp. 1999. Illustrated.*

Written in the same vein as *The Little Prince*, this is a tale about a child on a spiritual odyssey, his conscience his only compass. The plight of homeless Cambodian children and the fate of their turbulent country provide a backdrop for the tale. Full of allusions and ironies, this illustrated book is in effect a philosophical debate. Thought-provoking yet easy to read, it looks into the very nature of the human psyche.

**Boy, Doc and the Green Man** (also The Fire-eater, a short story)

*Anthony Aikman*

*4" 1/2 x 7" 1/8. 240 pp. 2000. Illustrated.*

The author translates what he had seen and been involved in at first hand as a medical volunteer in a remote part of North Sumatra into another moving story. *Boy, Doc and the Green Man* epitomises the recurring conflict between age-old rural community life and the demands of modern society. It graphically describes how the traditional way of life in a small village of farmers and fishermen is destroyed when they are forced off their land to make way for "development". It subtly shows how peace and harmony are replaced by hatred and despair as witnessed by a boy whose family has to migrate from the calm of the countryside with its folklore wisdom, to the chaos of city slums, mob riots and summary injustice.

◆◆◆◆◆